Praise for THE LOST SPRING

"Walid Phares has predicted the Arab Spring, has projected the rise of civil societies in the Middle East, and has also warned us about the Islamists' takeover and Iran's strategic expansion. But he has also accurately seen the comeback of the revolutionary democrats in Egypt and Tunisia and beyond. In his new, masterfully written book, *The Lost Spring,* Phares is telling us why the West lost a historic opportunity and what new policies are needed to avoid catastrophes and welcome a new Spring."

—Paulo Casaca, Socialist Member of the European Parliament from 1999 to 2009 and President of the European Parliament delegation to the NATO Parliamentary Assembly from 2005 to 2007

"Walid Phares is one of the leading geopolitical strategists in the world. His books, including *Future Jihad* and *The Coming Revolution,* have helped many members of Congress and the U.S. government better understand the forthcoming national security threats. In his new book *The Lost Spring,* Phares exposes the mistakes of our foreign policies in the Middle East, from partnering with the Muslim Brotherhood to abandoning the Iranian youth. His book is a historical, yet a future strategic reading, suggesting alternatives to forthcoming disasters in the region. A must read."

—Congresswoman Sue Myrick, Chair subcommittee on Intelligence 2011–2013, Co-Chair Anti-Terrorism Caucus, U.S. House of Representatives, 2007–2013

ALSO BY WALID PHARES AND AVAILABLE FROM PALGRAVE MACMILLAN

The Confrontation

Future Jihad

The War of Ideas

THE LOST SPRING

U.S. POLICY IN THE MIDDLE EAST AND CATASTROPHES TO AVOID

WALID PHARES

palgrave
macmillan

THE LOST SPRING
Copyright © Walid Phares, 2014.
All rights reserved.

First published in 2014 by PALGRAVE MACMILLAN® in the United
States—a division of St. Martin's Press LLC, 175 Fifth Avenue, New York, NY
10010.

Where this book is distributed in the UK, Europe and the rest of the world,
this is by Palgrave Macmillan, a division of Macmillan Publishers Limited,
registered in England, company number 785998, of Houndmills, Basingstoke,
Hampshire RG21 6XS.

Palgrave Macmillan is the global academic imprint of the above companies and
has companies and representatives throughout the world.

Palgrave® and Macmillan® are registered trademarks in the United States,
the United Kingdom, Europe and other countries.

ISBN 978-1-137-27903-3

Library of Congress Cataloging-in-Publication Data

Phares, Walid, 1957–
  The lost spring : U.S. policy in the Middle East and catastrophes to avoid /
Walid Phares.
  pages cm
  ISBN 978-1-137-27903-3 (hardback)
  1. Arab Spring, 2010– 2. Islam and politics—Middle East. 3. Democracy—
Middle East. 4. United States—Foreign relations—Middle East. 5. Middle
East—Foreign relations—United States. I. Title.
JQ1850.A91P46 2014
327.73056—dc23

                                                                2013038770

A catalogue record of the book is available from the British Library.

Design by Letra Libre

First edition: March 2014

10 9 8 7 6 5 4 3 2 1

Printed in the United States of America.

CONTENTS

ACKNOWLEDGMENTS

I WOULD LIKE TO THANK MANY PEOPLE WHO PLAYED A role in my life, in my professional career, and in the path leading to this book, those who actively supported me and those who came to the defense of my ideas. I owe gratitude to even more people than those mentioned here for their support, but in these acknowledgements I would like to select a few who walked with me during the journey to produce this book, each one in a different manner, whether knowingly or unknowingly.

First, I owe my family—my wife who consistently supported me all along and my son—tremendous gratitude for having consented to sacrifice the time I spent away from them to research, travel, discuss, and write this book. I appreciate not only their sacrifice, but they must know I also value their input when we discuss issues related to my thinking.

This book would never have found voice without my faithful and relentlessly successful literary agent, so I must begin my litany of professional thanks by extending them to Lynne Rabinoff, who since 2003 has been my bridge to the world of publishing, always encouraging me to continue my writing despite my many other endeavors. In this same vein, I wish to especially thank my publisher, Karen Wolny, who once again granted me the trust of Palgrave to add this book to the previous ones published by their prominent publishing house in New York. Her excellent editing team led by the very patient and professional editor Alan Bradshaw, helped me transform the manuscript into what will, hopefully, become a well-read book. My thanks also goes to publicity manager Lauren Dwyer-Janiec and editorial assistant Lauren LoPinto . In the writing of Lost Spring, however, I owe the greatest gratitude to my editing assistant Dorothy Logan, my former student in the 1990s and now a professor of political science and culture. Dorothy edited my work, word by word, day and night, until the manuscript was finished. She has been a pillar central to this writing project.

In the realm of public service, I would first like to thank former U.S. presidential candidate Mitt Romney, and his wife Ann, for trusting me to be his national security and foreign affairs advisor in 2011 and 2012. Mitt Romney's citing of my work in his 2009 book, and his endorsement of my own book of 2010 that predicted the revolutions in the Middle East, honored me greatly.

His decision to appoint me as a member of his presidential campaign's foreign policy cabinet bestowed upon me the ultimate honor of serving my country the best I could and triggered my decision to write this book. I also wish to thank former Congresswoman Sue Myrick, a chair of the Subcommittee on Terrorism, Human Intelligence, Analysis and Counterintelligence and the founder of the anti-Terrorism Caucus in the U.S. House of Representatives, for appointing me as an adviser since 2007 and trusting me to bring expertise to the U.S. Congress on terrorism and the Middle East. I would like to thank Congressman Jeff Duncan, member of the U.S. House Committee on Homeland Security and the co-chair of the Transatlantic Legislative Group on Counter Terrorism, and his defense assistant Rebecca Ulrich for their support. I thank Congressman Trent Franks and his foreign policy assistant, Stephanie Hammond, and Congressman Robert Aderholt and his chief of staff, Mark Dawson, for their tireless efforts on behalf of Middle East freedoms. Also, I value tremendously the research by and input from congressional fellow Tera Dahl, human rights activist Faith McDonnel, JD Gordon, Tom Harb, John Hajjar, Eblan Farris, "Major Thomas Knowlton," David Major, as well as the encouragements offered by Greg and Claudia Evans and Dr. Jim and Becky Davies.

My thanks in Europe go first to member of the European Parliament and deputy Chair of the EPP Jaime Mayor Oreja (Spain) and European Ideas Network director Guillermo Maria Cazan Martinez for their endorsement and support, as well as staffer Michael Valbuena for his diligent attention; I must also thank EPP member of European Parliament Kelam Tunne (Estonia) and former Socialist member Paolo Casaca for their relentless solidarity with the cause of freedom. I also wish to thank former Prime Minister of Spain José María Aznar, now president of the think tank FAES in Madrid, along with the latter's leaders for hosting me at their strategic seminars.

In the Middle East, I am grateful to seasoned journalist Karam Menassa for his regional research support as well as to Magdi Khalil and Adel Guindi from Egypt, Ibrahim Ahmed Beja from Sudan, and Sami Khoury and Roy Tohme from Lebanon. I wholeheartedly thank the many intellectuals and scholars who wrote in defense of my ideas when they were misrepresented, particularly Florida Atlantic University Professor Robert Rabil, National Review writer Mario Loyola, Shia liberal writer Mustafa Geha, Middle East Studies expert Cinnamon Stillwell, Harvard-trained scholar Charles Jacob, Egyptian writer for the liberal Elaph Essam Abdallah, and many others. And my thoughts go also to the departed abolitionist and writer Sam Cotton, Sudanese scholar Dominic Mohammed, Anglo-Swiss legal expert David Littmann, and Lebanese erudite Fuad Afram Boustany, with whom I have had decades of intellectual exchanges.

In the media, my warm thanks goes to chairman Roger Aisles, Bill Shine, and the dynamic teams at the wider Fox News family who continue to trust me as their Middle East and Terrorism expert. I would also like to thank the tireless Lou Dobbs at Fox Business Channel and Raymond Arroyo at EWTN and their teams. My gratitude also extends to my many friends at BBC, France 24, Russia Today, CTV, VOA, CBN, al Arabiya, Sky News, al Hurra, and national Arab and Middle Eastern TV networks, in addition to al Siyasa daily of Kuwait, al Watan Alarabi weekly from Egypt, and the many Mediterranean, European and Canadian sites as well. I thank writer Edwin Black, publisher of The Cutting Edge, Carol Taber, publisher of Family Security Matters, the History News Network, Newsmax Magazine, Political Mavens, as well as the many good anchors, producers, and friends I have met and conversed with through dozens of radio shows.

My global greeting goes to my many readers, fans and supporters on Facebook, Twitter, and in the blogosphere, whose encouragements are a constant boost to my writing. I have also found encouragement from and through foundations and institutes, including the CI Center, the Center for a Secure and Free Society, the London Center, the Heritage Foundation, The Bourse Toqueville, and many think tanks. And among my numerous friends, so many I cannot name them all, I want to salute two WWII heroes and their wives, Paul and Marylyn Cutler and Diane and Norm Elson, for the familial support they have extended to me. I must also acknowledge the wisdom of my university professors on both sides of the Atlantic, as well as the diplomats, military personnel and officers, scientists, NGO leaders, writers, bureaucrats, politicians, members of governments, and lawmakers I have had and continue to have as friends around the world and with whom I have exchanged views, which help me to enrich my analysis. This book has also been refined by discussions I've had at the defense, national security, and democracy agencies and departments who have been inviting me to offer seminars to their members.

And in the end, I cannot but send my warm regards to my sister, Liliane, always caring about my wellbeing, and my older brother, Sami, who shepherded my first teenager steps into the intellectual realm. Beyond our world, my thoughts go to those dear ones who left us, always too early, including furry companions. And until we meet again, I offer this book in the memory of my father, Halim, who shaped my ethics, and to my mother, Hind, who shaped my heart.

Washington D.C., January 3, 2014

INTRODUCTION

IT WOULD BE AN UNDERSTATEMENT TO SAY THAT U.S. foreign policy in the Middle East faces significant challenges today. In fact, America is involved in deep and unprecedented crises in one of the world's most dangerous and critical regions, stretching from North Africa to the Afghan borders with China. Since the Jihadi attacks of September 11, 2001, the United States has intervened in the region, waging wars, implementing sanctions, and sending foreign aid, all to ensure its own security in the homeland, to defend its citizens and interests as well as those of its allies in the Greater Middle East, and to maintain the regional economic stability that is needed by the world economy. Even before 9/11, Washington, D.C., had created an extensive web of diplomatic alliances and initiatives and maintained a strong military presence from the Atlantic to the Indian Ocean. Such measures, necessary during the Cold War to confront the Soviets and needed since the collapse of the Warsaw Pact to push the Middle East toward peace and progress, expanded multifold after al Qaeda's attacks in the first year of the third millennium. While many of the interventions of the past decade were deemed vital to strike back at global terror, the intended outcomes of the massive post-9/11 financial, military, and political efforts appear directly inverse to the actual results on the ground. The Arab world, Iran, Turkey, and the adjacent regions of the Sahel, central Asia, and the Horn of Africa have become battlefields, continually engaged in or on the edge of war. Significantly, they comprise a region where freedom and democracy are under constant duress. Ironically, over the past five years—a time during which considerable efforts have been made to stabilize the region—the Middle East has fostered the deepest crises ever faced by the United States.

America's image in the eyes of the region's populations has changed since 2009. The spread of anti-Americanism among surging Islamist movements has widened and deepened. Washington has argued that the elimination of terror leader Osama bin Laden has put al Qaeda on the path to decline. Reality refutes this assertion as well. Despite the killing of bin Laden in Pakistan, of Anwar al Awlaki in Yemen, and of other senior al Qaeda operatives by various means, the organization, and above all the movement, has prospered in the Arab world and other Muslim-majority countries. From Somalia to Mali and Libya, al Qaeda's networks have spread out and grown in immeasurable dimensions since the invasion of Iraq. The Jihadists have increased their strikes there since the United States withdrew in 2011. In Syria, the Nusra Front and "Dahesh" have infiltrated the opposition to the Assad regime and are supported by affiliates in Lebanon, Iraq, and groups linked to al Qaeda. The global Jihadi Salafi threat is far greater now in 2014 than ever before.

Americans were told repeatedly by their administration after 2009 that the Iranian regime has been kept in check, that economic sanctions are biting, and that Iran is more isolated than ever before. Furthermore, during the fall of 2013, Washington engaged the Khomeinist regime in a dialogue that encompassed building an agreement that would limit the nuclear ambitions of Tehran and move toward a possible normalization of relations. On November 23, a "deal" was announced whereby Tehran's regime committed to slow down its nuclear production in return for the lifting of some sanctions. The Obama administration claimed a success in its Middle East policy, yet reality on the ground again demonstrates otherwise. Despite what some see as a promising Obama-Iran détente, Tehran's ruling elite is still in place and the Iranian Revolutionary Guard, the Pasdaran (the hard core of the regime), is more powerful than ever and remains in control of the country's economy and political structure. Moreover, the ayatollahs continue to direct their networks to intervene in Iraq's sectarian fighting, particularly after the withdrawal of the American armed forces in 2011. They have been supplying the

Assad regime in Syria with men and materiel to combat the opposition. They have expanded their strategic support of Hezbollah in Lebanon, manipulated cells against Kuwait, Bahrain, and Saudi Arabia, and extended their reach to the Red Sea, West Africa, and the Americas. Iran's global influence in 2014 is much more dangerous than in the previous decade. Tehran's nuclear program, despite U.S. engagement, international talks, and the more recent "deal," has not been strategically and comprehensively stopped, and Russian and Chinese vetoes remain effective in defending the Iranian and Syrian regimes at the United Nations when these regimes are questioned about their human rights and terrorism records.

The greatest disaster for the region's nascent democratic movements, however, has been the systematic abandonment of its secular civil society forces as they confront both the dictatorships of the past and the rising tide of Islamist movements and regimes. Over the past five years, and despite the promise made by Washington to the peoples of the Greater Middle East after 9/11 to move freedom forward and stand with civil societies as they struggle for liberty, the U.S. administration has initiated the greatest retreat from supporting freedom since post-WWI treaties and arrangements undermined Woodrow Wilson's Fourteen Points. As we look around the Middle East since the explosion of what was called the Arab Spring, we see a transfigured region, with fewer secular dictators but with new authoritarian powers that are more totalitarian in nature, reminding us of the transition from empires to fascist states in the Europe of the 1930s. The irony of the Arab Spring was its mutation from blooming popular movements in the first month of 2011 to a full Islamist winter in 2013. Tunisia, Libya, and Egypt, with ripple effects in Morocco, Jordan, and Yemen, have been witnessing the ascendance of Salafist regimes and forces. And where the Salafis have failed, the other Islamists of the region dominate the scene, as in Lebanon with Hezbollah and in Iraq with the Mahdi militias.[1] In addition to Islamists dominating country after country, civil war continues to rage in Syria, terror strikes in Iraq and Lebanon, and civil strife spreads across North Africa and parts of Arabia.

The greatest disaster, then, is not the relentless war waged by the Jihadists against Western interests (for that is part of the 9/11 conflict, which, as predicted a decade ago, is and will be a long one). The true catastrophe has been that, in the face of genuine (and long overdue) civil society uprisings, Western democracies have intervened late (if at all) and with the wrong partners. In Egypt and Tunisia, Washington stood idle as the Muslim Brotherhood and the Nahda Party[2] stole the revolutions (as the Arab liberals described it and Secretary of State John Kerry admitted months later), yet continued to call the transformation of the region an Arab Spring.[3] In Libya, by not distinguishing clearly between secular and Islamist Salafi militias within the rebel forces, U.S. administration policies, in all practicality ignored the Jihadi militias' threat after the revolt, and a U.S. ambassador and three CIA employees paid the price in Benghazi. In Syria, three years after beginning to draw one red line after another, more than 120,000 Syrian civilians have been slaughtered and chemical weapons have been used, and America's foreign policy has been blocked at the U.N. Security Council by Russia and China. The surging Syrian revolt was practically abandoned, not just to Assad's brutal methods, but also to the claws of al Qaeda's affiliates. Instead of striking at the chemical weapons caches, as it promised it would during the summer of 2013, the U.S. administration backed off and resorted to a Russian diplomatic initiative, which has not yielded an end to the civil war. Liberals and democrats in the Arab world have grown extremely frustrated with Washington's flip-flopping on matters of human rights and liberties in the region. While the U.S. administration brags about its role in inspiring the youth in Arab countries to protest for change, these same youth regard it as a collaborator with the new authoritarians, the Islamists.

In Iran, a similar frustration has filled the hearts and minds of youth, women, and minorities. In 2009, two years before the Arab uprisings, an Iranian revolt, potentially the country's own and earlier political Spring, created waves in the region. In June of that year, more than a million men and women, mostly young, marched in the streets of Tehran to protest the falsified results of a presidential election. The movement mutated into a revolt called the Green Revolution and was in dire need of international support. Sadly, the Obama administration refused to stand by the protesters openly, thus appearing to validate the smashing of a movement that could have proven capable of wiping out the ayatollah regime two years before the Arab Spring. The Iranian revolution thus collapsed, and with that collapse, any hope for regime change to positively affect the region's stability and freedoms also died.

Within half a decade, two major revolutions—one in the Arab world and the other in Iran—could have weakened global terror and defeated Jihadi ideologies south and east of the Mediterranean. Unfortunately, Western policies, U.S. attitudes in particular, failed this rendezvous with history and assisted, either directly or indirectly, the rise of the Islamists, the spread of the Jihadists, and the survival of a few dictatorships. This was a damaging setback to secular democrats, the backbone of free civil societies in the region. More perturbing is the fact that current U.S. policy (and Western diplomacy in general) toward the Middle East lacks a comprehensive strategy, and in some cases the political will, to change the course of events. In short, without a dramatic reform of American and international policy toward the Arab world, Iran, and the adjacent regions, what lies ahead is even more dangerous. The failure to reform policy could lead that region of the world toward extreme peril, including genocides, and through a long, dark political age.

Between 2001 and 2009, the United States had a tremendous opportunity to invest its immense resources, or at least a part of its resources, in Iraq, Afghanistan, and around the world to counter al Qaeda and the Iranian regime and to build social and political resistance movements in North Africa, the Levant, the Arabian Peninsula, Iran, and other important subregions such as central and south Asia, the Horn of Africa, and the Sahel. The conditions were optimal for creating bonds with civil society groups, helping them form nongovernmental organizations (NGOs), and giving them a voice in the media and in international forums. Unfortunately, while the Bush presidency had a narrative that went along with the idea of pushing "freedom forward" and "spreading democracy," the Bush bureaucracy pushed back. From within the government, the bureaucracies within the State Department and Homeland Security, and the bulk of the administration's cultural advisers, aided by aggressive Islamist lobbies in Washington, sank Bush's support for the battle of democracy in the region. U.S.-based TV and radio channels funded by Congress beginning in 2003 and tasked with supporting democratic voices in the region's own languages defected and deviated from their mission. The region's liberals did not hear from America, and the American public did not see the region's liberals. There was no bridge built between the region's liberals and America even though the United States spent an enormous amount of money. In short, the campaign to partner with the forces of democracy was intelligently sabotaged from within by political pressures. Worse, the Islamist lobbies, with the Muslim Brotherhood and pro-Iranians competing within the Beltway, slammed the Bush administration with efficient accusations of "Islamophobia." These lobbies described as Islamophobic all efforts aimed at backing seculars in the Arab world and Iran, and thus at containing the Islamists. They said these efforts, by targeting Muslims, constituted religious and racial bigotry. They used America's political culture against America's national security with the full consent of the country's mainstream academia and media. By the end of 2008, the democracy offensive in the Middle East, funded and morally backed by the White House and its neoconservative supporters, was decelerated and eventually halted. The new era in Washington, beginning with the election of Barack Obama as president of the United States, abruptly ended U.S. backing of Middle Eastern democrats and unleashed support for the Islamists. Failure under Bush became policy under Obama.

After the terrorist attack in Benghazi in 2012 and the Boston Marathon bombing in 2013 by Jihadi terrorists, many called for a review of America's posture in the war against terrorism. Yes, a review was needed, but to achieve the best course correction for Middle Eastern policy, the realities of what was truly necessary first had to be recognized and addressed. The first decade of the millennia was crucial for pushing back against the Jihadists led by al Qaeda and the Iranian regime and the radical Islamists mobilized by the Muslim Brotherhood and funded by

Wahabi private circles. Under the Bush administration, from 2001 to 2009, billions of dollars were spent in the global War on Terror. Thousands of lives were sacrificed, and the American economy bled in order to support the effort. The direction of U.S. policy, its philosophy, and its goals were logical—to defeat an enemy and attempt to win the hearts and minds of the people in the region. But the war of ideas waged by the United States to turn its military achievements into political successes on the ground was doomed.

Why would I claim we need a correction to our foreign policy and to our perception of national security as it pertains to the Middle East, its limping revolutions, and its struggling civil societies? The war of ideas stalled due to political pushback during the Bush administration, but the succeeding administration performed an intentional and major strategic policy turn with catastrophic consequences for the region. In its first weeks in office, the Obama administration declared its intention to unilaterally end a war with combatants who had no intention of ending hostilities themselves. This meant a withdrawal from Iraq without having accomplished the ultimate strategic goals of the American presence there, a pullout from Afghanistan before defeating the Taliban, and a radical change in American political discourse on the confrontation with the Jihadists and, in general terms, with the radical Islamists.

After September 11, 2001, a new era had begun. America was gearing up to contain the Jihadists and support the democrats in the Greater Middle East. This determined optimism spread among youth, human rights activists, and minorities throughout the Arab world and Iran. Washington was seen by them as a beacon of hope after decades of abandonment during the Cold War and a rough decade in the 1990s. Though democracy had improved on all continents, particularly in the former Soviet bloc, this was not the case in the Greater Middle East. After al Qaeda's attacks on the United States in September 2001 and the unified American decision to counterattack less than a month later, the underdogs in the region felt their moment had come. It was a period reminiscent of the turning point for the resistance movements in Europe in World War II when the United States entered the war after Pearl

Harbor. The subsequent removal of both the Taliban in Afghanistan and the Baathist regime in Baghdad was celebrated by the forces of change in the region. Strategic efforts to connect the West with the oppressed civil societies in the Middle East went forward. But in 2009, with the coming of a new administration ideologically aligned with the existing apologist bureaucracy and partnering with the Islamist lobbies, American foreign policy was transfigured. The War on Terror was dismantled as a concept, the notion of a global Jihadi threat was negated, and the principle of intervening to assist secular democrats was demonized. The Obama administration created an ideological and radical shift. Though the Obama camp had not openly revealed what its changes in foreign policy would look like during the 2008 campaign, in the primaries or in the national election, it started to implement them immediately after moving into the White House, inch by inch, even without popular support. There was a cleft between the radical Middle East agenda of the new administration and the voters who supported the candidate. Only the far left and the Islamist lobbies supported dismantling the resistance to Jihadi terror and abandoning the democratic forces in the region. Most of the mainstream voters who supported candidate Obama wanted a withdrawal of U.S. military forces but did not necessarily advocate a partnership with the Muslim Brotherhood.

With the change of policy, the Islamist lobbies and their allies were emboldened. They initiated a series of campaigns attacking supporters of the opposing view, including lawmakers, think tanks, regional experts, writers, and dissidents based in the West. The first stages of the their campaign against national security experts who advocated counter-Jihadi strategies and partnership with secular democrats in the region started, almost invisibly, with pressure on government agencies, particularly those in defense and national security. The lobbies cut the latter's ties to speakers, academic lecturers, and analysts who advised for engagement with Middle East liberals and containment of Islamists. During 2009 and 2010, as the Obama policies dismantled the containment of Islamists and denied aid to Arab and Iranian liberals, those who advocated the opposite policy were quietly sidelined, often thanks to the help of campaigns waged by Islamist lobbies against those dissidents. With a congressional majority aligning itself with the administration on partisan grounds, at least until the congressional midterm elections in November 2010, and with backing from Islamist regimes in the Middle East, including Qatar and Turkey, Washington turned against the policies it had operated under since 2001.

From the outset, the Obama administration rushed to send strong signals to the region's regimes and Islamist movements that a change was on its way. The new president's very first interview in 2009 was with al Arabiya TV. He said then that U.S. foreign policy, like a giant ship, needs time and determination to change course. And indeed, in the next four years the Beltway realignment occurred. Two events indicated that the retreat from "freedom forward" was happening. President Obama, in a speech in Cairo, said that he would be "resetting the button with the Muslim world" and criticized America for an error of judgment and erroneous behavior toward Arabs and Muslims. In reality, Obama was courting the Muslim Brotherhood, an opposition movement in Egypt and in many other Arab countries, a movement that, with the help of Qatar's petrodollars, had a growing influence in Washington and other capitals. The Cairo speech sealed a partnership with the Ikhwan that carried through the Arab Spring.[4]

A few months later, Obama sent another hazardous signal, this time in the direction of the ayatollahs of Iran. In June of 2009, as noted, a million demonstrators protested the regime's manipulation of the presidential election results. The Green Revolution was close to toppling the regime. Yet, during a press conference with a foreign state guest, the president messaged the Tehran regime, assuring them that America "won't meddle in Iranian internal affairs." The message was clear: The protesters would receive no U.S. assistance. The new U.S. approach of accommodation with Iran was launched. It would have consequences inside that country as its secular democrats were crushed by the Pasdaran, and consequences regionally as Iran's influence leaped from Iraq to Syria and Lebanon and across the Persian Gulf.

Thereafter, the U.S. executive branch was in full control; it reshaped the conflict from confrontation with the global Jihadists to an innocuous notion of "overseas contingency operations." In reaction to the Fort Hood terror attack of November 5, 2009, the Obama administration, instead of identifying it as a "Jihadi attack" or a Jihadi-motivated act of terror (as admitted by the perpetrator, Major Nidal Hassan), identified the event as "workplace violence." Month after month, the war was minimized, limited to counterterrorism strikes against individuals or police operations against criminals. The big picture faded, and the public was gradually demobilized despite the fact that the Jihadist and Iranian efforts were expanding and becoming more serious. And as the enemy disappeared from the geopolitical map read by U.S. administrators, potential allies in the Middle East were also demoted. In Washington, new political dynamics pointed to a potential partnership with the Muslim Brotherhood and a renewal of negotiations with Iran's Islamic Republic. According to the Iranian opposition, President Obama wrote two letters to Grand Ayatollah Ali Khamenei, the last one in May 2009, calling for a mutual engagement of the two governments after decades of tension, and after Iran supported attacks on U.S. and allied forces in Iraq during the occupation. The United States went from a program of containment of the Iranian leadership and support for the opposition to a policy of outreach to the Khomeinist regime. It is no wonder that the added economic sanctions intended to pressure Tehran's regime to move away from its nuclear ambitions availed absolutely nothing. This U.S. position came fully to light in the fall of 2013 with the open "engagement with Tehran."

As the new administration immediately shifted away from advancing democracy and toward engagement with the Islamists, the bloggers, youth groups, and women's movements in the region were on a collision course with their authoritarian regimes. The Obama administration changed the pro-democracy direction of American policy, but it could not divert the drive for democracy or overcome the need for it in the minds and hearts of youth in the Greater Middle East. Between 2009 and 2011, there was a divorce between Washington and the democracy forces of the region, resulting in a chasm that ultimately set the stage for the Arab Spring. Protest groups in the Arab world were clashing with the oppressive systems, regimes, and Islamists.

The two years between the change of policy in Washington and the Arab Spring revealed the extent of Obama's shift. As the narrative of the region changed and mutated online in a manner that heralded the proximity of revolution, Washington dodged and abandoned the secular democrats and courted the Islamists instead. Encouraged by their new protector, the latter organized to seize the opportunity that the protests against tyranny would bring. The democratic civil society groups became frustrated with the retreating U.S. policy and decided to take the matter into their own hands. The regimes of the Arab world, secure for decades in their palaces, did not believe the West would let them fall. The dictators did not comprehend that a new ideological elite had been changing the course of events in Washington. The strongmen of the region did not think the reformers could prevail without significant support from the United States. And since the statements from America clearly signaled a change from the ways of Bush, the regimes could not envision the coming revolutions.

By early 2009, the United States was drifting away from almost a decade of attempts to plant the seeds of democracy in the Middle East. The new administration had already declared, during the campaign in 2008, that it would proceed toward a tectonic change in foreign policy, particularly regarding the Middle East and the Arab and Muslim world, though without detailing the substance of the new policies. The actual changes to be implemented in the following four years were revealed and clearly outlined by the end of that first year: The region would see Washington moving away from the commitments put in place after 9/11. The administration was set on disengaging from the War on Terror, quitting Iraq and Afghanistan and "ending all wars," intent on moving forward, or backward, to a pre-9/11 mindset. The Obama agenda took very little time to materialize into reality. It was on June 4, 2009, that President Obama gave the speech at Cairo University titled "A New Beginning." In sum, the leader of the free world

announced that his country was wrong. This was the official beginning of an undeclared partnership with the Islamists, even though the
authoritarian regimes were obviously not happy with the hints. Later
in the month, the president, as we noted, stated that the administration would not side with the uprising in Tehran. By the summer, U.S.-
funded media were toeing the administration's line, lowering their
criticism of the Islamists and minimizing the message of their regional
critics. In the following months, every move in Washington indicated
that a generalized retreat from the political and military battlefields of
freedom in the Middle East had begun.

Revolutionary spasms by civil societies in the Middle East had been
occurring sporadically since the collapse of the Soviet Union, and the
internet brought a new tool to the region's struggling communities in the
late 1990s. Home pages and websites were mushrooming in cyberspace,
followed soon by social media and chat rooms. Between 2001 and 2008,
democracy activists from the region flocked to Washington seeking support and advice, first after the collapse of the Taliban in Afghanistan,
then after the numbers of democracy-seeking cadres multiplied following the fall of Saddam in 2003 and the Syrian withdrawal from Lebanon
in 2005. They were received at the State Department, the Pentagon, the
National Security Council, and various offices in the White House—
including the oval one. A very busy democracy industry grew within
the Beltway with ramifications in Brussels and other European capitals.
The mood in the West was to invest in women, youth, minorities, and
all social forces opposed to the radicals in the region. This global Western approach to gathering the region's dissidents, democracy activists,
and intellectuals was epitomized in an international convention held in
Prague under the auspices of presidents Bush, Václav Havel, and Lech
Walesa in 2006. By 2008, many NGOs were operating in the region
from headquarters in Washington and Brussels. The mood among the
reformers was characterized by high hopes, and revitalized efforts were
bustling within civil societies. The Arab and Iranian Springs were on
their way, at least in the minds of freedom activists who met in the real
world and online. User-generated content on YouTube and Facebook,

chat rooms, and blogs defending democratic ideals and the various causes of self-determination and freedom peaked.

But the signals sent out in the first few months of the Obama administration chilled the Middle East's liberal and reformist community. The political change promised by the new administration inside America became a change for the worse in its foreign policy. The Cairo speech, destined to engage the Muslim Brotherhood and their Islamist allies in the region, announced the new American guilt problem in Middle East policies. The administration seemed to be apologizing to the Islamists, not to the democrats of the Middle East. The mood turned darker when Washington sent letters of accommodation to Iran's ultimate leader, Ayatollah Khamenei, in the following months, frustrating the Iranian democratic opposition. These two open moves by the administration were clear indicators of a new policy in Washington, but it was the failing of the Iranian Spring that stirred me to action. The administration had changed direction in a radical way. It was not a return to the Clinton years, as many feared, but rather a new political philosophy produced by the academics of the Middle East studies elites, themselves funded by petrodollars. The ballistics of such policies were easy to project. A race was on between the Washington foreign policy moving to partner with the Islamists and the democratic youth of the region moving to rise against the dictators. It was time to bring awareness of the real struggle in the Middle East to the public in the West.

The first and foremost battle in the War on Terror came in the form of a war of ideas. But the most important battle was the one raging inside our own democracies, as Tony Blair, prime minister of Britain, stated more than once. It was a matter of informing or misinforming the public about realities in the Middle East. It boiled down to one direction or the other. Either most Americans would capture the notion that there is a dual security threat with ideological underpinnings exploding out of the region with an impact on national security, or they would fail to see it and thus would favor a more isolationist policy. The corollary to this battle of ideas was the ability of Americans to understand that to push back against the menace, they needed to ally themselves with like-minded forces in the region's civil societies. But the American public was not even made aware of the existence of freedom forces ready to join the battle. Between 2001 and 2008, many in the Bush administration attempted to build that bridge by investing money and time and conveying legitimacy. Many more in Washington's bureaucracy, however, incited by the Islamist lobbies, acted against partnership with the seculars and liberals of the region and pushed for collaboration with the Muslim Brotherhood and its allies.

During 2012, as presidential campaigns clashed over American attitudes and steps taken in the Greater Middle East, the region's Islamist forces pressed on to score as many points as possible before the elections were over. In Tunisia, the Nahda Party and its allies secured a majority in Parliament and formed the cabinet.[5] In Egypt, the Muslim Brotherhood gained a parliamentary majority and, as liberals were abandoned by Washington, managed to install their leader as the elected president of the country. In Libya, Salafi militias expanded further across the country, solidifying their bases in the Benghazi and Darna areas. Furthermore, Jihadi militias crossed Libya's borders into the Sahel to establish bases in Mali and Niger. In Syria, the original civil society demonstrations that erupted in March 2011 receded and were replaced with militarized guerrillas fighting a regime using extreme violence, and the ensuing conflict caused tens of thousands of casualties. Moreover, Iran's regime was dismissive of U.S. sanctions and clamped down even more harshly on its internal opposition. Throughout the region, Islamist political forces rapidly pushed to secure power in preparation for the change in administration that might occur in November 2012. The American public, totally absorbed by the presidential election and its debates on domestic issues, lost sight of the region's swift decline at the hands of the Islamists. On September 11, a few weeks before election day, an al Qaeda–linked group, Ansar al Sharia, attacked the U.S. consulate in Benghazi and burned the facility down to the ground. The terror attack raised a red flag over the assertion that the Arab Spring was going well and cast doubt about the certainty that al Qaeda was on the path to defeat. The Benghazi crisis could have re-shifted the national security debate, but critics failed to challenge Washington's version of the disaster in time before the election.

Short of a major change in direction by Washington in early 2013, the Mideast and North African crises could not but grow and become ever more severe. In Egypt, President Mohammed Morsi engaged in repression of his own secular opposition in November 2012. That led to massive demonstrations against his regime in the first six months of 2013 that culminated in his removal from power in July. Toward the end of 2013, Egypt declared the Muslim Brotherhood a terrorist organization. In Tunisia, Nahda pushed forth its countersecularism agenda while Salafi Jihadis began establishing bases in the country. In Jordan, the emboldened Brotherhood initiated stronger opposition to the constitutional monarchy of the Hashemites. The Ikhwan also took on an aggressive stance toward the government of the United Arab Emirates, which prompted retaliatory action by the police chief.

In Syria, through the summer of 2013, Jihadist groups seized the opportunity to spread out provided by the lack of U.S. internationally led initiatives on the ground. The Nusra Front, the al Qaeda–linked organization, penetrated the Syrian opposition to a point where it would be difficult for any nationwide leadership of the anti-Assad forces to dislodge them without major foreign support. Also by mid-2013, Hezbollah forces, backed by Iranian auxiliaries and Iraqi operatives, moved deeper into Syria in support of the Assad regime. These moves generated an increase in al Qaeda strikes inside Iraq and the propagation of skirmishes into Lebanon. Syria moved closer to a humanitarian disaster and the region closer to a generalized war. Farther east, the Taliban, taking the offensive in Afghanistan, conducted almost daily raids on NATO and Afghan military personnel. In Somalia, the Shabab were back on the offensive against African forces.[6] In Mali, French and African troops were battling the Ansar al Din in the north. And in Nigeria, Boko Haram were conducting terror campaigns against civilians while clashing with the regular army.[7] The Jjihadi wave reached the Central African Republic by December 2013 and January 2014. The global war between the Jihadists and their allies (including the Khomeinists of Iran) and the

United States and their allies had mutated into a much wider conflict with areas of confrontation covering broad swaths of planet Earth.

My grand goals in this book are to ensure that the American public and international community are made fully aware of the global strategies of the Jihadi forces and how these forces take advantage of Western failures while the civil societies in the Middle East and Northern Africa yearn to live in freedom and democracy. America's use of its global power, at least its official policy, has always been on the side of the weak and opposed to the authoritarians. That has been the case from the Great War through the Cold War: fighting Nazism, fascism, and communism. Based on the same principles, after 9/11 the United States moved to counter the terror forces of the Middle East and encourage freedom activists to rise.

However, the change of direction in 2009 contradicted a century-long effort to back democracy worldwide. This change of direction has indirectly generated larger Jihadi forces from Mali to Afghanistan. It has also provided the Iranian regime with greater incentives to expand its influence throughout the Persian Gulf into the Mediterranean.

My first aim is to open the eyes of readers and policymakers to the dangers of retreat, both military and political, from the global battlefield with al Qaeda and its Jihadi allies and the Iranian regime and its associates. As Europeans learned in the 1930s and 1940s, retreating from National-Socialists and fascists led to a near-universal disaster. A similar retreat by the United States from Salafi and Khomeinist ambitions and advances will practically surrender the region to regimes and organizations following agendas bent on reducing and eventually eliminating democracy. This leads me to state the second aim of my writings: to obtain freedom for the peoples of the Greater Middle East. After decades of missed chances, a historical opportunity opened that would permit hundreds of millions of men and women to rise against oppression. One pane opened in 2009 in Iran and another in the Arab world in 2011. The United States failed to support both uprisings—the Green Revolution of Iran and the Arab Spring—and left the region to the mercy of oppressors and violators of human rights. Washington failed the region's first wave of democratic revolutions. Instead, it engaged the two regional counter-revolutionary powers, the Muslim Brotherhood and the Iranian regime. I intend here to further warn against the consequences of failing freedom. Until now, sadly, it has been a long but lost Spring, thanks to a mistaken policy of accommodating the Islamists. But the struggle is not over; the lost Spring can yet be recovered. Some encouraging signs can be seen, but U.S. policy must now begin to meet the aspirations of those living in the region. The historical change that was expected in the Middle East was halted by a political change in America. The reset button for freedom can still be pushed, but only if Washington changes course again, this time toward *better* policies. With this book, I hope to contribute to an enlightened debate about a change in U.S. foreign policy in the Middle East in the years to come.

In 2014, encouraging signs have emerged. Egypt has conducted a popular referendum for a new moderate constitution and has been pushing back against the terror of Jihadists and the urban violence of the Muslim Brotherhood, secular forces in Libya and Tunisia are on the rise, and resistance to the Ayatollah of Iran is spreading in the region.

CHAPTER ONE

WESTERN FAILURE TO PREDICT THE 2011 UPRISINGS

I FORESAW WHAT WAS TO BE CALLED THE ARAB SPRING. I projected the impending eruption of civil societies in the region—the uprisings, the forces of change coming together from numerical majorities and from ethnic and religious minorities—and the strong readiness of the Islamists, including the Muslim Brotherhood and the Iranian regime, to encourage and take advantage of the changes. I was convinced a revolution had to happen, and I wrote a book on its inevitability.

In mid-2010, I told my publisher, "The revolts are coming. There is no doubt. They have actually begun." I was referring to the 2005 Cedars Revolution in Lebanon and the 2009 Green Revolution in Iran. I added, "They are already on the internet, on YouTube, and on Facebook. They are happening, but governments are not seeing them because their experts are looking elsewhere."

As in Beirut and Tehran, the masses were ready to rise. Youth had been debating intensely the necessity of moving and demonstrating against the regimes in power and reforming them. It was not clear, though, even to these future revolutionaries, whether they would go all the way to regime change or if their quest would only eventuate in reforms, albeit vast reforms. Regardless of how far they might ultimately carry their message, the forces of civil society across the region were ready to support them. The countries of the Middle East had lost several historic opportunities to advance freedom and democracy. From the botched postcolonial era to the failed post–Cold War decade to the post-9/11 confusion, the peoples of the region had remained confined inside their nation-states under ideological elites that suppressed them. The swelling tide of civil society protesters was about to challenge (and later overthrow) the dictatorships. But other forces—authoritarians mostly within the Islamist movements—were preparing as well. It was crystal clear—at least to me—that the foreshocks in the region would soon develop into a fearsome earthquake. It was a matter of time and of circumstances, but all signs indicated that circumstances could change at any time in any of the Arab countries. I was monitoring the indicators, but my premonition convinced me that the earthquake would happen within a year. I was even wondering whether my book announcing a "coming revolution" would actually be published before the revolutions came. It was, in fact, very close. My book appeared in November 2010, a month before the early tremors of the Spring were felt.

After predicting the change, I saw it burst into reality, and I was able, as it was taking hold in the region, to further project outcomes. It would take me another book to describe this life-altering, historical experience. One main reality I have discovered was the lack of readiness in the West to project the initial fallout from the Arab Spring.

EUROPE'S CONFUSED PROJECTIONS

The European governments held high stakes in the sociopolitical developments taking place south of the Mediterranean. Years before the Arab Spring, the European Union, particularly under the leadership of French president Nicolas Sarkozy, had pushed the project of the Euro-Mediterranean Partnership. On the surface, the concept was about economic cooperation between the wealthier, more advanced economies of Europe and the poorer developing regions of North Africa. The cooperation was widened to include the Levant, Syria, Lebanon, the Palestinian National Authority, and Turkey. Israel's inclusion was a measure of peace acceptance by Arab countries around the basin. I did, however, detect in my briefings at the European Parliament and with the center-right European Popular Party, which controlled the majority in Brussels, another layer of interest among Europeans in the fate of the region's cultures and peoples. Shocked by the events of September 11 and by the Jihadi terror attacks in Madrid and London, European lawmakers and politicians took a closer look at the radical forces south of the Mediterranean. The rise of Salafism and extremism was becoming evident. Europe's think tanks knew that the Islamists were the force that would challenge the ruling regimes in the region. Conservatives and socialists were rushing to establish dialogues with the Muslim Brotherhood of Egypt and Syria and with the Nahda Party of Tunisia.

In the winter of 2010, I was invited by the European Popular Party to participate in a strategic seminar in Vienna with European think tanks and Middle Eastern experts to reflect on which sociopolitical wave to expect next in the region. The conference was clearly interested in engaging the Islamists and finding the moderates among them. I made the case for a possible uprising among civil societies in the Arab world but was met with skepticism. The southern Mediterranean countries were perceived from the northern shores as being ruled by authoritarians who could only be challenged by the Islamists. The European position was correct with regard to the challengers. The Salafists—the only global, organized, and well-funded force—were planning to crumble the regimes in North Africa and the Levant. The debates on al Jazeera and in chat rooms were filled with evidence of that intention. But the Europeans failed to realize that the Islamists had been trying to bring down these mostly secular and once-socialist governments for decades. I argued during the Vienna seminar—and in conferences in Paris, Brussels, Rome, Madrid, and other capitals—that liberal secular groups in the Middle East should not be omitted from Western strategic planning. I drew charts explaining that while the Islamists were the largest organized coalition of militants, the reformers could mobilize the masses and force change on the regimes ahead of the Islamists if they were well

supported. I underlined the importance of engaging the youth movements, women, minorities, and reformers in the different countries. I
expressly called on the European center-right parties to encourage Arab
and Middle Eastern reformers to build political movements and parties
and eventually partner with them. I argued that the Euro-Mediterranean project, the Sarkozy dream, could not be achieved with the Pan-
Islamists, but required the participation of secular forces.

The European politicians could not see the vision I advanced. They
simply could not visualize any players other than the authoritarian regimes and their Islamist challengers. Despite the examples of Beirut and
Tehran, they did not believe that young men and women would wage
massive protests in Cairo, Tunisia, Damascus, and beyond and call for
freedom and democracy. European elites were ready to measure the
power of the Islamist parties and negotiate the future of the region with
their leaders, but they were reluctant to sit down and interact seriously
with the representatives of the seculars.

I suggested to the European Parliament's largest bloc that it call for
a conference in Brussels to which hundreds of secular reformers could
be invited to discuss the future of a liberal Middle East, even though
the governing regimes would not see such a move as positive. Such a
global event, years or even months ahead of the Arab Spring, would have
united the early waves of protest from Morocco to Syria and formed a
regional democratic force. Instead, experts from the European Union,
on the Levant and North Africa, dedicated their energies and resources
to bringing the Islamists to Brussels and other capitals and engaging
them. Europe was already creating its future partner in the uprisings
to come—the Muslim Brotherhood and their allies—and neglecting its
natural partner and, in fact, its ally—the like-minded secular democrats. I knew Europe was going in the wrong direction and wondered
why the Westerners closest to the Arab world, and those assumed to be
the most experienced in the region's affairs, would choose to dialogue
with an authoritarian partner rather than a democracy-seeking one.

As in the United States, the oil-funded European academia and, by
ripple effect, the media's elite were penetrated by the Islamists. As I have

explained more than once, the eyes and ears of the West in the Greater Middle East are its political apologists. Interestingly, the apologist networks had a hierarchy of preferences. All regimes in the region were considered to be representatives of the legitimate anti-Western movement; hence they were protected by elite Western apologists. But socialist Pan-Arabist regimes such as Saddam Hussein's, Muammar Gaddafi's, and Bashar Assad's were seen as more in tune with their peoples than the mostly secular pro-Western governments of Hosni Mubarak, Zine El Abadine Ben Ali, Ali Saleh, or the monarchies of the Gulf. On a higher plateau, the apologists opted for the Islamist regimes, such as Saudi Arabia, Qatar, and Sudan, over the secular ones. It became clear that Western elites saw the Salafi Islamists, including the Muslim Brotherhood, as the ultimate partners of the West. Two reasons can be given for that choice. The first rests on the significant influence the intellectuals of the Brotherhood had developed inside Western educational and media organizations, influence that allowed them to convince decision makers that the only alternative to the dictatorships was a well-organized Islamist movement with which the West could do business. To European and Western politicians, this was a positive offer. It was pragmatic and corresponded to their perception of the Middle East. Since they did not believe in the actual existence of Middle Eastern reformers, Europeans and many of their counterparts in North America came to the conclusion that if a change should occur, it would come at the hands of the Islamists, framed as "moderates," not the seculars, perceived as ineffectual and in some cases Western-like, and thus not really native.[1]

There was, however, another (yet latent) reason that convinced European policymakers and bureaucrats of the necessity of an Islamist partnership if change should occur in the region. With the growth of urban Jihadism in Europe's cities and the terror acts committed in many European countries by Salafists, Brussels grew weary of enduring a transformation that appeared to loom over the continent's foreseeable future. Since the Muslim Brotherhood's organizations were the most prominent in Europe among Muslim communities, the conclusion was simple: If a deal was struck with the Brotherhoods of the Arab world, they would rein in the émigré communities in Europe and impose moderation and stability. The Europeans believed that if they partnered with the Brotherhood, the Brotherhood would deal with the extremists and eventually counter the al Qaeda types.[2] The secular democrats of North Africa and the Levant were deemed useless on both counts. The seculars did not have a regional representation and, according to Western experts, could not challenge the ruling regimes in the region. The logic was that if the Islamists were not able to trigger successful revolts against dictatorships, how could the liberals do it? The West was dead wrong on what would become the Arab Spring. As I argued in my warnings, the secular democrats *could* trigger the revolts, but they needed support to sustain them. The Islamists, I concluded, could not crumble these Muslim-majority regimes but would be able to seize the revolutions from the inside, especially if the West supported them. And sadly, that is exactly what happened in mid-2011.

By June 2010, there were no indicators in the West that governments and intellectual elites had yet detected the change of mood in the Middle East at the popular level, nor had they heard the increasing calls for freedom and democracy. Western failure to see the Spring coming had two causes: a distrust of the capacity of Arab and Middle Eastern masses to take to the streets and provoke a real change on the one hand, and a misperception of the readiness of the Islamists as a force that would seize the moment of the revolution and take over the reins of power on the other hand. Because of this double failure, the governments and experts in Europe and the United States and the West in general did not see the revolts coming.

U. S. FAILURE IN PREDICTING THE ARAB SPRING

The political establishment in Washington, D.C., was also ignoring these realities, both in the executive branch and in private think tanks. By the time President Barack Obama spoke in Cairo in 2009, his administration had already changed course from the Bush administration's "freedom forward" policy toward a "disengaging from the Middle East" policy. As soon as he took office, Obama and his team prepared for a general pull-out from the region and for a cessation of "democracy activities." The advisers within the White House and the State Department, but also at the main think tanks backing the administration, were pushing the notion that the region had two main players: the regimes on the one hand and the Islamists on the other. The forces of civil society and secular democrats were disregarded. And apparently, once the retreat from the Arab world was started, the partnership with the Muslim Brotherhood and other Islamists began. Diplomats, think tanks, and intelligence circles initiated programs to reach out to the various parties and organizations representing the Islamists in the region, from Morocco to Egypt, from Tunisia to Turkey. By doing so, the Obama administration ignored the forces opposing the Islamists, that is, the liberals and democracy groups. Obviously, one main reason for this sidelining of secular democrats was the influence the Muslim Brotherhood network had inside the Obama administration, particularly at the State Department, the White House, Homeland Security, and the U.S.-funded democracy agencies. It is logical to conclude that this influence barred the Arab liberals and seculars from obtaining support in Washington. Thus, when the youth took to the streets in Tunis and Cairo in 2011, the Obama administration had developed bridges only to the Islamist leaders in exile or to their militants inside these countries. Hence, when the Arab Spring arrived, Washington was not ready to meet its secular forces halfway. Instead, it partnered with the Islamists, meeting them more than halfway, even to the point of forming the new incoming governments.

During the fall of 2010, I looked at the annual national security assessment, a document produced by the director of national intelligence to evaluate all foreign policy developments worldwide that have potential impact on national security. I found no trace of findings that projected potential waves of uprisings in the Greater Middle East. The State Department's human rights documents and briefings also lacked indications that the region's civil societies were about to erupt. Throughout the year, seminars I offered were often attended by national security analysts from government and the private sector. Most of the participants seemed to ignore many aspects of the political dynamics inside Arab societies, such as the yearning for freedom and the existence of organized liberal groups opposed to the regimes and the Islamists at the same time. It was among the U.S. military and some of the intelligence services that I discovered a readiness to understand the possibility of political uprisings in the region.[3] Indeed, as I interacted with various military branches during my lectures and presentations, and particularly as I was finishing my book in 2010, I heard corroborating stories. These participants, having served on the battlefields of Afghanistan and Iraq and engaged civil societies there—particularly during what were called the surges in both countries—had had the chance to listen to women, students, workers, artists, and entrepreneurs who expressed their rejection of the fundamentalists. Many Iraqis of all backgrounds and Afghan workers in social and human rights domains have told U.S. soldiers, Marines, and local defense officials that the time for change has come and the time for representative democracies must begin. But under the Obama administration, attention had shifted to engaging the next landlords of the region, the Islamists. In Iraq, Washington was ignoring the secular and liberal alliance led by former prime minister Iyad Allawi. In Afghanistan, the U.S. administration was jumping hurdles to find takers from the Taliban quarters with whom they could engage. High-level American officials often hoped the conflict would be settled with a so-called moderate wing of the Taliban. Washington made no effort to organize and mobilize the small but determined nongovernmental organizations (NGOs) aiming at resisting the return of the Jihadists to Kabul.

And such was the scenario for the rest of the Greater Middle East. Officials of the Obama administration and the think tanks backing them were desperately seeking connections to the Islamists, from Morocco to Pakistan, while completely ignoring the forces of civil society. This attitude reflected the grand paradigm of the petrodollar-funded Middle East studies in North America. For while the region's civil societies were witnessing the development of a young and vocal liberal movement, U.S. policy was headed in the opposite direction. It did not see the Arab Spring coming because its advisers and experts were on the side of what they saw as the only alternative to Arab regimes, the Islamists, not on the side of secular democrats.

But the failure to predict the social upheaval in the region was not limited to the U.S. administration. Democracy agencies, think tanks, and other private sector organizations dedicated to the study of the region or the promotion of democracy also failed to detect the true nature of the foreshocks in the region. The leading government-funded agencies—such as Endowment for Democracy, the United States Institute of Peace, as well as international arms of the two major parties, the International Democratic Institute and International Republican Institute— had no findings by the end of 2010 that the region would go ablaze in 2011. However, after the uprisings began, officials from said agencies rushed to claim that it was their educational and training seminars that helped or prompted the youth in Egypt and other Arab countries to demonstrate. That was truly not the case. The training seminars instead prepared the attendees to work on reforming the government on long-term conditions, not to crumble the regimes in revolutionary fashion. The strategies of the democracy agencies mostly centered on partnering with the Islamists (as well as other groups) to bring about change *gradually*. That is what I heard and saw, and I argued the point with them during my participation in seminars, briefings, and meetings involving representatives of these agencies on both sides of the Atlantic. The agencies did not see the Arab Spring coming.

Interestingly, even those foundations that worked to support democratization in the Middle East did not perceive the social and political readiness in the region to take to the streets. Skepticism was deep. During December 2009, almost one year before the Tunisian revolt, I met with the leaders of my own foundation, which is dedicated to defending democracies, and thus democrats, in the Arab world and Iran, and had produced many efforts and publications toward that end. When asked about the subject of my next book, I told them the "coming revolutions in the Middle East." They smiled and told me: "Are you going to spend your time researching and writing about popular revolts in the Arab world? They won't happen. How can we convince our donors to fund your position?" At that point, I realized that Washington was not prepared to see what was already happening in the region. For if my own foundation, the best informed on this issue, refused to see what was going to happen, who could? A few days later, I resigned from the foundation and quit the world of think tanks. The millions of dollars dedicated to the promotion of democracy, both in the public and private sectors, could not even enable the diplomats or the activists to understand the subject of their assignment. It was impossible for the West to be ready for the future.[4]

THE FALL'S LAST WARNINGS

In November 2010, after one year of witnessing denial in Washington and Brussels, I felt the moment was right to issue strong warnings to the West that the East was about to experience a fundamental series of revolutions. I addressed several public audiences and briefed a few members of Congress to sound the alarm. The first main event was hosted by the Heritage Foundation in Washington, D.C. Having hosted the launching of three of my books since 2005, Heritage became—without planning to be so—the first think tank to give me a platform to predict the Arab Spring and its aftermath. Obviously, that day, the prestigious institution located near the U.S. Capitol was not gearing for a major political event, but for a simple lecture. The guests, however, many of whom I had worked with for years, included representatives from various Middle East communities and countries. The representation of Arab, Iranian, Egyptian, Lebanese, Syrian, Libyan, Tunisian, Iraqi, Kurdish, Coptic, Sudanese, and many other groups was highly symbolic. Middle Eastern women and youth were also well represented. The event took on the appearance of an omen regarding the developments that were to take place thousands of miles away in just two months. I presented my findings and concluded that civil societies in the region had reached their apex of tolerance with oppression and that revolts were coming. Giving the examples of Beirut and Tehran, but also the secession of South Sudan, I argued that Arab societies are not immune to democratic revolution.

Arab youth were online, and Facebook and YouTube were telling us about their feelings. The trajectory was crystal clear—if one measured the depth of the frustrations and compared them to the continuous oppression, the outcome was undeniable: uprisings. In reaction to my presentation, Arab and Middle East activists present at the event praised the findings and confirmed that in their own societies back in the region, human rights groups, dissidents, and civil society organizations had been escalating the struggle against dictatorship. Magdi Khalil, an Egyptian democracy activist, said, "Your briefings to Congress are the first shot in the revolutions to come. Our youth groups have begun to take to the streets. All that we're waiting for are the masses to respond." The Middle East dissidents knew that a movement had started but were not sure how the West would react.

The second event in Washington was a briefing to members of Congress and staff at a lunch on Capitol Hill. Reactions were positive on the principle of "freedom forward," particularly that the U.S. Congress had been supportive of Iranian, Lebanese, and South Sudanese liberation movements earlier in the decade. Most attendees were skeptical about the possibility of a mass movement on the "Arab street." The writings of Western intellectuals, particularly American journalists such as Thomas Friedman, had led most readers to believe that the so-called Arab street is a one-way street: faithful to the dictators despite the growing influence of the Islamists, or accepting of the latter if they dislodged and replaced the rulers. In short, Western academia had convinced the public that the peoples of the region were either with the dictators or with the Islamists. Arab liberals were portrayed as marginal in the eyes of the masses and disconnected from the feelings of civil societies. In the world of think tanks, there was no chance for regular people in the Arab world, if they were not connected to regimes, militaries, or Islamists, to rise against dictatorships. At some point, this attitude was borderline racist. Ironically, the progressive circles in the West were arguing that the peoples of the region cannot be progressives too. Left-wing media asserted that women, youth, minorities, and civil society across the Arab world were naturally inclined to accept authoritarianism and Islamism as part of their culture. It almost reads as if some races, ethnicities, or nationalities are not fit for democratic struggle. This wrong-headed assertion was reinforced initially by the notion of "cultural relativism," cultivated by academics such as Edward Said. The author of *Orientalism* had argued, generally, that Westerners should not meddle in framing Arab culture and should refrain from exporting liberal democracy into their midst, or else they would be acting as imperialists. But it was precisely this so-called anti-Orientalist position promoted by intellectuals like Said that convinced Western public opinion that "Arabs can't be democratic." A grave mistake because, as the Arab Spring proved, each civil society in the Greater Middle East has its democrats and its authoritarians. The outcome of the struggle between them will depend on historical circumstances and on the backing of the international community. Unfortunately, the West was disabled from understanding that secular democrats in these societies were representatives of the younger elements who could create better futures for these nations. Europe and North America failed to understand that the Islamists were *not* the only alternative to the secular authoritarian regimes and that the secular liberals were the real alternative to the Islamists. Hence, when the Arab Spring arrived, the West could not distinguish between the true freedom fighters and the usurpers of power on the streets of Arab cities. Eventually, and because of unpreparedness, chanceries confused the Arab Spring with the best-organized force on the ground and those best funded by petrodollars, namely the Islamists. This equation would lead the United States and Europe to hesitate when the uprisings started and to allow Islamists to take advantage of the shifting ground as the dictatorships collapsed.

The last event I addressed in 2010 was on Capitol Hill at the joint invitation of senatorial and NGO committees. The Center for Security Policy asked me to project major developments for 2011 in the region. I stressed that Arab societies would witness the beginning of upheavals that had been delayed for decades but that a race would ensue between the better-organized Islamists and the relentless younger liberals as dictatorships went down. I also projected that ethnic minorities across the region, emboldened by the general mood for change, would call for more autonomy than ever before, particularly in Sudan, Iran, and Algeria. As in previous events and seminars, participants were polite but skeptical. They did not, could not, subscribe to the notion that they were weeks away from cataclysmic changes in the Greater Middle East.

That year of 2010 was one of the most frustrating to me. I was predicting that earth-shattering events would hit an important region of the world while decision makers, analysts, and opinion makers were not yet able to see what I had seen. This experience is the equivalent of being above a giant chessboard by the sea, watching the moves on two sides, seeing a wave approaching the shore from afar, but being unable to convince the chess players that the tsunami is ineluctably coming. Ironically, I was intellectually relieved from this heavy responsibility only when the demonstrations hit Tunis and, later, Tahrir Square. My work was no longer a prediction with few believers. The revolution had become reality, and three years later it is seen as a veritable epoch in history.[5]

EARLY HESITATIONS

During the first weeks of the uprisings of 2011 in North Africa, one common characteristic of Washington's position regarding the demonstrations was . . . hesitation. The Obama administration, totally unprepared for the popular wave that was washing strongmen and regimes away in the Middle East, was taken by surprise. The Tunisian revolt happened so quickly that the United States did not have enough time to evaluate the situation and decide how best to position itself between its authoritarian ally and civil society protesters. Tunisian students, workers, and women filled the streets and acted within the norms of peaceful protests. The Tunisian army stood on neutral ground before it abandoned President Ben Ali and made it possible for the revolt to succeed. Washington, perhaps wary of the final outcome of the strife, slowly moved away from its hesitance and toward recognizing the results of the uprising.[6]

In Egypt, the Obama administration also tergiversated for many days between Mubarak and the protesters. As the demonstrations by Egyptian

youth hit Tahrir Square, Obama and his spokespersons called for calm
and for allowing the issues to be "settled among Egyptians," using words
reminiscent of the terms used by Washington during the peak of Iran's
demonstrations in June 2009.[7] But as the numbers of protesters soared in
central Cairo and civil society groups displayed determination in calling for the departure of Mubarak, the tone within the Beltway gradually
turned against the old ally. And as soon as the Muslim Brotherhood seized
part of Tahrir and their message was amplified by al Jazeera worldwide,
the White House shifted fully and also called on Mubarak to step down.
A mere reading of the evolution of U.S. statements during January 2011
clearly shows that the administration was not sure of the identity of the
demonstrators and their strength or of the particular participation of the
Islamists. Mubarak went from being a close U.S. ally to being treated as
an undesirable dictator in a matter of weeks. If anything, events in Egypt
demonstrated that the foreign policy establishment was not anticipat-
ing such an astonishing event. The establishment moved along with the
evolving facts on the ground but also made decisions based on previously
sought partnerships with the Muslim Brotherhood.

A similar equation emerged across the Arab Spring, from Libya to
Yemen to Syria. For U.S. bureaucrats, the forces of civil society were not
as well known as the key Islamist figures. During the early stages of the
revolts, public officials and commentators alike kept repeating, "But who
are these insurgents?" Unlike leaders of revolts in Eastern Europe, Latin
America, and Africa, the real leaders of the Arab youth movement were
unknown to both the American public and government officials. The
Arab youth's programs had not been debated in foreign policy circles or
forums.

In Libya, it took even longer to identify the protesters on the streets.
For days and weeks, the United States and Europe called them rebels
without identifying the political and militant forces on the ground,
even though it was clear to the Arab world that those who led the early
marches were students, former bureaucrats, judges, and diplomats as
well as dissident officers. The Salafists—including hundreds of Jihadists released from jails by Saif al Islam Gaddafi, son of Muammar, weeks

after the start of the Arab Spring in Tunisia and Libya—organized and joined the demonstrations, gradually mutating into armed militias. U.S. politicians and diplomats visiting Benghazi in the early part of 2011 could not distinguish between seculars and reformists. Similar situations occurred in Yemen and Syria, where Washington dawdled before it sided with the popular revolts, a delay that was used effectively by the Islamists to organize and seize control of the movements. Looking back at archives today, one can easily discern the hesitation and ambivalence of the United States toward the nascent and evolving Arab Spring. Some have argued that the Obama administration, or at least part of it, was cautiously moving parallel to measures taken by the Muslim Brotherhood, and what appears as hesitation was in fact coordination. We will address this theory later in the book, but on paper, and judging by statements and diplomatic activities, the general behavior of Washington's foreign policy establishment was one of surprise and disarray, with rapidly changing postures and ad hoc positions.[8]

In hindsight, both the administration and sympathizer think tanks within the Beltway praised the Arab Spring and the changes that followed. Often, over the years since the Tunisia revolt, many in the foreign policy establishment, particularly at the State Department, even took credit for the Arab Spring, almost hinting that the Obama administration was the inspirer of these revolutions.[9] Ironically, some in the opposing political camp in the United States argued in the same direction but for other reasons.[10] While governmental circles took somewhat abstract credit for helping Arab youth to rise for change, their critics in Congress, in the blogosphere, and on talk shows argued that the administration indeed was behind the Muslim Brotherhood in its attempted coup, organized to seize regimes in the region. The historical reality may lie somewhere else, as will be detailed later.

The fact is that before the revolts there were no indications that the Obama administration, or most academic institutions that provide advice to government, had projected—let alone predicted—the Spring. Not only was there no analysis in Washington and other Western capitals that drew strategic conclusions about what would actually develop in January 2011, but there was no serious research indicating that the forces of civil society were on the brink of revolt. The notion of an uprising was practically nonexistent on both sides of the Atlantic. The idea that youth, women, minorities, and activists for democracy would unite and eventually lead a successful popular movement to unsettle or even openly challenge an authoritarian regime was not a mainstream notion. Furthermore, unlike during the Cold War, when the names of Soviet and East European dissidents lit up the headlines of the press and the newscasts, the Middle Eastern reformers, leaders, student organizers, human rights activists—in short, dissidents—were not considered celebrities and were anonymous in the West. In a sense, the hesitation of the U.S. administration regarding the first waves of the Arab Spring emanated from two phenomena. One, ignorance of who was who in the region's freedom struggle; and two, effective lobbying by the Islamist pressure groups in the West, which succeeded in eliminating all their secular and liberal opponents from American and European debates on the region. The real question, which we will address later, remains: What caused the Western failure to predict the Arab Spring?

CHAPTER TWO

THE ARAB SPRING

FIRST WAVES

THE YOUNG TUNISIAN MAN MOHAMED BOUAZIZI walked into traffic and set himself on fire on December 17, 2010, to protest his abuse by authorities. The mood in his country had already reached a critical mass of frustration because of economic and political suppression.[1] The self-immolation of the young man is to the Arab Spring what the assassination of Archduke Ferdinand of Austria was to World War I: the trigger. But the spasms preceding the trigger were multiple and deserve notice.

In late 2010, demonstrations were taking place all across North Africa. In Algeria, Tunisia, and Egypt, the cause was high prices. In Libya and its diaspora, criticism of Gaddafi's regime had already reached significant levels. Meanwhile, in Yemen, opposition to its president, Ali Abdallah Saleh, was widespread. In many Arab countries, protests against police brutality, political suppression, and human rights abuses had increased significantly in the previous decade. In Egypt, the April 6 Movement and other similar civil society groups emerged to criticize arbitrary arrests and torture. In short, the ideas of the Arab Spring had already been spreading for years, but their expression in mass movements had been impeded by fear and divisions among activists.

The Bouazizi incident, however, set a spark to highly flammable social tinder.

Discontented ethnic minorities were also very active and moving toward their own spring. The Amazigh of Algeria had already organized several protest marches in their province of Kabylie under the leadership of the Movement for the Autonomy of Kabylie. One of their noted leaders, Ferhat Mehanni, told me that December that "the Kabyles cannot go back now; they will renew their spring." I answered that I hoped the Amazigh and other ethnic communities would eventually be helped by an Arab Spring led by democratic forces among Arabs. The year preceding the Arab Spring also witnessed a rise of activities internationally among Kurdish groups. Sherkoh Abbas, the U.S.-based Syrian Kurdish activist, informed me that "something has been going on inside the northeastern part of Syria where Kurds and Assyrian and Syriac Christians formed a local majority." I also met with Iranian Kurdish activists in Washington; they too were in political effervescence.[2]

With blogging and Facebook posts spreading everywhere, the virtual map of the Middle East by the end of 2010 was very different from the visible one. The authoritarian regimes did not see a serious threat coming from the Islamists and dismissed civil society activists as incapable of organizing a real revolution. The Islamists ignored the seculars and liberals while still fearing the regimes. The democracy activists did not believe they could actually trigger an all-out revolt and crumble regimes. Their highest expectation was a series of reforms by the rulers. And as we described in the previous chapter, the West was not ready to absorb the reality of a rapidly unfolding political change that would sweep through the Greater Middle East in just a few weeks. This strange and unusual situation in which none of the players expected that revolts could or would happen so quickly was representative of a world in denial. By mid-December 2010, the spasms multiplied in North Africa and the Levant. The revolutions were indeed coming. Small demonstrations were taking place in Algeria, Tunisia, and Egypt while dissidents were intensifying their internet struggle and organization throughout the region. The first major push for freedom, however, came from Sudan.

SOUTH SUDAN IS FREE

Indeed, the first dramatic development in the Arab Spring was the historic achievement of the people of southern Sudan. In 1924 while under British rule, Sudan was basically split into a northern Arabic-Islamic region and a southern African-Christian majority region. Since the 1956 independence of the Sudanese state, the African southern populations inside Sudan have been claiming self-determination and revolting against the Arab regime in Khartoum, culminating in a war that lasted from the late 1950s until 1972 and was rekindled in 1983. More than a million people were killed and millions more were displaced, yet the southern rebellion was ignored by the West. This conflict escalated after the 1989 coup led by Hassan Turabi and Omar al Bashir in Khartoum, which resulted in a Jihadi regime that waged a holy war against the non-Arab ethnicities of southern Sudan. It was only after the Soviet collapse that the southern rebels, led by the Sudan Popular Liberation Movement, were able to gain momentum. During the 1990s, significant political support for the movement grew within the United States, led by human rights activists and African American churches. After decades of bloodshed between the Arab North and the rebels of the South, Sudan's dictator, Omar al Bashir, was indicted by the International Criminal Court for genocide in Darfur (Sudan's western province) and the regime accepted the South's secession.[3] Thanks to the efforts of the Bush administration and the stubborn resistance of the African population since 1956, on January 9, 2011, through a long-overdue referendum on self-determination, the Republic of South Sudan was finally created. The referendum of January 2011 was the final reward for a half-century-long resistance.

The process was monitored by thousands of nongovernmental organizations and international observers. A nationwide vote on official separation from the North was organized, incorporating the cities and villages of what were considered simply several southern provinces of the Arab Republic of Sudan. South Sudanese living abroad, including those in the United States, had the right to participate in the referendum. At the celebration of the historic referendum at the main polling station in the greater Washington, D.C., area in northern Virginia, I saw hundreds of émigrés from southern Sudan, all happily casting their vote, and met with historic figures of their struggle, particularly Simon Deng, who had advocated the cause in the United States for years. During those joyous hours of the early days of 2011, the feeling of freedom sweeping the region was there, but with it was also the expectation that the Islamists would not let this opportunity to obtain power slip by.

The loss of southern Sudan, through the creation of the Republic of South Sudan, was an enormous blow for the Salafists and the Muslim Brotherhood.[4] That week on al Jazeera TV, Sheikh Yusuf Qaradawi, international mentor of the Ikhwan, was haranguing his viewers: "This is an utter defeat of the Islamic umma, to the Jihad of generations. Khartoum is responsible for failing to keep that land, and the Arab regimes are responsible for allowing Sudan's Islamist government to be defeated by the West." He added: "This is not the first time we lost Islamic territories. We lost al Andalus [Spain] and we lost Palestine, and now a large territory in Africa." Qaradawi was intimating that every time a minority or a nation on perceived Islamic lands or lands once belonging to the Caliphate declares itself a non-Muslim state, it would be considered a loss to the umma, or global nation. Other Salafi ideologues went into the blogosphere and were often on satellite television to call for a Jihad purposed to bring down the unqualified "apostate regimes" that "lost the land of the Caliphate to the infidels." Ironically, it was the success of minorities and nationalities in self-determination that fueled the energy of Islamists and Jihadists toward crumbling the authoritarian regimes in Muslim-majority countries. After South Sudan's successful bid for self-determination, Muslim liberals and other minorities also joined in the cause of more freedom while Islamists actively sought to block that very freedom.[5] However, during the fall of 2013 and early 2014, an internal power struggle in South Sudan threatened the stability of the young republic to the delight of the Islamists in the region.[6]

THE EVE OF THE ARAB SPRING

Between the early weeks of December 2010 and the first week of January 2011, youth and liberal activities online were increasing in the Arab blogosphere. I identified several rights groups calling for demonstrations aimed toward releasing political prisoners in Egypt, Tunisia, Yemen, Algeria, and Syria, to name only the major countries. In Egypt, the April 6 Movement had formed among university students and human rights activists during 2010. The group originated in response to police brutality and was calling for the release of detainees. In Tunisia and Yemen, similar activities had been going on for the previous few years, but thanks to Facebook and other social media, they had increased in 2010 as well. The issue of torture and the question of political detainees were triggering points for activists to organize protests. The number of people arrested for their political *opinions* throughout the Arab world—and not only their activism—was at that point among the highest in the world. I often illustrated this reality on al Jazeera and other Arab media with this slogan: "There are more political prisoners in the Arab world than people living in Gaza." The human rights networks were, among all the sectors of society, the readiest to lead the early waves of protests in 2011. In almost every country that participated in the Arab Spring, the first waves of protests were launched by youth groups working to release prisoners or to stop torture in jails.[7] Even though the trigger varied from country to country, the very first cadres who posted online, who blogged, and who took to the streets arose from the internet generation, the same social class that had triggered the demonstrations of the Cedars Revolution in Beirut in 2005 and the Green Revolution in Tehran in 2009.

Weeks before the demonstrations in Tunisia launched the Arab Spring, economic protests were under way in Algeria. As I heard from my contacts in the region, the flashpoints were reached over a variety of issues: rising prices of food, political prisoners, minority suppression, and more. The citizenry had been suffering for far too long, but protest networks were finally becoming very active. The marriage between the breached tolerance level within civil societies and the level of social mobilization reached by youth groups, particularly online, detonated the uprisings. The explosive ingredients had long existed, and could have been set off by one or more of the triggers. Egypt seemed to be ready for its revolution because of the many youth groups active in politics.

Algeria had the Kabyle problem, and a number of liberal groups were dissatisfied with the distribution of wealth. Libya had unsatisfied factions in the eastern part of the country, particularly in Benghazi. In Syria, the reformers had become louder and louder on the internet and in international forums. Other countries also experienced a rise in social and political tensions. Morocco's and Jordan's political oppositions were escalating their protests, both on socioeconomic grounds. Yemen's situation was not a surprise to observers. The South, by early 2011, had developed the Hirak al Janoubi (Southern Action) to secede from Sanaa, and a stronger northern opposition had already been developing. In Bahrain, liberals had formed opposition associations even though their majority was Shia. Kuwait's opposition—which has been vocal for years—was also becoming highly active by the end of 2010.

Note that, as the activities by secular groups increased, the Islamists across the region were readying themselves for action. Observing the seculars and reformists organizing, the Muslim Brotherhood of Egypt, the Nahda Party of Tunisia, and the Salafists of Libya and other Arab Sunni countries were waiting for the results of a possible forthcoming clash between the seculars and the regimes to decide on their own plans of action.

These trends were becoming more and more apparent—and much easier to define—in the cyber universe. The Arabs seemed to be living in two worlds: In one lived the authoritarian regimes and the Islamists, and in the other lived civil societies and liberal groups.

TUNISIA: THE JASMINE REVOLUTION

From the least-expected quarter of the Arab world came the vanguard of the Arab Spring. Tunisia was not thought to have an authoritarian regime that could be brought down simply by popular demonstrations. But, in fact, it should have been the first revolution expected. Although repressive, the regime was not as bloody as others, such as the Assad and Gaddafi regimes. The army was not highly ideological, and in fact it did not respond to orders to repress demonstrations. And the secular

forces were rooted in old traditions dating to the time of French colonial rule. After decolonization, Habib Bourguiba, the great Mujahid
for independence, was hailed as the father of the nation. His authoritarian secular party, al Destour, ruled the country for decades. During
the rule of Bourguiba (1957–1987), women were granted equal rights,
secular traditions gained respect in parallel with religious beliefs, public
secular education was assured, and cultural relations with France were
maintained. However, Bourguiba was an authoritarian leader. His police
shut down the opposition. Ben Ali, his deputy, succeeded him in 1987
in a palace coup and preserved the authoritarian method of governance.

The Ben Ali regime was a classical Arab nationalist government
with populist tendencies. It maintained a strong security service to
contain the opposition, and its political pillar was the Destour Party
founded in the 1920s and reorganized in the 1950s as a neo-Destour led
by Bourguiba. The army continued to support the regime but did not
subscribe to a specific ideological program. A variety of political parties, from the Communists and Socialists at one extreme to the Islamist
Nahda Party at the other and all the centrist parties in between, make
up the Tunisian political spectrum. Tunisia had known organized political movements and parties for decades, but civil liberties were limited
by neo-Destour and Bourguiba dominance, though a desire for liberties had played a central role in the struggle for independence against
colonial rule. As many other authoritarian leaders had done, Bourguiba
and Ben Ali played the card of ultranationalism, and their resistance to
the previous Western occupation transformed this creed into long-term
authoritarian rule. Like many other Arab dictators, Tunisia's rulers asserted that their struggle for independence granted them the legitimacy
of "protecting the revolution" and thus they should not be challenged.
In practice, this meant that those who led the struggle against the outside occupation could not be challenged by domestic opposition. While
European countries such as France and the Netherlands had national
heroes (General Charles de Gaulle, for example) who fought against the
Nazi occupation, these World War II heroes did not convert their victories into one-party systems dominating national political life ever after.

Like Algeria, Morocco, and other countries, Tunisia had to give up its democratic freedoms to the elite that fought the battle for independence. After Bourguiba's demise, his successor, Ben Ali, made few changes but continued the Destourian rule at the expense of democratic growth.

One social force in Tunisia having no real equivalent in other Arab countries was the National Labor Union or, in Arabic, Ittihad al Shoghl. This Tunisian workers' union, closer to the left-wing Socialist parties in other Mediterranean countries, has historical roots in decades of labor struggles, and many of its members have ties to the Tunisian workers' community in France. The union was a core entity of the movement there; it sought social and economic advantages for its hundreds of thousands of members in France as it had in Tunisia during the Bourguiba and Ben Ali eras. The Tunisian army, mostly trained by France and having good relations with the United States, was not educated ideologically. Hence, unlike those in Iran, Syria, and Iraq under Saddam, Tunisia's armed forces were not controlled by a cabinet-level security agency or by an SS-like corps inside its institutions. Hence, the country's secular movements, its labor unions, and its armed forces were pivotal for the success of the demonstrations turned revolution in January 2011.

Bouazizi's self-immolation was followed by a cascade of demonstrations, growing in size and spreading from the countryside toward the capital and from neighborhoods to downtown Tunis. At first, the Ben Ali regime deployed its police and security forces, but they were unable to contain the demonstrations. A number of Tunisians were killed and wounded, and in reaction, the youth and civil society NGOs mobilized multiple simultaneous demonstrations in several avenues and towns and overwhelmed the security apparatus. To stop the popular uprising that had reached the main arteries of the capital, the regime then unleashed the armed elements of its ruling party. More demonstrators were shot by the regime's thugs, triggering a massive call by the labor unions to strike and protest against government institutions and the presidential palace.

Labor unions and liberal groups were instrumental in mobilizing greater masses, of a size unseen on the streets of Tunis since the fifties' battle for independence. The pressure on Ben Ali grew stronger. As a last resort, he called in the army to defend the palace and the regime. But the Tunisian military, mostly secular and not indoctrinated with radical ideologies, sympathized with the people. The soldiers fraternized with the demonstrators. This was the equation that brought down the government of Tunisia without massacres or a civil war.

Viewing the bigger picture is important to an understanding of the very first wave of the Arab Spring. Several elements and precise conditions had to exist in order for the Jasmine Revolution to succeed in Tunisia. There needed to be a growing youth and liberal movement connected by modern technologies such as the internet, cell phones, Twitter, Facebook, and more. There was a large labor union not controlled by the regime and an army free of doctrine and friendly to the West. The incident that triggered the revolt will remain symbolic in history, but it was the will of the youth to provoke a change that made all the difference in the outcome. The fact that the revolt was led and organized by the forces of civil society, to the exclusion of violent extremists—at least in the early stages—drew the support of the international community and the neutrality of the army.[8]

The opposition to Ben Ali included the Islamists, those close to the Muslim Brotherhood, Nahda, and those more radical, the Salafists and Hizbul Tahrir,[9] who called for an immediate establishment of a Caliphate. The Islamists, led by their historical leader, Rached al Ghannouchi, attempted several times to rise against both Bourguiba and Ben Ali. But the Islamists, at times backed by Gaddafi and in the last years supported by Qatar and the international organization of the Muslim Brotherhood, were not able to provoke, let alone lead, a massive uprising against the authoritarian but secular power. In their majority, Tunisians are secular, even though most are devout Muslims. But Nahda is a fundamentalist organization aiming at erecting the Caliphate. The Islamists waited to see if the civil society demonstrations would be successful before committing themselves to the uprising. This pattern of wait-and-see and enter gradually was prevalent throughout the Arab Spring. Indeed, not until the protests appeared to be irreversible did Nahda plunge into the uprising, positioning itself as the main political player of the Arab Spring in Tunisia.

With the collapse of the regime and the exile of Ben Ali, the Jasmine Revolution moved to the next stage: eradicating the institutions of the regime, drafting a new constitution, and electing a new government. By March 2011, while the fire of the Spring was engulfing other countries, the alliance of insurgents broke down into its two basic components: on one hand, the secular democrats, including old political parties, labor unions, women, and youth; and, on the other hand, Nahda and its Salafi allies. The Islamists, who were helped tremendously by the very influential al Jazeera broadcast during the uprising, rushed to organize themselves and call for rapid elections. They knew they were better organized and better funded than the secular political parties. The sooner the election was held, the more their rise to power would be guaranteed. The seculars were divided, and the younger generation of youth activists was disorganized and poorly funded. The first post–Ben Ali election gave Nahda enough seats to form the government in 2011. The next stage in the Tunisian Arab Spring began.

CHAPTER THREE

EGYPT'S FIRST REVOLUTION

DURING THE EARLY WEEKS OF JANUARY 2011, AS DEM-
onstrations were under way in Tunisia, Egyptian youth started to organize protests in Cairo. The April 6 Movement, launched by liberal
students and bloggers the year before, was the first to go nationwide
and call for the release of detainees in Mubarak's jails and for an end
to torture. According to human rights reports, Egyptian authorities
had been acting harshly against critics for many years. Egyptian liberals had attempted to push for reforms in the country, but the Mubarak
regime stood firm on its position and resisted democratization, particularly regarding free elections, free speech, and forming free political
organizations. According to the Egyptian opposition and many international observers, all elections under Mubarak, and those under previous presidents, had been manipulated by the regime. Even though there
had been elections in Egypt since 1954, liberals and left-wing opponents
of government, including the Islamists, had been unable to sufficiently
mobilize the public to wage massive protests until January 2011. Two
elements had strengthened the regime in power. Mubarak was the successor to two national heroes: Gamal Abdel Nasser, who led the first
republic from 1954 and into war with Israel in 1967, and Anwar Sadat,
who launched the 1973 war with Israel and recovered the Sinai via a
peace treaty. Mubarak, a former commander of the air force and vice

president under Sadat, was a nationalist Arab but secular leader who led modern Egypt with the help of a heavy bureaucracy backed by strong intelligence and security services.

THE CLASSICAL OPPOSITION

The classical opposition to Mubarak's government on the eve of the revolution included the traditional left and secular parties ranging from the Socialists, Nasserites, Progressives, and seasoned liberals to conservatives such as the Wafd party. These political forces, arrayed to the left of the regime and rarely united, constituted the largest gathering of political forces in the Arab world, for Egypt has the largest Arab population. The "seculars and left" bloc all demanded more political freedoms, but differed among themselves on other issues, ranging from domestic economics to relations with Israel and the West.

A second component of Egypt's classical opposition was the Muslim Brotherhood and its Salafi allies. This Islamist bloc was the most united and best integrated of all political forces in Egypt. With the exception of the Wafd party, the Muslim Brotherhood, founded in the 1920s, has a longer history than any other political group in Egypt. Under Mubarak, the Islamists had a dual experience. On the one hand, they were banned from forming an official political party because they had staged coups and assassination attempts against Nasser in the 1960s, and it was Gamaa Islamiya, a group launched by offshoots from the Muslim Brotherhood in the late 1960s, that assassinated Sadat in 1981. In fact, Gamaa Islamiya increased their numbers after the 1973 war and served as an umbrella to Jihadist factions, such as the Egyptian Islamic Jihad. Regardless of past tensions and subversive activities, however, the Mubarak regime allowed a space for the Islamists to "breathe"—that is, to spread their ideological indoctrination. The regime aimed at keeping a balance between this and its pro-American policy and commitment to the Camp David agreement in return for significant U.S. financial aid. It decided to allow some room in the public sphere for the Islamist movements to express their anti-Israel and anti-Semitic feelings. The Brotherhood and the Salafist groups took advantage of the Mubarak policy of "do it, but not officially," meaning they continued their indoctrinations and ideological network organizing. The Brotherhood, partially funded with the petrodollars of the Gulf states and with growing political connections to the Obama administration, gradually became one of the largest organizations in Egypt, second only to the armed forces, and qualitatively superior to the ruling Hizb al Watani (National Party) of Mubarak.[1]

The dialogue between the Muslim Brotherhood and the Obama administration grew stronger after the U.S. president delivered speeches in Istanbul and Cairo in 2009. With these ties, the Islamist movement of Egypt felt strong enough to start challenging Mubarak's regime. For decades, the Brotherhood had been unable to topple the Socialist and military elite in Cairo, and it could not mobilize the masses and other political parties in a civil society surge or gain recognition by accepting international norms. The Brotherhood's failure to launch a revolt of its own was due primarily to the fact that its ideology was unacceptable to most other Egyptians. Moreover, the Egyptian armed forces, mostly secular, were loyal to the regime and respected the power of the United States. Then, in January 2011, the Islamists were given a historic opportunity.

Since the coup of 1952 that deposed King Farouk, the main power broker in Egypt has been the Egyptian army. Under Sadat and Mubarak, its leadership, later known as the Supreme Council of the Armed Forces (SCAF), was the backbone of the regime and of the country. While it was the General Security Agency that maintained political order, the SCAF was the powerful institution that backed the security forces and protected the national borders. Through the largesse of U.S. financial aid amounting to billions of dollars, the regime was assured the continuous funding of the army and its economic projects across the country. To both the secular and the Islamist oppositions it seemed impossible to challenge a regime backed by a well-paid army and good relations with the United States.

THE YOUTH

But a third force, both Islamist and progressive, emerged between the regime (and its security and military apparatuses) and the opposition.

It was the youth, *al shabab*—the educated, revolutionary, and independent youth who saw the post–9/11 Middle East evolving and used modern communications and information technologies. Internet savvy and connected across Egypt and the Egyptian diaspora, *shabab* triggered the January 2011 revolution. Having already been mobilized against the candidacy of Jamal Mubarak, the dictator's son, the liberal youth movements were the first to organize sit-ins, strikes, and press conferences in 2010. Three developments were said to have launched the Facebook explosion that triggered the revolution.

As I noted earlier, the demonstrations in Beirut in 2005 and in Tehran in 2009 had great psychological effects on the student and youth groups in Egypt. Years of uploads on YouTube and Facebook pages dedicated to the first two post–Cold War democratic revolutions in the Middle East mobilized the younger souls along the Nile River.[2] "We thought we could do it too," said Cynthia Farahat, a young member of the Council of the Egyptian Revolution of January 2011. Farahat, whom I met in Washington, D.C., in 2012 after she sought political asylum, told me, "Young men and women in Cairo and Alexandria, who followed the Cedars and Green Revolutions, felt they could also rise up for freedom and started to organize groups aiming at social and political mobilization." But it was the victorious Tunisian marchers who convinced the Egyptian liberal revolutionaries that "it could actually work." The Muslim editor of a liberal publication, while in Washington during the summer of 2012, told me that "the mere sight of tens of thousands of Tunisians hurtling into the streets of their capital was the last straw." It encouraged their Egyptian counterparts to prepare to take to the streets.[3]

THE COPTS: WEAK LINK OF THE SPRING

According to observers who have studied Egypt's revolution, in early January there was another development that hastened the street demonstrations and proved to many among those who planned the protests that the regime was weaker than before: attacks on the Copts, the largest Christian group in Egypt, and the reactions of the group's youth.

A series of attacks on Copts by Salafists in 2010 left many dead and wounded. Then, on January 1, 2011, a car bomb blew up in front of a large Coptic church in Alexandria. It killed dozens and destroyed the street. Thousands of Copts in Alexandria and other towns rose up. In Cairo, for the first time, Coptic students staged a loud protest on a university campus. It lasted for hours, but security forces did not intervene.

Mubarak's regime, embarrassed by such terror attacks on Christians and concerned about a backlash in the United States by a Congress very sensitive to Christian persecution abroad, permitted the Coptic youth to express their anger. By doing so, the regime was opening a Pandora's box, as all other political forces were now indirectly encouraged to test the readiness of the Mubarak regime to confront demonstrators. Ironically, it was the weakest segment of Egyptian society that sent the signal that a revolution was possible, that the planets were rightly aligned, and thus that larger demonstrations were a "go." The Coptic students' protests resembled those of the Iranian youth and the Cedars Revolution. They were composed of boys and girls with signs and cell phones who were videotaping the event and later uploading the footage to YouTube and Facebook. This was the model to follow. The Copts were the first spark of the revolution's youth trigger. The West was worried about the safety of the Christian minority, and Mubarak stepped back. The liberal youth stepped up. Mubarak attempted to stop them, but he was stopped by the West. Historians will look into the archives years from now and conclude that the weakest links in societies are eventually those who make things change.[4]

REFORM OR REVOLUTION?

The liberal youth movements, however, were not ready to advance the idea of a regime change; their only notion was to reform the existing regime.[5] But the torrent of events rushing through Egyptian civil society broke the dam, and the demand for reform translated into a demand for regime change. The movements that started the Tahrir Square demonstrations initially sought the release of political prisoners; a greater number of freedoms including the right to protest freely, run for election, and manage campaigns without government control; and additional liberties for the Coptic minority. They also opposed the presidential candidacy of Jamal Mubarak, the choice of the National Party and son of the president. But once the masses met in the open, they became conscious of their power, and the revolution was under way. It all started with a Facebook page, an appropriate symbol for an era of change.

THE FACEBOOK PAGE THAT CHANGED EGYPT

As our Western-based freedom NGOs were monitoring the Tunisian demonstrations, the launch of an Egyptian Revolution Facebook page by several liberal youth groups in early January 2011 caught my eye. While observers in the West did not pay enough attention to it, I consulted with Egyptian liberal activists both in the West and inside Egypt and understood that these youths were seeking to initiate demonstrations similar to those in Tunisia. I kept reading the posts and comments and concluded that we were watching something radical. The writers and bloggers within Egypt and overseas, excited by the success of the Tunisian wave of protests, were seeking to emulate the Lebanese and Iranian street events. They were planning a massive gathering in the center of the Egyptian capital to provoke a significant political change.

In only forty-eight to seventy-two hours, the Egyptian Revolution page on Facebook scored more than 85,000 likes, an indication of a tsunami in the making. The posts multiplied by the thousands, and groups began to organize in virtual space. By the time the adherents reached 100,000, it became technically impossible for the security forces to arrest all participants. Egypt did not have enough agents to arrest and jail all the Facebookers, even though the faces, personal information, and attitudes of almost all participants were clearly posted.

For the first time in the Arab world, probably in the entire world, a nonviolent Facebook revolt was successful. In Beirut, it had been impossible for Syrian and Hezbollah security to arrest or kill a million people gathered in Martyrs Square; the Cedars Revolution won. In Tehran, it had been impossible for the Pasdaran and the Bassij[6] to detain or massacre a million Iranians marching together; the Green Revolution survived for weeks. In Cairo, the mass movement targeted the most symbolic public square in the Republic: Tahrir Square, the beating heart of Egypt. From among the hundred thousand likes on the Facebook page *al Thawra* ("the revolution" in Arabic), tens of thousands headed to Tahrir, the number peaking on January 25. Once ordinary Egyptians saw their students, youth, and human rights activists braving security forces and camping in the square, they started to hurry downtown. In a few days, civil society mobilized as never before in Egypt, forgoing their association with traditional political parties.[7]

THE TAHRIR REVOLUTION

Middle-class people—lawyers, journalists, teachers, women, artists, comedians, students, public servants, shopkeepers—as well as peasants and labor unionists, descended on Tahrir in a show of popular force unparalleled in Egyptian history, but reminiscent of the Beirut and Tehran rallies and with the same vigor as Tunisia's marches. As the masses in Tahrir Square grew to the hundreds of thousands, the political parties of Egypt started to gather and catch up with the forces of youth and civil society. The left wing, the centrist Wafd, and the Nasserites rapidly organized and joined the chanting crowds to demand radical reforms. The Muslim Brotherhood, watching the congregation from afar, refrained from joining early on for fear of failure and of being suppressed harshly by the regime. The Islamists, shrewd tacticians and seasoned urban militants, knew Mubarak's security apparatus inside and out, having had several experiences over the decades, and delayed their entry into the fray. They had an undeclared understanding with the regime: They were permitted to run for office in the legislative elections and maintain their doctrinal schools of Sharia if they didn't cause too much trouble. Their leadership wanted to measure the power of the uprising before risking their position. Their tactic was to first ensure that the demonstrations would survive before throwing their weight behind the movement. For days, the Brotherhood sent its youth to join the liberal youth in solidarity, yet refrained from officially entering the fray.

As the number of demonstrators grew day by day and their diversity revealed their revolutionary nature, the international community drew closer to the students, women, artists, and ordinary citizens at Tahrir. The key to Western support was the civil society nature of the uprising. As with its predecessors in Beirut, Tehran, and Tunis, international public opinion quickly sided with the demonstrators. Had the uprising been organized by Islamists, it would have been less likely that the West would have supported their Jihadi slogans. Tahrir's slogans were pro-democracy and free from anti-Semitism, anti-Americanism, and Salafi narrative. Viewers in Europe and North America connected with the boys and girls in Cairo's public places. As, in fact, did Egypt's larger society, which supplied the protesters with added thousands of citizens, creating the famous *malyuniyya* (million-strong rallies) that called for Mubarak to resign. The unleashing of the regime's thugs on the unarmed demonstrators just days after the start of the protests created greater worldwide support, and American backing of the Egyptian dictator waned. The equation of power changed rapidly over three weeks' time. When Mubarak understood that the West would not allow his security forces to crush the masses, he attempted to use his last resort, the army. But the army—as nonideological as its Tunisian counterpart and in this case having significant, decades-long friendships with members of the U.S. military—refrained from sending tanks against the Egyptian people. (Arab armies were of two kinds in 2011: those who followed the dictators blindly and lost their power after their leaders' demise and those trained and funded by the West, who survived.) By siding with the demonstrators, Egypt's SCAF might be considered the actual cause of the collapse of the Mubarak regime. From the moment the military, led by Field Marshal Tantawi, stated that they would not follow the president's orders to stop the demonstrations, the revolution had already won.

Upon realizing that the United States had pressured Mubarak to resign and the military to work with political forces on the transition, the Muslim Brotherhood entered the battlefield of Egyptian politics. It poured members into Tahrir Square and took the lead in the negotiations with the armed forces for the formation of an interim government. As the single largest political organization in Egypt after the disbanding of Mubarak's National Party, more populous than the left-wing and liberal factions combined, the Brotherhood maneuvered itself away from the sidelines of the revolution into its center. As days passed after the arrest of the Mubarak family and the SCAF took power through a newly formed cabinet, the Islamist alliance between Ikhwan and the Salafists rose to become the next power in Cairo. The liberal youth—the initiators of the revolution—were marginalized and divided, isolated from the political game.

U.S. POLICY TOWARD THE REVOLUTION

Another factor helped the Muslim Brotherhood in its course, and that was the sympathy of the Obama administration. With many advisers in its bureaucracy close to the Brotherhood, the administration shepherded the Egyptian revolution in a manner advantageous to the Islamists. That is how many critics in Washington described U.S. foreign policy during the Arab Spring. According to some, Washington's diplomacy dealt carefully with the events in Tahrir Square, maneuvering from one stage to the next in order to land the Brotherhood at the top of Egyptian power.[8] Indeed, when the Copts were attacked, the Obama administration expressed its concern but took no action—as had been the case for the previous three years. When liberal youth took their demonstrations to Tahrir Square and their gatherings grew stronger, the Obama White House stated that it was monitoring the situation and wished the crisis to be resolved between the Mubarak regime and its opponents. If one follows the statements made by Washington's officials from day one of the uprising, it is clear that until the Brotherhood took full part in the uprising, the United States refrained from asking Mubarak to step down. By staying almost neutral between the dictator and the liberal youth, the White House slowed international support for the revolution and gave the Brotherhood enough time to join forces. The Brotherhood became a full partner in the Tahrir movement, and the Qatar-funded al Jazeera boasted how the role of the Islamists in Egypt's revolution had transformed them into the leading force. A thorough analysis of the sequence of the diplomatic ballet between Washington and Cairo shows that the United States was not expecting the Egyptian youth to succeed in triggering a mobilization of civil society. Once the youth uprising in Tahrir was an irreversible fact, the White House delayed the outcome of the revolution—the removal of Mubarak—until the Islamists moved in. Tharwat al Kharbawi, a former leader of the Muslim Brotherhood, confirmed the partnership in several media statements during 2012 and 2013. Egyptian secular opposition leaders (including youth leaders such as Ahmad Douman, who was imprisoned by the Brotherhood regime during 2012) asserted in retrospect that "only when the Islamists were part of the revolution did Obama let go of Mubarak." Douman told Egyptian media that youth leaders were waiting for Washington to ask Mubarak to leave, but that U.S. statement came only "after the Muslim Brotherhood were well installed in the center of Tahrir Square."[9] The undeclared partnership between the United States and the Brotherhood transformed the Egyptian revolution from a liberal youth uprising to a co-ownership among the youth, the Brotherhood, and the army. The second phase of the revolution, particularly beginning early in 2012, would be a race among these three associates in Egypt's Spring.

CHAPTER FOUR

THE ARAB SPRING'S CIVIL WARS

THE ARAB SPRING WAS BLOODIER IN SOME COUNTRIES than others. The revolutionary goals of civil society in the Middle East most likely did not include two heavily armed factions engaging in violent conflict with one another, resulting in massive civilian casualties. Regardless of internal or international expectations, however, the Arab Spring produced two full-fledged civil wars in which both sides were militarily armed.

LIBYA

Between Tunisia's uprising and Tahrir's revolution, Libya's opposition caught fire and started to mobilize toward similar protests. But the dictatorship of Muammar Gaddafi was radically different from the other authoritarian regimes in North Africa. The ruler whom many in the Arab world, including Anwar Sadat, once referred to as "*al fata al Majnun*," or "the crazy kid," was the longest-ruling and most eccentric oppressive leader in the Arab world. Cartoonish stories about Gaddafi had made their way across the region, and pictures of the leader with female bodyguards at international conferences were well known. Emulating the older Colonel Gamal Abdel Nasser of Egypt, whom he admired, Colonel Muammar staged a coup in 1969 and removed Libya's monarch, King

Idris Sanussi. He then closed the U.S. air bases there. Gaddafi created a third-world brand of socialism, tying it to Islam. (He termed it "Islamic Socialism.") The Libyan dictator became a client of the Soviet Union during the Cold War and supported a good many terror organizations while financing factions among Palestinians and during the Lebanese civil war. In 1986, however, after President Ronald Reagan ordered air strikes on Gaddafi's headquarters in retaliation for his role in the downing of Pan American flight 103 over Scotland, Gaddafi moderated his international stance but maintained an oppressive regime against his own people for two more decades, surviving the end of the Cold War.

During the George W. Bush years, a number of Libyan freedom activists found refuge in the West; I met a few of them, in Washington as well as at European conferences, such as one in Prague in 2006. These freedom activists represented a larger force opposed to Gaddafi, but not the only one. Over the last decade, the Libyan regime had two main opponents, the liberal elements and the Islamists. The latter, mostly Salafists and the Muslim Brotherhood, were omnipresent in eastern Libya, particularly in Benghazi and Darna. Many of Libya's Jihadists joined al Qaeda's ranks in the Afghan war against the Soviet Union and in the U.S. war against the Taliban in 2001. Among the most notorious was Abu Yahiya al Libi, the military commander of al Qaeda, who was killed by a U.S. drone in 2012. The secular opposition to Gaddafi ranged from communists, socialists, and monarchists to socio-democrats and liberals. Gaddafi suppressed these opponents, including critics in his own regime. Like Saddam Hussein and Bashar Assad, Gaddafi used secret police who tortured and killed political dissidents. As in Tunisia and Egypt, Libyan dissidents and reformers used the internet as a tool to coordinate and mobilize the struggle against Gaddafi. The Salafists opposed him but directed most of their activity overseas to avoid the dictator's wrath. To please Washington, Gaddafi arrested some al Qaeda supporters, but like Mubarak, he gave the Islamists some room to survive. As a "socialist Islamist" he did not want to risk an open confrontation with the Jihadists. Like Yemen's leader Ali Abdallah Saleh, Muammar played it safe: He suppressed the Jihadists just enough to be in the camp of the post-9/11 antiterrorist campaign, but tolerated the Salafists and, from time to time, released Islamist detainees to their families, particularly in East Libya, as a merciful measure.

This strategy ultimately proved insufficient. As in Egypt, Libyan youth and liberal cadres, inside the country and out, were excited by the winds of change in the region, those blowing from their east in Lebanon and Iran and those blowing from their west in Tunisia. Almost at the same time as Egypt, the Libyan opposition rose rapidly against Gaddafi in the first months of 2011. The posture of the West, which was seen as supportive of the Arab Spring, encouraged the Libyan liberals to launch similar internet calls for demonstrations. Similarly, the Salafists regrouped to seize the opportunity in Libya as well. Ironically, immediately after the success of the Egyptian demonstrations in Tahrir Square, Libya's dictator ordered the release of hundreds of Jihadi fighters from his jails, including members of al Qaeda. Saif al Islam Gaddafi, Muammar's son, said the release of these "fighters for Islam" was to defend Libya against the enemies of Allah. The Gaddafis' strategy was to split the opposition between liberals and Islamists. They thought that since it was the liberals leading the demonstrations in Tunisia and Egypt, in the first stage, and since the West would side with them, the dictators could use the Jihadists to fight the "infidels." The logic was that the Islamists would prefer Islamic dictators with anti-Israel rhetoric over reformers and liberals with a secular narrative. But the strongman of Tripoli was wrong. The Islamists of Libya and those of the region in general had a strategy of their own. They knew all along that Arab dictators would use them against a liberal outburst, only to come back and crush them as a way to satisfy a West frustrated by the elimination of the liberal movements. Hence the Islamists of Libya chose the side of the secular revolt, advertising themselves as "revolutionaries" like all other Libyan democrats.

THE DEMONSTRATIONS SPREAD

The pro-democracy demonstrations marched across most Libyan cities, from Benghazi to Tripoli, led by youth, rights groups, former

bureaucrats, judges, professionals, and workers. The protesters believed that emulating civil society's gatherings in Tunisia and Egypt
would be as successful and peaceful. As Libya's ambassador to Washington, Ali al Oufali, who defected from Gaddafi's regime, told me
that year, "Our people thought that Gaddafi would fear America's reaction if he were to use violence with his own citizens. We saw that the
U.S. had used its clout to pressure Mubarak and Ben Ali out of power.
We thought Washington could do the same with Gaddafi." But Gaddafi was a bloody dictator who financed his own security services and
army from his regime's oil production income. Libya was no Egypt or
Tunisia. As in Syria later, there would be violence against civilians followed by a raging civil war.

Indeed, as soon as demonstrators took to the streets of Libya's
coastal cities, Gaddafi sent in his police, then his security brigades, and
at last his army. Segments of the demonstrators—former military and
Islamists—rushed to control the vehicles descending upon them and
take over police stations and checkpoints. Gaddafi, intolerant by nature,
ordered air raids on the rebels. His fighter jets bombed demonstrators
as well and triggered a Western, soon to become an international, reaction. Events in Libya rapidly deteriorated. Civilian marches redoubled
in the capital and other cities such as Misrata and Benghazi while the
military wing of the rebellion was forming across the country. Gaddafi
dealt with the whole movement as a single threat. He used his entire
security apparatus, including the infamous Gaddafi Phalanx. In a few
weeks, after attempting to pressure the regime for reforms, the protesters were instead met with weapons and mass arrests, with participants facing jail, torture, and, in many cases, execution. Gaddafi was
attempting to choke the revolt before it could live, before its reach got
beyond the leader's ability to control it. He had seen the fate of his two
neighboring states and had decided not to be the third dictator to fall.
Thus the Libyan Spring, originally led by civil society forces and bureaucratic dissidents, descended into chaos and violence, opening the
path to military resistance.[1]

THE ARMED STRUGGLE FOLLOWS

Two forces rose rapidly against Gaddafi: dissidents and breakaway units among the Libyan armed forces on one side and Islamist Salafi militias on the other. The fury of the conflict became apparent as the rebellion spread through the country.

Libya's military was monitored by Gaddafi's elite forces. The dictator did not trust his regular forces but only those that hailed from his tribe or region or were directly linked to his ruling party—the only party—the *lijan sha'biyya* (Popular Committees). Hence, he sent the Security Brigades, the equivalent of Saddam's Republican Guards. These units were later called the "phalanges of Gaddafi" (*Kata'eb el Qathafi*) by al Jazeera and the Libyan Islamists.

The breakaway regular units of the Libyan army were led by General Abdel Fattah Younis, one of the highest-ranking officers in the military. The heaviest gathering of the "regular rebel" units occurred in Benghazi, where officers were joined by former bureaucrats, diplomats, judges, and other public personalities. The Benghazi forces seized large areas of the city's military compounds and depots and began marching toward other locations in Cyrenaica (East Libya) and along the borders with Egypt. Shortly thereafter, the Benghazi leadership formed an interim national council to act as a rebel government overseeing liberated areas.

The Islamist Salafists rapidly joined the interim council and used the influence of Qatar—backers of the Muslim Brotherhood in the region—to seize a large proportion of seats inside the interim rebel government. At the same time, however, the Salafi Jihadists, led by commanders trained by al Qaeda and many who were freed by Saif al Islam Gaddafi from Libyan jails, set up their own training and staging centers to ensure their influence in the post-Gaddafi era.

From the start, the dictator's forces attempted to crush the rebellion in Benghazi. They deeply penetrated the city and threatened the very existence of the interim council. But the diplomatic pressures deployed by the United States and France extracted a resolution (Chapter VII, number 1973) from the Security Council of the United Nations, allowing military action against Gaddafi.

Although Russia and China opposed the notion of military action by NATO in Libya, the vicious violence by Gaddafi against the Libyans, aired on television, brought significant pressure on the United Nations. Moscow and Beijing allowed the use of military action to defend the civilians only after the regime forces bombarded large areas in Benghazi and were about to invade the city. But Washington and its allies, encouraged by Qatar, moved from striking at advancing Gaddafi forces to providing air cover to advancing rebel forces. NATO air forces, including American, French, and British, operating mostly from Italy, wrecked Libya's airfields, missile forces, and radar. They then pounded Gaddafi's tank divisions and degraded his communications system to a point where the fight on the ground became a conflict between two almost equally matched forces. NATO acted as an air force for the rebels while its battleships tightened the blockade on Gaddafi's ports.

As the regime's heavy weaponry became degraded by NATO, the rebel forces started to move from Benghazi along the coast toward Misrata on the way to Tripoli. The balance of power between the rebels and the regime started to shift, and the Islamist militias began to focus on the post-Gaddafi power grab. As the fighting raged on between the two parties engaged in the civil war, the military chief of the rebels, General Younis, the man who could have seized power from Gaddafi and helped rebuild the Libyan army on secular grounds, was assassinated in Benghazi. His supporters accused the Islamist militias, arguing that this was their preemptive strike to behead the secular army opposition and seize the uprising on the ground. In fact, after the elimination of Younis, the Salafi-armed groups penetrated and controlled most areas of Libya and were able to keep command of operations. One of their commanders, who trained with al Qaeda and served in Gaddafi's prisons, was Abdelhakim Belhaj. He soon rose to prominence on the national scene and ended up leading the Jihadi forces, becoming the military commander of Tripoli after the fall of Gaddafi.

Within a year, the rebel forces and air support by NATO crushed the forces of Gaddafi. Tripoli fell to the insurgents, followed by Misrata, Bani Walid, and Sirte, the regime's tribal capital. After the gruesome killing of Gaddafi and his supporters at the hands of Jihadi militias, a new interim government was installed in Benghazi before it was moved back to the capital. The composition of the new ruling body reflected the forces that struggled to bring down the dictatorship, including both seculars and Islamists. The Jihadi militias, however, remained in place despite the interim government's commitment to NATO to disband militias and decommission their weapons. The next stage in the Libyan revolution was a race for power between the two contenders found in the aftermath of each Arab Spring conflict: Islamists and seculars.

SYRIA

One of the most violent of all Arab Spring uprisings was Syria's. The revolt there turned abruptly into a civil war, one that has been threatening the region with an even wider military confrontation. The opposition had tried several times over the decades to dislodge the tyrants, both the father and the son. But the regime was so well entrenched in security layers that all attempts had failed. Even as I projected that revolution was bound to happen in Syria, the region was undergoing massive political changes. The ruling elite in Damascus was already nervous when Ben Ali left Tunisia and Mubarak quit power. The last Baathist power in the Arab world after the collapse of Saddam felt its turn was coming, particularly in that it had experienced previous revolutionary spasms in the eighties. But the Arab Spring was of a different nature. This time, as of mid-2011, it was evident that the Assad regime would never again rule Syria entirely, if at all, as the masses surged.

Over the years, I had established a good rapport with Syrian dissidents, human rights activists, and opposition figures, mostly in the secular liberal circles and with ethno-religious minorities. In 2010, Syrian reformers told me of the readiness of their society for a change, as did reformers from other Middle East countries. The Syrian dissidents, who have for years consistently worked against the Assad regime, were emboldened by the Iranian and Lebanese demonstrations but frustrated by the Obama administration's unsupportive attitude toward the opposition. Some repeated the slogan used by Secretary of State Hillary Clinton that "Assad is a reformer." Others were skeptical of the American foreign policy that had abandoned the Iranian and Lebanese oppositions and the Iraqi anti-Iranian secular leaders over the previous two years. Only Syrian Kurds expressed a continuing optimism about resisting the Baathist regime of Damascus. I argued then that when the civil societies in the region finally took action, they would encourage each other. Even Syria's embattled opposition—the Damascus Declaration, a loose coalition of liberal intellectuals—would motivate other entities to move. It was difficult to imagine in the autumn of 2010 how an uprising could be successful in a country ruled by an iron fist.

EFFECT OF THE CEDARS REVOLUTION

One harbinger of a Syrian Spring was the immediate impact of the Cedars Revolution. As was the case in Eastern Europe, where the rapid collapse of Communist regimes in formerly Soviet Europe in 1989 provoked ripple effects inside Russia that led to the collapse of the Kremlin in 1991, the massive demonstration in Beirut forced the pro-Syrian cabinet of Prime Minister Omar Karami to resign. That opened the path for Western powers to pressure Bashar Assad into calling his troops out of Lebanon.

Such was the earthquake whose ripple effect hit the Syrian hinterland: The unarmed demonstrators of Beirut in 2005 inspired the unarmed demonstrators of Syria in 2011. Syrian opposition forces saw their colleagues in Lebanon marching with courage against Assad's occupation in Martyrs Square in downtown Beirut. They then saw the regime's army returning home to Syria. And with the formation of an anti-Assad government in Beirut headed by Fuad Seniora then later by Saad Hariri, Syrian opposition leaders and cadres fled to Beirut and began voicing their criticism of Assad II from there. In this way, the Cedars Revolution unlocked a door for the Syrian opposition inside Lebanon, despite Hezbollah's omnipresence. In the summer of 2005, Assad's Syrian critics unleashed media and blogosphere campaigns from Lebanon. For six years, the Syrian opposition in exile in Lebanon, backed by the anti-Assad coalition March 14 Alliance (named after the date of the Cedars Revolution in 2005), fed its underground operatives working under Assad's regime in Syria with information and support. This Lebanese "connection" encouraged the human rights and activist networks inside Syria to organize. As Syrian citizens could easily cross into Lebanon, dissidents and reformers went to Beirut and from there to the outside world, and they came back with ideas and technologies and a renewed political will.

INTERNET GLOBALIZATION

As in the rest of the Arab world, but even more so in Syria, online activism ignited the Syrian revolution. During the fall of 2011, multiple Facebook pages and blogs surfaced that began calling for reforms in Syria. Following the Tunisian and Egyptian revolts, the Syrian opposition increased its activities online, emulating its sister movements in North Africa. By February 2011, the historic Facebook page *Al Thawra al Suriyya* (Syrian Revolution) was launched. In just a few days, as was the case in Egypt, the page had thousands of likes, and many posts on the page announced a call for demonstrations across Syria.

The Syrian regime was much bloodier than those in Egypt and Tunisia and had a long history of successfully crushing revolts in Syria and neighboring Lebanon. As soon as the Syrian Revolution page appeared on Facebook, Assad's security services went on the offensive. They attempted to bring the page down and to find and arrest the founders of the page and those who joined it. They found it was not as easy to crush a cyberrevolution as it was to crush demonstrations in the streets. Tanks and jets cannot be launched into cyberspace.

By early March, multiple Facebook pages and blogs waged an online rebellion against the Assad regime. While the revolts against three Arab dictators were peaking in Cairo, Tripoli, and Tunis and brewing in Sanaa in Yemen, oppositional Facebookers in Syria were widespread and well implanted in many cities, and they were backed by Lebanese colleagues and activists throughout the Syrian diaspora. The Facebook explosion could not be contained. The confidence inspired by this first wave of the Syrian revolution led more citizens to step out of the ether and into the physical world, to make their presence known.

REVOLT OF THE TEENAGERS

The first clash occurred in Der'a, a poor, mostly Sunni city in the southern tip of Syria.[2] There, in March 2011, some teenagers were caught inscribing anti-regime graffiti on the walls. The teens were arrested, interrogated, and tortured, and a few died. The description of the torture in this incident inflamed the feelings of the ordinary people of Syria, who were already oppressed by years of the regime's ruthless behavior.

The Der'a killings were to Syria what Bouazizi's self-immolation was to Tunisia and the arrest and torture of students were to Egypt: the trigger. The ensuing riots by Der'a teenagers represented a response to the calls of the Syria Revolution Facebook page that initiated the popular uprising. The seemingly stable Assad regime was now collapsing. And as in the other countries experiencing revolt, the youth were the first to demonstrate. The explosion in Der'a first aroused the province, then the fire spread across the country. The people of Der'a demonstrated en masse. Assad's security forces met them with violence. The protests grew stronger and spread. Then Bashar Assad ordered his thugs (called *Shabbiha*) and security forces (*Mukhabarat*) to crush the mounting protests.[3]

RISE OF SYRIAN CIVIL SOCIETY

With this, Syrian civil society mobilized from north to south. Liberal groups organized small- and medium-sized demonstrations in neighborhoods and small towns and broadcast their marches on YouTube. Authorities rapidly ordered international media out of the country in order to cut off news of what the Syrian people were doing. Assad's forces were disciplined and followed the regime's orders closely. They made thousands of arrests, kidnapped hundreds, and killed many. As the number of victims multiplied day by day, demonstrations burgeoned. The clamping down by the regime's security apparatus only fueled the uprising and, just like a fire fed with more kindling, it grew. Homs, Hama, Edleb, and the Kurdish northeast joined the uprising. Students, workers, shopkeepers, professionals, women, and many others rose up and protested. The Syrian demonstrations, in contrast to those in Tunisia and Egypt, took place in several cities and towns instead of concentrating on the capital, as happened with Beirut, Tehran, and Cairo. The opposition quickly split into several branches. The most active were the youth and liberals who took the struggle to its zenith and called for the resignation of Bashar Assad. Another faction included the opposition "from inside the system," meaning those who did not call for the demise of the regime but for their participation in government as the political opposition. A third faction, the Muslim Brotherhood, played it safe and inserted themselves gradually. As in Egypt, they waited for the liberals and seculars to move first; they then moved into opposition with the logistical help of other Islamist forces in the region and were backed by Qatar and Turkey. In addition, traditional opposition, such as dissidents to the regime or former bureaucrats, also rallied around the uprising, but only when they were persuaded that the revolution was viable. However, in the center of the popular uprising were the forces of civil society, some of which had formed coordination councils inside the country while collaborating with reformist groups overseas. The Syrian revolution, initially launched by the secular youth, was only possible as a widespread national movement because large sectors of the population joined in. For several decades, many different factions, including the Muslim Brotherhood and outgrowths of the Baath Party, had tried to remove the Assad regime; but only when civil society as a whole, led initially by secular youth and reformers, took to the streets, signaling a point of no return, did the revolution became viable.

THE FREE SYRIA ARMY

By the end of summer 2011, the demonstrations had spread throughout Syria, but they had not shaken off the regime of Bashar Assad, though the protests occurred daily and in multiple locations. Many coordination councils emerged and seemed to be leading the movement. The Assad regime feared an irreversible spread of protests that would eventually fill the country with urban uprisings and draw an international outcry to end his regime. Bashar remembered the combination of demonstrations executed by the Cedars Revolution in Syrian-occupied Lebanon and a coalition between Washington and Paris that led to the withdrawal of the Syrian forces from Lebanon. What had been taking place inside Syria since March 2011 was a reminder of that combination, but on a much larger scale, and this time the goal was to bring down the Assad regime itself. The decision by the regime to launch a swift military and security crackdown on the opposition and the marches was based on their own assessment of the strength of the uprising. According to the former vice president of the Syrian Arab Republic, Abdel Halim Khaddam, Bashar's intelligence assessment was that the revolt across Syria had a real chance of undermining the regime. Khaddam explained,

> We know how the regime thinks; I served as foreign minister and vice president under the father [Hafez Assad] and the son [Bashar] for thirty years. When dissidents act, the regime can suppress them easily. When a demonstration takes place, the regime can still contain it and even launch a bigger pro-regime demonstration. But when protests explode across Syria, and not all led by the traditional opposition such as the left-wing or Muslim Brotherhood, the regime knows it is a revolution. And after what happened in North Africa, Bashar knew that the future of these demonstrations, if successful, is the end of his own regime, maybe also his own demise.

Khaddam was one of the most seasoned leaders of Syria to leave the regime to date; his words held historical weight.

When the Assad security machine began what the international community saw as a slaughter of peaceful demonstrators, many members of the Syrian armed forces could no longer tolerate the bloodshed. Though we do not have an exact date for the launch of its operations, we know that by the end of summer 2011, a collection of splinter groups from Assad's forces had emerged as a "Free Syria Army" (FSA). The two main leaders of the military rebels were Colonel Riad al Asaad and Colonel Malik al Kurdi. They appeared on Arab television and called for more defections to occur. In the last months of the year, more soldiers and even some officers joined the FSA and began to engage in guerrilla warfare against the regime's brigades. The first targets of the FSA were the infamous Shabbiha, who had killed most of the protesters.[4] The rebels first attempted to protect the demonstrators as they marched, but the Mukhabarat promptly used lethal force to mow down the marchers. The FSA's volunteers moved to create safe zones for the uprising in towns and cities, but Assad responded by deploying the army with its tanks, artillery, and special forces. By the end of 2011, the Syrian army was heavily involved in the fighting. In opposition, the FSA quickly took the place of the small demonstrations. It spread out across Syria and struck back against the regime forces in guerrilla style.[5]

THE BROTHERHOOD OF SYRIA

The Muslim Brotherhood of Syria is one of the oldest Islamist networks in the Middle East. In the early 1980s, the Brotherhood had attempted to break the regime of Hafez Assad, the father of Bashar, but was severely suppressed, particularly in the city of Hamas in the winter of 1982. The Ikhwan relentlessly maintained their violent opposition to the Hafez Assad regime for two decades but were not accepted or respected by the other, more secular wings of the opposition.

The early waves of the new uprising, though made up of ordinary people, soon became organized by the left wing and the progressives. In the first months of the confrontation, the Brotherhood still operated backstage of the movement, attempting to measure their steps and in some instances secretly talking with the regime. Two major developments led to their leadership's decision to end their negotiations with Assad. One was the progress made by Syria's civil society in its upheaval.

The regime was incapable of crushing this revolt as it had done in 1982. This fact convinced the Islamists that this revolution was irreversible; thus any agreement with Assad was virtually meaningless. But the other development that sent the Syrian branch of the Brotherhood onto the battlefield was the outcome of events in North Africa. By the end of 2011, the Muslim Brotherhood in Egypt was leading the political process there. The Islamist Nahda Party had taken leadership of Tunisia's government. Even in Libya, the Islamists were gaining influence in the country, and the Jihadi militias were spreading quickly and entrenching themselves in most cities, particularly in the Benghazi province. The rise of the Islamists in the Arab Spring countries inspired enthusiasm in the Syrian Brotherhood. Add to this the U.S. administration's undeclared support of the Islamist components of the Syrian opposition, and there was no reason to continue making deals with Assad.

Zuhdi Jasser, head of Save Syria Now, and Sherkoh Abbas, head of the U.S.-based National Assembly of Syria, had been trying to establish communications between the secular and liberal elements of the Syrian opposition and the Obama administration for the first nine months of the revolt—with no success. Abbas told me, "It is clear that with the influence of Qatar and the AKP government in Turkey, the U.S. administration is partnering with the Muslim Brotherhood of Syria at the expense of the seculars, liberals, and minorities of the country."

Abbas's projections were correct. By the end of 2011, the main international representation of the opposition overseas was slowly moving in the direction of the Brotherhood. "They are received at the White House and at the State Department more than others," Ahd al Hindi (a member of the Syrian National Council, the leading Syrian opposition body) told us.

With growing support from Washington, Ankara, and Doha, the Syrian Islamists rushed to seize as much control as possible of the military uprising. The FSA's leadership remained mainly secular, but armed groups on the ground became increasingly Islamist as cash and weapons flowed from Turkey and Qatar, both ruled by Islamist governments. By early 2012, the Syrian opposition to the Assad regime included both seculars and Islamists, but the latter held the optimal position, being the international interlocutors and partners with the three major players: Qatar, Turkey, and the United States.[6]

IRAN AND HEZBOLLAH

As I had projected years ago, the Iranian regime and Hezbollah, two staunch allies of Syria's Assad regime, came to Bashar's rescue when he faced the armed uprising. Since Tehran and Damascus have had a strategic treaty of cooperation binding them since the early 1980s, a treaty they continuously renewed from Assad the father to Assad the son, an attack against one ally is an attack against the other. In this case, Syria's regime was under duress, so the sister regime in Tehran came to its aid. It is important to note, however, that beyond the formalities of written agreements, there was another more fundamental reason for Iran's intervention in Syria. A collapse of the Assad regime in Damascus would potentially undermine the single most fundamental element of Iranian foreign policy and strategic survival in the region. The Iranians had for decades used Syria as an aerial bridge to connect with Hezbollah's forces in Lebanon. Without Syria's airports, Iranian logistical support for its Lebanese Shia ally would have to sail through the Indian Ocean, onto the Red Sea, through the Suez Canal, and head to the eastern shore of the Mediterranean under Israeli eyes in order to reach Lebanon's seaports. Losing Assad would mean that Iran's ayatollahs would lose Syria, and that would cut the regime off from Hezbollah and from the Mediterranean, both crucial to Iran's westward expansion.

The Syrian bridge became even more important in the eyes of the mullahs when the U.S. coalition withdrew from Iraq in December 2011. With the Obama administration abruptly leaving Iraq that month, a wide and accessible space opened between Iran and Syria. In Baghdad, a government friendly to Iran, headed by Prime Minister Nour el Maliki, would not stop the Pasdaran from crossing and traveling to Syria's hinterland. Iraqi politicians opposed to Iran's regime, from all ethnic backgrounds, including Sunnis, liberal Shia, and Kurds, told me in Washington and Brussels during 2011 that Iran was waiting out the United States. "The day U.S. Marines are out is the day the Pasdaran are in," they warned. In fact, during the Syrian uprising of 2011 the Iranian regime was planning to help Assad regardless of the U.S. presence in Iraq. Iranian military advisers, intelligence, and logistics arrived in Damascus via flights from Tehran, notwithstanding the U.S. presence in Baghdad.

But the most significant support the "axis" sent to Assad would be the fighters of Hezbollah. By late summer 2011, reports circulated in the Arab world that hundreds of Hezbollah militiamen were crossing into neighboring Syria to fight the rebels. It was easy for the pro-Iranian network in Lebanon to join Assad's security forces from their bases inside the Bekaa Valley, which is contiguous with Syria. They simply had to cross the borders, which were in their hands. Body bags with Hezbollah fighters killed in Syria started to be returned to Lebanon in the autumn of 2011. Some say before. The skills of Hezbollah's militiamen as urban fighters were needed by the Syrian intelligence in order to wage the type of guerrilla warfare these militia had become familiar with while fighting in South Lebanon against the Israelis.

By early 2012, Syria had become a battlefield contested by the regime and its opposition; and the latter was divided as the race for leadership between seculars and Islamists heated up. Qatar, Turkey, and the regional Muslim Brotherhood came to the support of the Islamist components of the rebels while Iran, Iraq's government, and Hezbollah in Lebanon rushed to help Assad. At the Security Council of the United Nations, another stalemate took place as the United States attempted to pass a resolution in favor of U.N. action against the regime, while Russia and China used their veto power to block it.

CHAPTER FIVE

THE WINDS OF UPRISINGS IN ARABIA

THE ARABIAN PENINSULA WAS ABLE TO CATCH UP with the Arab Spring during its first year. The last subregion to feel the winds of change, it nevertheless followed the course of North Africa and the Levant. The monarchies of the Persian Gulf were wealthy enough to satisfy their middle class, social scientists thought. Saudi Arabia had a hermetically sealed system of power, wrapped tight in Wahabi Islamism; the mere formation of opposition was unthinkable there until 2011. The United Arab Emirates, Qatar, Oman, and Kuwait had monarchies, providers of services and cash to their people, thus lessening the menace of revolutions. True, Bahrain had had a clear problem with Iran for years, but it was under Saudi protection. Only Yemen was ripe for trouble. Its own modern history was filled with coups, civil unrest, and terrorism. The winds of the Arab Spring, ravaging North Africa, fed the flames of that poor country's already explosive situation.

YEMEN

In April 2011, popular demonstrations against the rule of authoritarian president Ali Abdallah Saleh exploded in Yemen. The country's precarious political structure and powerful internal players added peculiar dynamics to the revolt. As indicated earlier, the southern part of the country, brought under the banner of the north in 1992 by military force, was in a state of civil disobedience against Sanaa authorities. The Hirak al Janoubi (Southern Action), representing the organized political forces centered in Aden, was already mobilized due to the previous years' conflict, but with the Arab revolts crumbling the Tunisian and Egyptian regimes and challenging Gaddafi and Assad, the Yemeni revolt grew. However, unlike past southern demonstrations, which had been quickly suppressed by a stronger northern regime, the new protests contained a northern opposition to Saleh as well.

Over the next few months, most cities and towns in Yemen experienced massive demonstrations calling for the resignation of the president and the introduction of reforms within government bureaucracies. Saleh, like the rulers in other countries challenged by the Arab Spring, sent his security agencies to put down the demonstrators. They killed and wounded dozens of civilians and jailed and tortured hundreds. During the first stage of the revolt, Yemen's armed forces remained somewhat loyal to the dictator. The organizational structures of the military and security apparatus were largely controlled by Saleh's tribe, the Sanhan, and their allies.

However, as casualties mounted, many officers in the army joined the rebels. In Washington, I had a sense that it would take a great deal of unrest and suppression for the Yemeni army to start abandoning its president. From Yemeni officers who were training in Washington, I understood that the tribal structure within all institutions would play a role in the shrinking of Saleh's support, but the strongman's failure to bring about reconciliation among the tribes through federation would lead to the demise of the president's powers. Indeed, even as Saleh rejected most political initiatives for reconciliation, including several propositions made by his friends in Saudi Arabia and by the United States, more demonstrations took place in the streets and rebels emerged in towns across the country. To rein in the revolt, Yemen's leader resorted to armed responses, and more demonstrators were killed and wounded. These deaths provoked the demonstrators' tribes to seek revenge against the tribes whose soldiers were serving in the military units. As the tensions harmed the precarious tribal structure of the country, the dynamics changed in favor of revolt. More soldiers quit the army to join their tribes, and more tribes decided to not engage in violence against other tribes just for the sake of Saleh. By the end of 2011, large segments of the armed forces had switched allegiances to the rebels, and high-ranking officers formed an alternative command. Saleh was gradually isolated but maintained his control over a hardcore component of the army and his praetorian guard.

A collection of diverse political forces made up the opposition to Saleh. Southern separatists, northern left-wing and reformist groups, and liberal networks were the initial constituents. The Islamists soon became a growing component of the demonstrations. In addition to the military dissidents, the opposition gained traction among the tribes opposed to Saleh. The Salafists, the largest coalition among the Islamists, soon broadened their representation to the point that they became inseparable from the movement.

Concern grew in the West about the connections of Southern Action to al Qaeda, which meanwhile had penetrated areas in central Yemen. Saleh used this Western anxiety to favor his cause. He claimed his forces were fighting al Qaeda among the rebels and if he lost the fight, al Qaeda would take over. In fact, al Qaeda's cells did take advantage of the fractures in Yemen to invade villages, recruit among the tribes, and gather weapons. Anwar al Awlaki, the American-born terrorist of Yemeni parents, used the opportunity to mount operations that penetrated into Africa while attempting to trigger attacks within the United States. But the rise of al Qaeda, although perhaps delaying the placement of international pressure on Saleh, did not change the course of events in Yemen. The imminent pressure was increasing in his own ranks. One year into the uprising, Saleh was battling for his political and personal future.[1]

BAHRAIN FACES THE WINDS OF CHANGE

In the early months of 2011, as Egypt and Tunisia were producing their versions of massive political change, and as Libya underwent its descent into irreversible violence, the island-kingdom of Bahrain faced its own protests. The Bahraini opposition was composed mainly of Shia citizens who felt disenfranchised by the mostly Sunni regime. The sectarian division between a slight Shia majority and a large Sunni minority had always been in the background of political tensions in the oil-rich country. But the new explosive uprisings in the Arab world emboldened Bahrain's opposition to seize the moment, particularly because the international community was watching closely and siding with the protesters. By mid-2011, opposition groups organized demonstrations against the ruling al Khalifa family, calling for deep reforms, while more militant factions sought full regime change. The government responded with police actions and made arrests. The turbulence in Bahrain took a different direction than in North Africa. The sectarian divide overtook the politico-economic crisis. While most sociopolitical claims were legitimate, the movement appeared to be Shia in its essence and the government was perceived as quintessentially Sunni. The sectarian complication deepened as regional forces entered the confrontation: Iran's regime seized the historic opportunity for a social Shia upheaval on the island and infiltrated the community with its own sympathizers. The Iranian factor in the Bahraini opposition drew a Saudi intervention. To assist the government in Manama, which feared a pro-Iranian coup, Riyadh sent military convoys and forces across the causeway to support the Bahraini forces.

Bahrain's Spring was botched precisely because of the Iranian attempt to use the popular discontent arising from political and social grounds to seize power and influence in the kingdom and overthrow its government. Tehran's meddling provoked a Saudi counteraction and transformed the crisis from civil society versus government into an Iranian-backed uprising versus a Sunni-Gulf counterforce. Bahraini military personnel who were training in Washington, D.C., at the time feared Iranian manipulation of militant groups inside the Shia community— a Hezbollah presence had already been detected by Bahraini authorities. Shia Bahrainis whom I met then were true reformers and had a political agenda for change. During 2011, Bahraini officials and the opposition both realized that the two parties could have accommodated a

democratic process had Iran not pushed for the radicalization of the social struggle. Within the Shia community there were authentic reformers, but there were also pro-Iranian elements; there were also circles
pushing for reform within the Sunni community. My advice to both
sides was to form a common Shia-Sunni reform coalition to head off
Iran's radicalization of the movement and at the same time avoid inter-
ference in Bahrain by the Gulf states.[2]

THE KINGDOM BRACES FOR ITS KHAMSIN

The winds of the Arab Spring did not spare Saudi Arabia, the self-
declared Wahabi Kingdom, but it may be the last monarchy in the region to be challenged by a violent revolution. The country has been seen
as immune to mass uprisings or military coups, and for good reason: Its
power structure makes it quite difficult for a popular movement to be
organized and gain a space in civil society before it is dismantled. There
are no activist NGOs in the kingdom and no political parties. The only
well-organized entities are the clerically approved religious networks,
which are Salafist and thus opposed to any change coming from seculars or non-Wahabi quarters. Yet, as noted in an earlier chapter, those
advocating there for human rights, women's rights, and other reforms
had been active for years before the blossoming of the Arab Spring. The
king has responded, though slowly, to the emerging pressure from those
moderate groups by allowing more space for women in the public arena
as well as by relaxing codes of conduct, but he has encountered pushback from the hard-core clerics. As demonstrations brought down authoritarian presidents in North Africa, the Saudi royals moved to offer
more rights to their citizens, particularly the most marginalized group:
women. During the year 2011, King Abdallah authorized Saudi women
to vote and run as candidates in municipal elections, a significant move
toward granting gender rights but still a long way from equal political
rights for women.

Regardless of any reforms permitted by the king, the tremors in
Cairo, Tunis, Tripoli, and Damascus warn that instability may come to

the country, perhaps even impacting its government. The rapid fall of Ben Ali and his subsequent exile in Saudi Arabia signaled the possibility of revolution-based regime changes in the Arab world at a scale that might affect the kingdom. When Mubarak left power in Egypt, a major ally of Saudi Arabia was lost. The Egyptian strongman, also an ally of the United States and a foe of Iran, had been a major undeclared ally of the Saudis. The rise of youth and reformers in Egypt, and behind them the Muslim Brotherhood, could not have been less thrilling news for Riyadh because of the many unknowns in Cairo's political future. If liberals took over, they would, with time, influence Saudi youth by the power of example. But if the Muslim Brotherhood were to seize power, the Egyptian Islamists would eventually turn east to obliterate the rich kingdom. In contrast, the downfall of Gaddafi, who had incessant quarrels with the king of Saudi Arabia, came as a relief to Riyadh. But in Libya there was also the issue of who would be in charge: seculars or al Qaeda–inspired Jihadists? Both were trouble for the Gulf state. As for Damascus, the Saudis had been at odds with the Assad regime and systematically backed the mostly Sunni opposition. This in turn drew the ire of the Alawi regime, of Hezbollah, and, more important, of Iran's ayatollahs. For the previous few years, Saudi Arabia had been at odds with the "Shia axis" extending from Beirut to Baghdad, and the Syrian civil war heightened the tensions between Tehran and Riyadh, already exacerbated by the Iranian nuclear threat. The ripple effects of the Arab Spring announced a coming Khamsin blowing toward the kingdom.

As noted above, the first Iranian wind heading to Saudi Arabia was felt in Bahrain. Riyadh perceived the uprising on the island to its east as an Iranian attempt to seize the small ally and transform it into an advanced Iranian military and propaganda base for campaigns against the Saudis. Such was the reason for the Saudi intervention in support of al Khalifa. But more concerning to the monarchy were Iranian activities in the eastern Saudi provinces with large Shia communities. The areas of Qatif, Dammam, and al Ihsa', like Bahrain, witnessed both Shiite political activism on the one hand and Iranian-backed militant activities on the other. For Riyadh, the sudden rise in violence in the east, where the nation's oil reserves are located, was caused by the Khomeinists.[3]

Last but not least of Saudi concerns is the menace of the Shia Houthis guerrillas on Yemen's northern borders. They have a potential to spill violence over onto the Saudi side at the southern edges of the Hejaz. The Arab Spring, ironically, had activated a chain reaction that led to an all-out Iranian assault on the kingdom. But that was not the only hot wind blasting against the royals. As Yemen was dividing into zones and the regime of Ali Abdallah Saleh was weakening, another enemy of the ruling al Saud grew in strength: al Qaeda.

With scores to settle against the king and his emirs because of the suppression of al Qaeda inside Saudi provinces, the Jihadists jealously eyed the regime again. The Arab Spring in Yemen opened another stream of threats, this time from the south, and Riyadh had to ensure a solution inside Yemen that would guarantee Saudi Arabia's southern security and contain the resurging al Qaeda menace.

The Arab Spring Khamsin is putting pressure on the kingdom. Its future is difficult to foresee. The country is solidly held by a powerful security apparatus, but neither of the threats on its borders, from Iran or al Qaeda, is likely to recede. This has created an opportunity for two opposing forces inside Saudi Arabia. The pro-regime Salafists have mobilized in defense of the Wahabi regime against an "apostate Shia Iran" and its allies inside the Peninsula. At the same time, Saudi dissidents have increased their activities, albeit most of them in online and international forums. The Arab revolts in the region seemed to have shaken off the foundations of a system established in the 1920s. The liberals may be the least harmful, as other forces—the Iranian regime and the Muslim Brotherhood—have been seeking not the liberalization of Arabia but its control by different Islamist movements.[4]

GULF DEVELOPMENTS

Although most of the dramatic developments generated by the Arab Spring took place in Yemen, Saudi Arabia, and Bahrain during 2011, other countries in the Peninsula were touched by the waves of challenge, though in varying degrees. Kuwait—still living under the protection of the United States and its allies since liberation from Saddam's invasion in 1991—witnessed a rise in opposition. On the one hand, also encouraged discretely by Iran, a Shia protestation began demanding greater political participation in the political system, which was perceived as being fully in the hands of the Sunnis. This mounting pressure triggered further Salafist counterpressures to demand the implementation of Sharia. On the other hand, liberal groups increased their activities in accord with youth protests in the Arab world. The geopolitical positioning of the small principality—between an Iranian-influenced Iraq, Saudi Arabia, and the ayatollahs' regime across the waters—has compelled Kuwait to enter the arena of dramatic choices. As for the rest of the Peninsula, all three forces of change are simultaneously putting pressure on the ruling dynasty, the House of Sabbah.

The United Arab Emirates also felt the pressures of confrontations taking place on the Arabian Peninsula during the first waves of the Arab Spring, but the federation of wealthy monarchies did not experience serious challenges compelling their governments to mobilize. The heavy concentration of businesses and investments in the Emirates played to their advantage, at least in the first year or two of the region's uprisings. Liberal forces did not have political incentives to move, and Salafi networks were contained and satisfied with the UAE's backing of the rebels in Libya and Syria. Most important, Iran's regime had invested widely in the Emirates' financial institutions. The UAE's stability became subject to challenge only toward the end of 2012, when the Muslim Brotherhood, having secured its gains in Egypt and Tunisia, began meddling in the federation's internal politics.

Oman, bordering the UAE, remained the Gulf country most removed from the Arab Spring. Events in Yemen will soon catch up with the peaceful Arab Sultanate on the Indian Ocean. In this country, a race between Salafi Jihadists and supporters of Iran, not to mention liberals, will demand that unusual policies be adopted.[5]

QATAR AND AL JAZEERA, AN ISLAMIST SUPERPOWER

In the Arabian Peninsula, one country surged from being simply a rich oil and gas producer and exporter to becoming a leader in the Islamist sphere of influence worldwide. At the onset of the revolts, the al Thani dynasty had already scored significantly in expanding its political and media influence in the region and beyond. The main tool of influence has been the al Jazeera television network, which grew to become the primary ideological and communications hub serving the Muslim Brotherhood in the Arab world. Through this popular channel, Qatar's elite positioned itself as a pillar of influence in Arab and international politics. During 2010, the U.S. Congress, the European Parliament, and many think tanks in the West invited me to debate the role of al Jazeera in influencing events. The question was whether the channel had enough clout to actually provoke political changes. In most forums, there were two schools of thought: One argued that al Jazeera has limited influence on events in the Arab world; the other school argued that it can actually provoke events. I argued that the answer was somewhere in between. Based on my monitoring of the editorial line, guest speakers, ideologues, and the responses by audiences over fourteen years, my projection was that al Jazeera has significant, if not ultimate, influence on a sector of Sunni societies, particularly the Islamists, and more precisely the Muslim Brotherhood and Salafists. I had no doubts that, once the revolts began, al Jazeera TV, with Qatar behind it, would become a major player in directing the Islamists in their interaction and steps taken throughout the Arab Spring. That was exactly what happened in Tunisia, Egypt, Libya, Yemen, and Syria in 2011. The network played a tremendous role in focusing on the Islamist forces and pounding the regimes until they crumbled. When Sheikh Yusuf al Qaradawi, the station's mentor, appeared on al Jazeera, he delivered the final blows to Ben Ali, Mubarak, and Saleh by legitimizing an Islamist resistance against the dictators.[6]

However, as I also argued, al Jazeera was caught off-guard by the initial rise of civil societies. The ideological elite of the network invested in Islamists and Jihadists and projected that they would lead future revolts against the rulers in the region. Al Jazeera's analysis did not predict that the uprisings would happen so soon or that secular reformists would be the ones to trigger and lead the initial wave. I appeared several times on al Jazeera over the years leading up to the Arab Spring and was always rebutted for arguing that youth, women, workers, and minorities would rise against the dictators and, after them, against the Islamists. My take was dismissed as "pro-American" and in some cases "pro-Israeli." Those who debated me counterargued that the masses were in harmony with their leadership's fight against the Zionists and for the liberation of Palestine, and that no revolution could supersede these central themes. As the events of early 2011 demonstrated that the masses of the Arab world are first concerned with their own oppression, al Jazeera had to adapt to reality. It navigated shrewdly, cautiously supporting the revolts of the youth and skillfully focusing on the Islamists throughout the revolutions.

Al Jazeera and Qatar saw the creation of South Sudan in January and had to digest it as a loss to the Arab and Islamic identity. They blamed Khartoum for the defeat. And as soon as demonstrators took to the streets of Tunis, and later flocked to Tahrir Square, the Islamist hub in Doha focused on the "forces" leading the revolts, not the identity of the masses marching against the dictators. The full power of television coverage elevated the Nahda Party in Tunisia, the Muslim Brotherhood in Egypt, and the Salafi militias in Libya to a level of international recognition that led the West to believe that all or most of the rebels were Islamists. In a few months, partially thanks to Qatar's funding and al Jazeera's heavy campaigning, the Islamists of the Arab Spring supplanted the seculars and the liberals. Qatar was at the top of a regional web of Islamist forces that were rapidly on their way to seizing power in several countries within the following year.[7] However, as counterrevolutions began to brew against the Islamists in North Africa, particularly in Egypt and Tunisia in 2013, the network and Qatar were severely criticized by secular forces.

CHAPTER SIX

U.S. AND EUROPEAN ATTITUDES TOWARD THE SPRING

BY THE END OF 2011, THE SHAPE OF THE ARAB SPRING was already defined by the paths of the first revolts. The picture was grim. The results were earth-shattering in the region, but the movement was not over. In fact, in its second year, the Arab Spring itself was exploding. Let us take a quick overview of the Arab world map during that second year.

Egypt was now without Mubarak, who was in jail awaiting trial, while the revolutionaries, both secular and Islamist, were locked in a delicate balance of power with the military over the inheritance left by the former dictator. The second-year events in Egypt were really about who would seize power.

In Tunisia, the revolution had ousted Ben Ali and seized the country's institutions, but the struggle to determine the political future of the first country of the Arab Spring continued. As in Egypt, Islamists, seculars, and the army were maintaining an equilibrium of force.

Libya moved quickly into a seemingly more stable postrevolutionary position. After Islamist rebels killed Gaddafi in October 2011, a new government emerged that included both seculars and Islamists. The Salafi militias did, however, remain in control of large swaths of land, particularly in the east.

In Yemen, Ali Abdallah Saleh resigned in November 2011. He left behind a precarious government with a southern secession still alive and a resurging al Qaeda.

Bahrain remained in crisis mode with an entrenched Sunni government and a determined Shia opposition.

The bloodiest battlefield in the first year of the Arab Spring was Syria. The country was engulfed with killings, kidnappings, and occasional massacres. The Assad regime turned gradually to using regular troops in addition to security forces and ordering air raids when needed. Assad's opposition had produced a military uprising, but Islamists were seizing more and more ground from the seculars.

In other areas of the Middle East, unrest was growing, often explosively. In Morocco, the Islamists of the Justice Party won the legislative elections in December 2011 and set themselves up to form a cabinet in 2012. Algeria's Islamists, encouraged by their kin's victories across North Africa, reorganized amid the nervousness of the mostly secular and authoritarian regime. In Sudan, Omar al Bashir, although indicted by the International Criminal Court for genocide, survived the Arab Spring of North Africa and repositioned himself to reemerge on a regional scale. Months after South Sudan obtained full independence in July 2011, Bashir's forces pounded the Abiei area with shells and the Khartoum air force resumed its raids on regime opponents.

In the Sahel, armed Salafi groups roamed the desert, shipping weapons from southern Libya to Niger, Mali, and Mauritania, a trend that would culminate the following year in an al Qaeda military advance in northern Mali.

In Iraq, the pro-Iranian factions were waiting out the American military withdrawal scheduled to end in December 2011, and the developments in 2012 that followed the U.S. pullout were ominous, warning of things to come.

Last but not least, in Lebanon, Hezbollah consolidated and tightened its grip on power during the first year of the uprisings while Salafi armed groups, emerging from the Sunni areas, extended their support to the Syrian uprising against Assad.

The big picture of the revolutions at the end of 2011 was dark. After the glory days of popular demonstrations à la Bastille, from January to April 2012, from Tunis to Cairo, Tripoli to Damascus, the uprisings quickly turned into bloody repression, military uprisings, Jihadi penetration, and, as in Syria, full-blown civil war with regional ramifications.

In reality, the first waves of the Spring never died, for the youth and forces of civil society continued to press forward; for they believed in the final democratic goal of the upheavals. But to that first wave another was added, led by the Islamists. In fact, by the end of the first year of the revolts, there were two distinct waves clashing for political change: a secular push and an Islamist pull.

The Arab Spring did not end with the fall of the secular dictators; it was instead torn between the two waves and pounded by undaunted surviving dictators, such as Assad of Syria and Bashir of Sudan. However, the real game changer was the positioning of the international community. It would make all the difference to the fate of the Arab Spring whether or not the West in general and the United States in particular decided to pressure the remaining dictators to step down. If the West chose to accelerate the dictators' isolation, their choices for new partnerships regarding the parties replacing the crumbling regimes would also impact the final fallout from the Spring. This is why the policies of the United States and Europe during the movement's first months—and the role these policies played in the aftermath in 2012—are key to understanding the unfolding events there.[1]

During 2011, as an adviser to the U.S. Congress on terrorism and then as a senior adviser on foreign policy and national security to presidential candidate Mitt Romney in the fall, I engaged with lawmakers, diplomats, military commanders, and representatives of various civil society groups in the Greater Middle East about the future of these revolts. Across the board, the main concern I detected among my interlocutors was the position of the United States. Activists from Egypt, Libya, Tunisia, Syria, and other countries, immersed in the upheavals, along with the Western politicians, were constantly asking about Washington's position on the Arab Spring and the forces involved in it. In fact,

since day one of the revolt there was an "American issue": On whose side
was the United States?

U.S. POLICY AND THE ARAB SPRING

In his speech at Cairo University in 2009, President Barack Obama addressed an audience consisting of supporters and opponents of President
Mubarak. The dominant analysis at the time was that the U.S. president
aimed to change America's image in the eyes of what was then considered to be the Muslim world. The ambiguous approach in world politics
taken by the Obama presidency was to reduce the existing relationship
between the United States and the peoples of the region to a bilateral relationship between the American government and a worldwide religious
community, the Muslims. Aside from that, international relations in the
post–World War I era and under the United Nations have always been
between nation-states or between international organizations and nation-states, not between religions or between nation-states and religions.

The new Obama approach to engaging the Muslim world reduced
relations with the Middle East to the currents, movements, and parties
known as Islamist and who perceived themselves as representatives of
all Muslims. The speech in Cairo, the product of a new U.S. policy,
assumed that the region is Islamic and that its representatives are Islamists. Obama's assertion was that since the West in general and the
United States in particular were perceived as aggressors in the Islamic
region, a change had to be made in relations with the region's representative religion. That would entail a major shift in its diplomatic posture.
Washington would sound a global retreat from the Greater Middle East,
end the two ground wars in Iraq and Afghanistan, terminate the War of
Ideas waged after 9/11 by the George W. Bush administration, end the
propagation of Western-style democracy in the region, and partner with
the one dominant force in the Arab world and surrounding regions, the
Islamists. The Cairo speech was preparation for the Obama partnership
with the Muslim Brotherhood—two years before the advent of the Arab
Spring.[2]

The new policy toward the Arab world had a direct effect on the outcome of the revolts as they exploded from Tunisia to Egypt. Washington's foreign policy bureaucracies were readied to engage with the Islamist movements and parties, not with the seculars and minorities—as the previous administration had at least attempted to do. As previously noted, the uprisings during the first year of the revolutions clearly demonstrated a pattern of U.S. favoritism toward the Islamists over the seculars. Across North Africa, the Obama administration timed its pressures on shaky regimes with the positioning of the Islamists—the Nahda, Brotherhood, and Salafists. Far from being presented as an official policy, the partnership with these movements was subtly presented as "backing the rebels." In Tunisia, U.S. pressure grew on Ben Ali as Nahda was resurging and securing its position in the country. Its leaders received access to policymakers in Washington while their secular colleagues were offered zero visibility. When the dictator left the country, the Islamists—the largest, best organized force—were in position to seize the revolution and run for election. In Egypt, a similar scenario took place, and on a much larger scale.[3]

The Obama administration dealt carefully with the events in Tahrir Square. It increased pressure on Mubarak only in proportion to the growth of the Muslim Brotherhood's participation in events. When the Islamists were solidly at the center of the movement, Washington abandoned Mubarak and asked him to step down. Later, as the best-organized and best-supported movement in the country, the Brotherhood completed its control of Egypt's institutions.

In Libya, a similar scenario shaped U.S. patronage of the Islamists. NATO support of the "rebels" profited the Salafi militias, the largest body of insurgents against Gaddafi. As the rebels took over the regime's positions and cities, increased U.S. aid was largely directed to the militias, most of whom were Islamists. The country was slowly falling to the omnipresent armed groups chanting for Jihad under the command of leaders who trained and fought with al Qaeda. This U.S. policy of fraternization with the Islamists did not openly aim to encourage the Jihadists to seize power. Perhaps the policymakers were led to believe by their advisers that by partnering with the "political Islamists" they would be creating an Islamist dam against al Qaeda and its nebulae, but this was a miscalculation. As historical analysis clearly shows, Salafists of all genres eventually move from their interim agendas to the global agenda of creating an Islamic state. Ignoring history demonstrates utter failure in U.S. projections. Throughout 2011 and 2012, the "political Islamists" who seized power with the West's assistance in turn helped the more extreme elements enter the political system, and the latter maintained their links to al Qaeda. From Tunisia to Egypt, the Nahda and the Brotherhood seized parliaments and governments and formed an alliance with a network of Salafists, who moved under the umbrella of the mainstream Islamists but maintained strategic relations with the Jihadists, including al Qaeda. U.S. strategies did not work to ameliorate the fallout of the Arab Spring. Instead of moderating the political Islamists, they legitimized the radical ones.

The Arab Spring strategies of the Obama administration also encountered obstacles in Yemen, Bahrain, and, most important, Syria. In Yemen, Washington worked hand in hand with the Saudis to pressure President Saleh out of power, but because of the strong partnership with the Salafists within the opposition, the post-Saleh era failed to witness a serious move toward secular democracy. Furthermore, the empowering of Salafists led to a wider spread of al Qaeda in parts of the country. Yemen was yet another example of Western mishandling of the Arab Spring. For instead of using the opportunity of a major political change in a country ruled by autocrats and intimidated by Islamists to support civil society, U.S. policymakers opted for a rushed move to satisfy the Islamists without empowering secular forces. Toward the end of 2012, Yemen had a post-Saleh regime with the exact same problems faced under the dictator: a secessionist south, a divided north, and growing power in the hands of the Salafists.[4]

In Bahrain, U.S. policy attempted to balance the Sunni regime, which was an ally to Saudi Arabia, and the Shia opposition. However, Washington failed to identify the most secular components of the

Shia, leaving the pro-Iranian elements to overly influence the opposition. This failure led the United States to an undesirable option: either support the regime in friendship with Saudi Arabia—or support the Iranian-penetrated opposition, thereby extending an advantage in influence to Tehran. The sympathies with the Islamists were not limited to the Sunni Salafists in Washington's Middle East policy quarters. In North Africa, U.S. foreign policy opted for the Brotherhood and their allies; in Bahrain, Washington chose to give equal attention to the Islamist components of the Shia opposition and the Saudi-backed Sunni government. The Obama administration should have identified the secular components of the Shia opposition and paired them with the most liberal among the Sunni NGOs before attempting to mediate between a friendly government and a liberal opposition. Bahrain by 2013 was still in a stalemate between state power and its opposition.[5]

The U.S. choice to partner with Islamists instead of with liberals and seculars also played a catastrophic role in Syria's civil war. When nonviolent demonstrations erupted against the Assad regime in March 2011, Washington failed to identify the secular elements and invite them to dialogue. Instead, the administration reached out to representatives from or close to the Muslim Brotherhood of Syria, and so lent its support to the coalitions led by the Muslim Brotherhood. The Americans made another mistake by subcontracting Syria's revolution to regional players also governed by Islamists, such as the AKP government in Turkey and the Qatar government. Instead of building a direct channel between Washington, Brussels, and an inclusive Syrian opposition (with both its seculars and Islamists), the United States shepherded the Islamist-led Syrian opposition and encouraged its regional Islamist partners to back them at the expense of liberals and civil society groups.

By the end of 2011 and into early 2012, the Islamist armed elements in the Syrian opposition had grown rapidly. They had seized several strategic positions across the country and had become indispensable to the opposition and to civilians desperate for help and protection from the Assad forces. This opposition organized itself as the Syrian National

Council and obtained official recognition from the Islamist governments of Turkey, Qatar, Libya, and Tunisia as well as an endorsement by the United States.

The American position on the Arab Spring as a whole, though led by the Obama administration, was not a unified one in Washington, D.C. A majority of Congress, particularly in the House of Representatives, was clearly opposed to empowering the Islamists, including the Muslim Brotherhood. Among the many legislators who expressed these concerns were Senator Joseph Lieberman and representatives Sue Myrick, Chris Smith, and Frank Wolf. Lawmakers who spoke at Coptic conferences in Congress, including Trent Franks and Frank Wolf, insisted that the Brotherhood was not the right partner for America. Congressman Ed Royce, who spoke at the annual Conference on the Copts of Egypt in June 2012, and who became the chairman of the Committee on Foreign Affairs of the U.S. House of Representatives in January 2013, told me, "It is a grave mistake to subcontract Egypt and the countries of the Arab Spring to the Islamists and Salafists." But in American politics, it is the executive branch under the authority of the president that manages American foreign policy. The legislative branch can influence, pressure, and guide the administration in world affairs, particularly by funding or refraining from financing projects, but it cannot lead relationships overseas.[6]

EUROPE'S POLICIES TOWARD MIDDLE EAST REVOLTS

While the West in general had initially placed high hopes in the uprisings hitting the Arab world in 2011, Europe approached the revolt with a different bent than the United States. First, there was no ideological agenda in dealing with the so-called Arab Spring. Unlike the Obama administration, the governments of the European Union were not under a direct influence of the Muslim Brotherhood per se, though they eventually fell into the same trend followed by Washington, and also served to empower the Islamists in the region. Second, Europeans held higher stakes, as the continent's economies relied profoundly on Libyan oil, and the proximity of North Africa and the Levant made it crucial for Europe to secure influence over the post–Arab Spring regimes. Third and more important, the migration of North African and Near East peoples into Europe posed a greater challenge to social and cultural integration than it did in America. Whichever elements controlled the Arab world after the revolt would also influence the radicalization process inside Europe's Arab and Muslim communities. It could go either way; that is, the communities could become more radical or more moderate. These concerns were related to me by European parliamentary groups and leaders at conventions in Brussels, Madrid, Berlin, Budapest, and Bucharest. These meetings, organized by the European Popular Party (EPP), which had a majority in the European Parliament, were attended by prime ministers, presidents, ministers of foreign affairs, and many lawmakers.

During my several briefings in Brussels, these lawmakers expressed their hopes and concerns. Tokia Saife, a French member originally from Algeria, said to me, "This is a great opportunity for the peoples of the region to free themselves and engage in a Mediterranean dialogue." Parliamentarians from Italy, Germany, and Sweden also expressed positive feelings. They felt that the rise of the youth in Tunisia and Egypt and of protesters in Libya was a sign that a massive change could happen south of the Mediterranean. In Brussels at the end of March 2011, two different tunes were resonating among the people. One group of lawmakers was excited by the events in the region and wished its governments to engage the "rebels" or demonstrators. British, French, and Swedish legislators were among this bloc. But another group was more skeptical and feared the better-organized Islamists and eventually Jihadists might hijack the movement. Among those concerned were Spanish, Italian, and Cypriot members of the European Parliament. Ioannis Kassoulides, deputy chair of the EPP group at the European Parliament from Cyprus, told the briefing session that "while it was clear that youth and democracy activists were driving the demonstrations against the regimes in the region, one can see the second wave behind them, made of Salafists and other Islamists, seizing the historic opportunity to establish their Caliphate." In this early stage of the Arab Spring, both European groups were right. The uprisings were producing, at the same time, both political species: liberal youth and Islamists. And as I had been arguing since before the revolts and during their eruption, the West was in a unique position to help one at the expense of the other.

Regrettably, Europe's governments, led by the United Kingdom and France, followed the U.S. administration's rush to assist the "rebels" without making the vital distinction between seculars and Islamists. Europe's proximity to North Africa and the Levant had significant consequences for the policy of providing assistance to the rebels. In Libya, France and Great Britain moved quickly and correctly, along with the United States, to stop Gaddafi's forces from taking back Benghazi from the opposition by launching very successful air strikes that degraded Libyan strategic weapons to a point where ground opposition forces could march toward Tripoli. But the Europeans made a grave mistake through their inability or unwillingness to distinguish between the two components of the Arab Spring. They supported the opposition in general instead of ensuring a specific partnership with the secular and liberal forces of the insurgents or the demonstrators.[7]

In Tunisia and in Egypt, Europe's representatives endorsed the protests but ended up meeting with and backing cabinets dominated by Islamists. The Europeans argued that the Islamists' political clout was helpful in stabilizing the region after the Arab Spring. In other words, since the Brotherhood and their allies were organized and had engaged the Europeans in previous years, they were trustworthy enough to form successor governments if they won the elections. In Libya, European military action took place under NATO, but the French and British took the lead in air strikes and other naval operations. Encouraged by Qatar and Turkey, the Europeans tolerated the presence of Salafi militias in their guise as rebels. These Islamist armed elements, however, quickly seized installations and neighborhoods across the country and maintained a high level of influence in Benghazi and the adjacent areas. The European Union as a whole (with a few exceptions, including the Italian prime minister Silvio Berlusconi) pressed for a rapid ousting of Gaddafi in Libya and a swift transition in Tunisia and in Egypt.

On Syria, the European position fluctuated but followed the same general path. Throughout 2011 and 2012, Paris admonished the Assad regime and threatened intervention. Both President Sarkozy and his successor, President François Hollande, condemned the brutal oppression of Syrian civilians, but as the revolt mutated into a civil war in early 2012, France and Great Britain moved from open calls for Assad to step down at once to carefully crafted statements still condemning the regime but hesitant to arm the opposition. As the Arab Spring spread across the continent, I felt that European leaders and diplomats had a difficult time distinguishing the good from the bad. However, European legislators held more subtle views.

During the winter of 2011 the European Ideas Network, the main think tank of the European Popular Party, organized a forum on the Arab Spring in Madrid. There, lawmakers from Bulgaria, Italy, and Spain expressed concerns about the uncertain future of the region if liberal democrats could not be found to partner with. As a speaker at the forum, I encouraged the Europeans—the democracies closest geographically to North Africa and the Levant—to lead the exploration of this idea in order to find political forces with which the West should associate. I warned, though, that the Islamists would have the advantages of organization and funding from the outset. Both currents, I emphasized, stood in opposition to the dictators, but the Islamists were unified and receiving funds from the Gulf states while the liberals were disconnected from one another, unable to coalesce and organize. That same year, the center-right party at the European Parliament held its summer university conference in Bucharest. The event—one of the largest annual gatherings of lawmakers, politicians, ministers, prime ministers, and presidents—dedicated a panel to the Arab Spring. As one of the panelists, I drew the audience's attention to an emerging reality of the uprisings: The early stages of the revolutions were triggered by youth and reformers, but as it became evident that the demonstrations could take and hold ground, the Islamists were sneaking to the forefront.

One interesting finding I made during the Bucharest conference concerned the varying reactions to my analysis by Western and Eastern Europeans. Participants coming from the United Kingdom, France, Germany, Belgium, and the Scandinavian countries seemed to be skeptical of the assertion that the Islamists were making inroads inside the movements opposed to the dictators. Officials from these countries and some of their political think tanks seemed to be excited about the rise of a political opposition, regardless of its ideological coloration. Dutch, British, and Scandinavian members argued that the Muslim Brotherhood and Nahda, as political parties, "may have learned lessons from being suppressed in the opposition and will behave as new democrats once in power." The remoteness of many Western European politicians from the reality of Islamist tactics was probably due to the effective lobbying by oil interests in Europe. For years, the Brotherhood had been working to convince the bureaucracies of Western Europe of the legitimacy of political Islam. Most of the lawmakers knew about the ideology of the Islamists, but tended to believe that the uprising would change their behavior. This pragmatic attitude was sharply expressed by members of the committee on Middle Eastern affairs. They promoted the notion of "new Islamists who can deliver democracy and stability."

Politicians from central and eastern Europe had a distinctly different attitude toward the Arab Spring. They were able to distinguish Islamist movements from secular liberal ones. The minister of culture of Romania, Kelemen Hunor, told me she was interested in hosting a conference of dissidents and democracy activists from the Middle East to launch a Euro–Arab Spring partnership. "Most of us were dissidents under Soviet and Communist domination," she told me. "We know how to distinguish between civil society activists and ideological militants. Eastern Europeans could help in the dialogue with Middle East freedom activists. We both struggled against totalitarian regimes and their secret polices but also against the Communist networks and their militias." I received the same assessment from Polish, Czech, Slovak, and Slovenian participants. The Bucharest conference of 2011 showed a divide in Europe. There were those who wished to partner with any force, including Islamists, who would settle for political stability across the Mediterranean even at the expense of freedom in the Arab world. Others believed that the revolutions had to continue until a real democratic force could shape the future of these countries.

The ambivalence toward the Arab Spring had yet another rationale: domestic terror and émigré violence inside Europe. After the terror attacks in Madrid and London and the many other attempts in France, Sweden, Italy, Belgium, the Netherlands, and Germany, countering the radicalization of young Muslim immigrants or their descendants became a central issue on European policy and security agendas. Here again, the Arab Spring was seen from two different angles. One perspective hoped the political Islamists of the region, once they moderated their attitudes as they seized the governments in North Africa and the Levant, would moderate the positions of the Islamists and even Jihadists operating in Europe. Roland Freudenstein, the director of the research arm of the majority party at the European Parliament, participated in many engagement events (organized by the European Parliament both before and after the Arab Spring) with Arab activists, including the Islamists. He confirmed to me that, "There are many in Europe who believe that the Arab Spring is a movement that will transform the Islamists into Islamic-democrats, just like Christian-Democrats in Germany, Holland, or Italy." Freudenstein, who is one of the leading strategists in Brussels regarding the relationship with the Islamic countries, understands the strategies of the Islamist movements, but he also knows how European politics toward the southern Mediterranean works. "The idea that Islamists can be partnered with is not [held] because Europeans prefer them over liberals; it is because the latter cannot be found as organized and efficient parties [that] we can work with. European decision makers want to work with political forces that exist, not with forces they have to assist to become political parties."

This tactic—to work pragmatically but cautiously with the Islamists if they display tendencies to support pluralism and moderation—was also asserted by the president of the EPP, former prime minister of Belgium Wilfried Martens. During several seminars organized in Vienna,

Brussels, and Washington that focused on engaging the south Mediterranean countries, Martens told me he "was personally intrigued by the possibility that political Islamists may mutate into a comparable movement to Christian-Democrats but in the Islamic culture instead." In the seminars we participated in, he told of discussions he had had with Turkish prime minister Recep Tayyip Erdogan. He had asked the Islamist leader if indeed the AKP is an Islamic-democratic party. Erdogan refused to admit that secular democracy can be found in "political Islam" but asserted that "Islamist parties can perform in a democracy." The European leader of the center-right felt this was sufficient to find common ground. On the other hand, European socialists and other left-wing parties, though more concerned about the secular component of liberal democracies, also endorsed the idea of cautiously partnering with the Islamists in the Arab world, as long as they accepted the principle of democratic elections. The European left had a partnership with the Arab left, but the latter was either in power and acting undemocratically in the region or was in the opposition and unable to confront the more dynamic Islamists. What I learned from the years preceding the Arab Spring and those immediately following the revolts was that Europe's political parties knew more about the essence of the Islamist ideology than their American counterparts, but they have been betting—out of fear or out of pragmatism—on a rapid liberalization of the Islamists in the region.

Europe missed a crucial rendezvous with its real liberal and secular partners in the Arab world in 2011. But in 2012, European lawmakers and think tanks began to realize that the Islamists of Tunisia and Egypt had double-crossed the West: They had seized power, received foreign funding, and were in the process of installing full Sharia law. And with the attack on the U.S. consulate in Libya on September 11, 2012, Europeans started to realize that the forces they supported (at least a large segment of the Libyan rebels) were in fact Salafi Jihadi militias. By early autumn 2011, the mood had changed among European lawmakers and many members of the executive branches. In the annual summer conference of the European Parliament's think tank, held in Berlin and attended by European leaders, the Arab Spring was addressed in a plenary session, but impressions had already shifted. More lawmakers expressed concern for the rise of fundamentalism across North Africa and the Levant. During the debates, the president of the International Republican Institute (IRI), Lorne Crane, addressed the closing in Egypt of the U.S.-funded democracy agencies, including IRI, the Democratic International Institute, and Freedom House. Europeans began to realize that the Islamists had used Western support to get rid of the dictators only to replace them with their own brand of authoritarian regime. During this conference, Kassoulides, who was originally skeptical of the success of the Arab Spring because of the Islamist factor, admitted, "We as Europeans lost the Arab Spring." He repeated a slogan popular in the American media: "It has now become an Arab Winter." (He became foreign minister of Cyprus in 2013.)

Europe's attitude toward the Arab Spring had a significant effect on the evolution of the revolts and civil wars in Africa and the Middle East. As noted earlier, although Europe is considered the West, it is much closer to the Middle East. In short, it is a geographical neighbor with direct economic and demographic ties that cross the Mediterranean. During a strategic assessment seminar of the Arab uprisings held in Madrid in July 2012 by Spain's national conservative think tank FAES (Fundación para el Análisis y los Estudios Sociales), politicians and scholars from across Europe focused on how their countries could best assure a successful transition. I argued that direct partnerships between the European Union and its many NGOs and the region's civil societies was the best and fastest way to empower secular democrats in the region. Former prime minister of Spain José María Aznar argued similarly: "If the United States doesn't partner with Europe in reaching out to the seculars and moderates in the region, and continues to partner with the Brotherhood, Western efforts to salvage the Arab Spring will collapse." Many agreed with Aznar's assessment. A Romanian member agreed, "If we don't develop a Western unified policy toward Middle East dissidents in the same fashion the West morally backed our Eastern European dissidents during the Cold War, the Islamists will seize the region and we will be facing a new Cold War, a more dangerous one." Madrid's representative, the executive director of FAES, Alberto Carnero, reminded me: "Unlike most Americans, most of us Europeans know all too well the threats of the Jihadists. They are closer to us: they are among us. But America is the bigger kid on the block. If Washington doesn't lead the Western efforts to contain the Islamists and support the liberals in the Middle East, the revolutions will be crushed, as were the revolts of Budapest, Prague, and Gdansk. We will be looking at a very dangerous region for decades."[8]

CHAPTER SEVEN

BREAKDOWN OF THE SPRING

BY THE SUMMER OF 2012, MOST OF THE ARAB REVOLTS were breaking down and liberal forces were being driven to the periphery. In every country, Islamists, led by the Muslim Brotherhood, were at the forefront in the forming of the new governments or in expanding their presence inside the opposition, as seen in Syria. In Tunisia, the Nahda Party was able to form a coalition cabinet with Islamists and Arab nationalists and began to endorse a rapid Islamization of bureaucracies and society despite robust secular opposition. In Egypt, the Muslim Brotherhood secured a win in the legislative elections and ruled in Parliament, then won the battle of the presidency, placing its leader, Mohammed Morsi, in the country's executive office. The Ikhwan also moved to attempt gradual Islamization, but not without encountering strong popular resistance. In Yemen, the Salafists secured influence within the post-Saleh republic.

In two important countries, Libya and Syria, the Islamists pushed for control on the ground. In Libya, the Salafi Jihadist militias deployed in Cyrenaica, the eastern region, with a strong presence in Benghazi, facing off with the moderate post-Gaddafi government in Tripoli. The terror attack in Benghazi in September 2012 uncovered a sour reality about the Arab Spring in Libya: It was penetrated by Jihadists, and bad news loomed on the horizon. Last but not least, while many in the West were jubilant about the Syrian popular uprising against the oppressive Assad regime, a growing number of observers in the international community started to realize, as of mid-2012, that al Qaeda had landed in Syria in the form of the Nusra Front and was competing with the Free Syria Army (FSA) for leadership of the revolution.

Elsewhere in the region the forces for democracy were in retreat. In Lebanon, the once-rising March 14 Alliance, which was attempting to consolidate the Cedars Revolution, was pushed back. Hezbollah had not only strengthened its control of Lebanon's national security, it had replenished its reserves with missiles and weapons from Iran. By the summer of 2012 it had sent thousands of its own fighters to support the Assad regime in its war against the Syrian revolution. In Iraq, 2012 was the year in which the post-American geopolitics exploded. There was a significant rise in Salafi terrorism in the Sunni triangle, and Shia militia activities sharply peaked. In short, the second year of the upheavals, and most of 2013, witnessed a collapse of the so-called Arab Spring, and it had almost cataclysmic consequences on international security and stability.[1]

THE BENGHAZI FAILURE

Perhaps one of the greatest shocks to the American public since the blowing up of the U.S. embassy and Marine barracks in Beirut in 1983 was the terror attack waged by the Jihadi militia Ansar al Sharia on the American consulate in Benghazi on September 11, 2012, a few weeks before the quadrennial presidential election. The Benghazi affair shook Americans' confidence in the ability of their government to defend its diplomatic missions and interests worldwide. The issue was not the ability to stop every single terror attack. In a war, this is practically impossible. But the public was confused by the inability of their diplomats to understand the threat, identify the force behind the attack, and take action against it afterward. The statements made by the State Department immediately after the killing of the ambassador and security staffers linked the incidents to a so-called spontaneous reaction by angry demonstrators to a satirical YouTube video of the Prophet Mohammed. The facts were otherwise, as was later admitted by the State Department in an internal review given to Congress.

The attack in Benghazi was conducted by a Jihadi militia linked to al Qaeda and was part of the movement's relentless campaign against the United States and its allies. In Egypt and other Muslim countries, Salafists had organized a protest of the video in front of U.S. embassies; in Libya, Jihadi Salafists mounted a military operation meant to massacre the diplomats. It was part of a strategy to remove American presence and influence from the country and was a prelude to seizing the regime entirely. As a result of the Benghazi attack, which became part of the presidential election debate in October, a wider debate opened in America about the Arab Spring in general, starting with Libya.

The first shock to the American psyche came when it was learned that the Obama administration had not mounted an immediate military operation to rescue the beleaguered consulate. The second shock arose in debate over the first: U.S. officials explained the violence as unforeseen and blamed the attack on a videotape instead of identifying it as a Jihadi military activity. The third issue raised in the controversy over Benghazi was the nonmilitary response against the militia perpetrators. These issues were hotly discussed in a series of congressional hearings at the end of 2012 and in May 2013. The Republicans accused the Obama administration of failing in the War on Terror while claiming before the presidential election that al Qaeda was on the path to defeat after the killing of Osama bin Laden. The Democrats defended the administration on the grounds that no one could have prevented this tragedy; the Republicans were politicizing a national security issue, they said. The Benghazi drama, however, revealed more than a partisan divide in the United States; it disclosed a much larger crisis in American foreign policy than was previously apparent, a crisis with dimensions as vast as the Arab Spring itself: There was a need to understand the revolts and their players. The real issue, I argued in my briefings to members of Congress, their staffers, and the media, was much deeper. It was about Washington's perception of the identity of the forces on the ground, not only in Libya but everywhere in the Arab world.

In April 2011, I had posted on my Facebook page (and noted on Fox News and in radio interviews) that al Qaeda flags were being flown on buildings in Benghazi by armed men who chanted Jihadi hymns similar to the ones chanted on YouTube by members of the bin Laden network. In September of that same year, I noted the spread of these flags to several other locations as well as the appearance of Jihadi literature on many rebel websites in Libya. The presence of al Qaeda–linked Salafists was evident to observers months before the collapse of Gaddafi's regime. By early 2012, I signaled to lawmakers in the United States and Europe, as well as to the foreign policy team of presidential candidate Mitt Romney, that Islamist militias were expanding inside Libya, spreading in and around Benghazi and Darna and across the eastern provinces of the country. My projections warned of possible terror attacks on American or Western interests in Libya. And on France 24 television, I warned of drives to export Islamist militias to the Sahel, including to Mali and Niger. By reading the ideological and political narrative of the Salafist militias in Libya, I was able to determine, as did a few other analysts, that the Jihadists had penetrated the Libyan rebellion from day one: marched with the revolutionary seculars and dissidents against Gaddafi; adapted their speech to one of "rebels against the regime"; profited from NATO strikes, support, and training; received Qatari funding and media support; and, after the demise of the dictator, established dozens of bases around the country.

The Jihadists partnered with the secular Libyan rebels until the fall of the dictator and his death at the hand of militias. Once Enemy Number One was eliminated, the Islamist militias operated quickly. Some sources believe that the militias linked to al Qaeda eliminated influential members of the secular opposition, including General Abdel Fattah Younis, as the war was progressing to ensure the domination of Islamist militias after the revolt was over. In any event, by early 2012, armed Jihadist networks were strongly rooted throughout the country, including in Tripoli and Benghazi.

When asked about the Islamists' goals by members of the U.S. Congress and the European Parliament, I projected three possible future tracks. One was to consolidate their presence inside Libya and connect with their Salafi partners in Egypt, Tunisia, and Algeria. Another was to move toward the Sahel, starting with Mali and Niger. And third was to target Western and American interests in Libya, forcing them to leave. None of the three projections was exceptionally theoretical, as they were all discussed in chat rooms and online. All three objectives materialized in 2012 and continued to develop in 2013. The Algerian-based al Qaeda in the Islamic Maghreb (AQIM) reached out to the Libyan Jihadists and integrated them. The unified North African Jihadists armed and equipped bands of Salafi militias from Libya and Algeria and sent them to occupy the northern part of Mali in the summer of 2012, and on September 11 of that year, Ansar al Sharia—a Jihadi group also linked to al Qaeda and part of the nebulous but armed Salafi presence in the region—waged a terror attack on the U.S. consulate.[2]

I had seen the attack coming, or more accurately, "an" attack against U.S. or Western sites in Libya. It was doomed to happen. In fact, reports have indicated that prior to the Benghazi September raid, British convoys were assaulted and other European interests intimidated. As soon as Salafi demonstrations took place in Cairo and then spread to other cities, a more attractive opportunity could not have presented itself to al Qaeda in Libya for scoring a solid victory while claiming it was a reaction to a silly satirical video of Mohammed. As was eventually uncovered by Congress and some media, the bloodshed was a full-fledged operation conducted by an al Qaeda linked group on a U.S. target. What complicated Washington's stance in September 2012 were statements by the American president at the United Nations and by Susan Rice, U.S. ambassador to the United Nations, apologizing for the anti-Islamic video. They ignored the real Jihadi threat on the ground. In 2013, it was revealed that the embassy in Libya had contracted another Jihadi militia, the 17 February Brigade, to protect the consulate in Benghazi. This armed group and the attackers belonged to the same Salafi network allied to al Qaeda. Americans were shocked to see their government confused about its security partners. The question raised in Congress was about the lack of response by the Obama administration. The larger question I continued to raise, from September 2012 until the writing of this chapter, was, Why did the U.S. administration not identify the Libyan Jihadists as a threat? My question addressed the greater issue of how the Obama administration perceived the rebels as a whole. Based on the fact that the State Department and the White House did not distinguish between Islamist militias and seculars when it strategized for that country, their policies were very revealing. It was unequivocally confirmed that the Obama administration had looked at the Islamists in general as "partners" unless they were proven to be part of al Qaeda. Toward the end of 2013 and in early 2014, U.S.-based journalists sympathizing with the Islamists came back to the thesis that while the attack was conducted by Jihadists, it was not connected to al Qaeda and was triggered by the online video.[3] *The New York Times* report, authored by David Kirkpatrick (who was criticized by Egyptian seculars for siding with the Brotherhood and the Islamists), was debunked by Libyan reformers who circulated a comprehensive analysis establishing that local Jihadists in Libya are in fact affiliates of al Qaeda.[4]

This is where the United States had grossly miscalculated and made its most damaging strategic mistake of the Arab Spring. The administration was badly advised by scholars and lobbyist groups. It was told that political Islamists were thoroughly different from al Qaeda terrorists and that they could be trusted as partners. This assumption became U.S. policy in North Africa and the region as a whole. But when it was tested in Libya, the error in analysis was readily revealed. Washington had been induced to make this same strategic mistake since 2009. Instead of focusing on the secular segments of Arab societies to befriend them, it zoomed in on the Islamists, from Tunisia to Egypt. Benghazi was a clear demonstration that the Salafists, a main component of the Islamist movements in the Middle East, can mutate into Jihadists when conditions favor their ascension.

In June 2013, the adviser to the Libyan president on foreign affairs and international cooperation, Dr. Fathi Nuah, whom I met in Washington, told me that the United States and Europe should have moved faster to fill two voids. "One was to train and equip the new Libyan armed forces and have them as an entity that could confront the militias, or the al Qaeda–linked groups. Second were the Libyan NGOs, very vibrant but isolated inside and outside the country. By moving on these two fronts," argued Nuah, "we would have been able to preempt the rise of Salafi militias." The presidential adviser was right, as clashes multiplied in Libya between the young new army and the multiplying Jihadi armed groups.[5]

A benchmark was reached when a leading politician opposed to the Islamists was executed in Benghazi by Jihadists on July 25. The *Financial Times* wrote: "A prominent Libyan political activist and outspoken critic of his country's version of the Muslim Brotherhood was shot dead on Friday in the eastern city of Benghazi, according to the country's official news agency."[6] Abdul Salam Mohamed Mismari, a lawyer and a leading figure in the secular democratic movement, "was seen as a threat to the Islamist militias aiming at the regime; he was taken out by them," I was told by a civil society activist who specialized in Jihadi movements in Libya. "Like in Egypt and in Tunisia, a democracy uprising will challenge the Terror Islamist organizations," he projected.

TUNISIA'S RACE: ISLAMISTS VS. SECULARS

The electoral win of Nahda and its allies in Parliament in 2012 allowed the Islamist movement to form a cabinet, and that gradually set the stage for the Islamization of the state. The first wave of the popular revolt was a mix of secular youth, progressives, liberals, and Islamists. As argued previously, the Islamists were able to reorganize and move publicly after years of suppression by a regime of strongmen because the secular forces of civil society in Tunisia provided a moral and political umbrella. The revolution was initially ignited by the poor and common people; it was mobilized and organized instantly by women's groups, students, and workers, particularly Ittihad al Shoghl, Tunisia's national Labor Union. However, the Islamists, inspired by their longtime charismatic leader Rached al Ghannouchi, seized a significant portion of the political representation of the revolution, larger than their actual presence at the onset of the uprising, and with this prize sailed through the rapidly unfolding elections.

Why did the Islamists win Tunisia's first post–Ben Ali elections, even though the seculars were omnipresent in Tunisian society under the previous regime? Two factors can be cited. First was the fact that the regime had suppressed the political institutions of the democratic opposition for many decades, disabling its ability to reorganize quickly and form effective coalitions, whereas the Islamists had already organized in the underground during the authoritarian period. The interim period for reorganization of democratic and secular parties was too short. In addition, Nahda and the Salafists were obtaining funding from the Gulf states, including Saudi Arabia, but mostly Qatar. Tunisian Islamists, whose leadership was operating mostly in exile and free there to prepare for its political future, and whose networks inside the country were camouflaged under religious activities, were ready to launch their activities as soon as Ben Ali's regime collapsed. The Islamists were faster and better coordinated. They cornered the seculars, already divided, with the argument that elections had to be held immediately. It was important for Nahda and its allies to secure power before the seculars could organize an effective opposition. Besides, the Islamists of Tunisia had the financial and media support of the Gulf, or at least of Qatar. They were better positioned.

The other unseen reason for the rapid win of the fundamentalists in the first Arab revolution was the tacit U.S. support provided by the Obama administration. Throughout 2011 and 2012, Nahda leaders and their allies were given access to the State Department, the White House, and the U.S.-funded democracy NGOs in Washington. They skillfully used it to promote themselves as the most credible political force to assume government responsibility in a postrevolutionary Tunisia. A Tunisian liberal politician whom I met in Madrid during a European forum on the Arab Spring in 2012 told me, "The civil society forces in Tunisia are profoundly secular and have been around for decades, but their struggle against the Bourguiba and Ben Ali regimes denied them a full organizational capacity. The secret police went after democracy activists for years, so when the Ben Ali regime crumbled fast, these forces found themselves disorganized, dispersed, and divided. The only main organized political force on the scene ready to move was the Nahda." Mahmoud May, now deputy secretary general of the Social Democratic Party, is among leaders pushing for a reorganization of the democratic forces in Tunisia to avoid a full descent into a Sharia-based Islamist state in 2014.[7]

But the most troubling factor in the Tunisia Islamist recuperation was the Jihadi terror. By early 2012, elements of the al Qaeda–linked Salafi factions were emerging at an alarming rate. The radical Islamists benefited from the formation of an Islamist government under Nahda auspices. Nahda was backed by a large political movement known as Salafists, including Hizb al Tahrir, the old Pan-Islamist movement rejuvenated by the fall of secular dictators.[8] Secular politicians and activists began to increasingly complain about the exactions by Jihadists in early 2012. Counterterrorism experts in Tunisia told me then that the fall of Gaddafi and the spread of Jihadi militias from Libya into the Sahel and Tunisia had caused the creation and expansion of terror pockets in the south of the country. The Salafists, protected by the ruling Nahda, covered for the Jihadists, who were joining militant and terrorist organizations. Along with powerful propaganda material, including hundreds of YouTube videos that called for joining the Jihad in Africa and the Middle East, the al Qaeda–linked factions enjoyed two shields: above them, the Salafi movements that moved in the streets and, above those, the ruling Islamist Nahda Party. The latter claimed it was ordering the security forces and the army to go after the terrorists, but in fact the army refrained from launching massive operations against the Jihadi fighters.

As they do in the other countries of the Arab Spring, Islamist regimes claim they fight terror, but in fact and in practicality they do not and never would use military action to kill or arrest Jihadists at a strategic level.[9] Instead, one dramatic result of Tunisia's falling into the hands of Islamists and the rise of al Qaeda's offshoots in several spots inside the country was the export of Tunisian fighters to Syria to join the Salafi militias there, particularly the Nusra Front. This internationalization of the Jihadi fight peaked with a unique phenomenon known as the Jihad al Nikah, whereby Salafi ideologues issued fatwas allowing Tunisian women, and women supporting the Jihad worldwide, to join the fight in Syria and serve the sexual needs of the Jihadi combatants. According to media, "Reports have spread on the internet calling for girls to offer themselves to fighters." Tunisian media affirmed, "Thirteen girls traveled to rebel-held Northern Syria influenced by Islamic preachers."[10]

But resistance to the Islamists in Tunisia advanced in 2013, particularly after the assassination at the hands of Islamists of Chokri Belaid, a leftist progressive leader of the secular opposition to Nahda. His supporters accused the Islamist regime of masterminding the killing and pledged to stop the Islamization of the country.[11]

According to Jilani Hammami, spokesman for the Tunisian Workers' Party, a pillar political force of Chokri Balaid's Popular Front, "The new government had to start again from scratch. So there was no recovery program. It pursued the same course as Ben Ali, counting on Qatar and Saudi Arabia and getting nothing." According to its critics, Nahda's agenda is about reasserting the "Islamist-Arabist" identity, not establishing a secular democracy.[12] Across Tunisia, a wind of opposition to Nahda and the Salafists is blowing. It will be a long struggle before Tunisia's real revolution materializes.[13]

In my meetings with the president of the al Joumhouri Party (Republican Democratic), Ahmed Nefer Chebbi, during his visit to Washington in June 2013, he confirmed the view that Tunisia's civil society is generating a new type of democratic movement, "which by coming together may well obtain future majorities in the Parliament and form a Tunisian government representing the real goals of the initial Arab Spring of 2011." Chebbi, a seasoned opposition leader who was persecuted by the Ben Ali regime, is a credible candidate for the presidency of the republic, and could in the future become an alternative to the Ghannouchi Islamist leadership. In Chebbi's view of the future, the old secular generations who fought for liberalization under the previous regime will fuse with the younger liberal generations who are struggling under the Nahda regime to seek a secular and democratic lifestyle in Tunisia. Tunisian youth, though, may well engage in a democracy movement to regain the country from the Islamists earlier than expected. On July 3, 2013, as the Muslim Brotherhood was removed by a popular coalition with the armed forces, political activist Mohammed Bnour and his supporters launched Tamarod Tunisia (Tunisia's Rebellion), a movement aiming at staging civil uprisings to stop the takeover by Nahda and the Islamists. The second revolution had begun.[14]

But as Tunisian secular revolutionaries were preparing for a popular surge against the Nahda regime, a prominent opposition politician was assassinated, along with his bodyguard, on July 25. Mohammed Brahimi, a member of Tunisia's legislative assembly, was a critic of Nahda's agenda. His killing prompted a wide protest among civil society forces and secular opposition in Tunisia, among whom many vowed to bring down the regime.[15] Dozens of lawmakers resigned from the legislative assembly and a growing popular protest targeted the regime's ruling party and its founder, Rached al Ghannouchi. The Tunisian democratic revolution against the Islamists was marching in parallel to the Egyptian multimillion demonstrations against the Brotherhood.

SYRIA AND WESTERN HESITATIONS

Two years and three months after the start of the Syrian revolution and its subsequent transformation into a full-fledged civil war, the United States and Europe stood at a historic crossroads: intervening with the goal of bringing down the Assad regime and erecting an alternative power in Damascus, or backing the opposition to a point where the regime has no other choice than to negotiate via the Geneva talks, a gradual exit from power that would surrender the country to a combination of political forces that would satisfy all regional and international players. In mid-June 2013, the Obama administration stated that it would begin the process of arming the trusted opposition and could consider many more measures, including a possible limited no-fly zone over the beleaguered country. France followed suit.[16]

But even at that point, the U.S. endgame in Syria remained unclear. The administration had yet to explain its regional strategic plans for Iran and Hezbollah on the one hand and the Salafi Jihadi militias fighting on the other hand. Sending weapons to the opposition, though legitimate in order to fend off the advancing Assad forces, raised significant questions. Who in the opposition would receive the arms and be responsible for their use? What would be the next steps after the opposition was armed and supplied? Would it be a long war between two equal forces with thousands more civilian casualties? Would the equipping of the Free Syria Army (FSA) create a new balance of power that would lead both sides to realize that a military solution was not going to happen and that negotiation in Geneva was the only remaining choice?[17]

The stark reality in the country revealed that the Assad regime was unwilling to accept a balance of power with the opposition as a basis for political negotiations and the Russian leadership would not pressure its allies in Damascus and Tehran to accept real power sharing. This stance was what prompted Washington and its allies to beef up the capacities of the anti-Assad coalition and explore the more lethal options, such as no-fly zones over the country. In short, there was no apparent path to a real political solution in Syria that excluded one or the other of the fighting parties. Faced with this reality, the United States should have contemplated new strategies for ending war in Syria even if that meant reshaping its entire Middle East policy.

At the beginning of the Arab Spring, Washington followed the strategy of shepherding the rebels as they made progress against the regimes in North Africa and Yemen. In Tunisia and Egypt, the protesters obtained the moral and political support of the Obama administration, and that enabled them to bring down the pro-American but repressive regimes. The best-organized among them—the Muslim Brotherhood—were able to form new governments. In Libya, Gaddafi had no regional allies and was far from Russian logistical supplies. The Obama administration obtained U.N. resolution number 1973 from the Security Council that permitted joint military action under Chapter 7 of the Charter and launched NATO strikes against the regime until it collapsed. The strategy worked. In Syria, however, the Obama administration decided to let the revolt brew, as it had done in Egypt during 2011. It hoped that the mass demonstrations would topple Assad or would at least psychologically convince sectors of the army to move against its own commander in chief. It was an erroneous assessment, and a precious year was lost. During the early stages of the revolution, the movement was led mostly by liberal and secular forces organizing demonstrations, marches, and protests in Damascus and several other cities. That year, U.S. forces were still deployed in Iraq and along the borders with Syria. A quick action coordinated with Turkey, Jordan, and other partners, in the interest of an erupting civil society, would have most likely forced Assad to quit power and seek refuge inside the Alawi region or in Iran. President Obama should have put an end to this quagmire before he pulled troops out of Iraq. The United States military was already deployed along the border with equipment, an air force, and, more important, a heavy strategic deterrent against Iran. Assad was practically surrounded; Iran was kept at bay, and Turkey was yet untouched by its own protests. Even more significantly, al Qaeda, via the Nusra Front, was not yet deeply deployed across the Syrian opposition. The first year of the Syrian crisis, from April 2011 to April 2012, was a major U.S. failure. By not using its resources already in place in Iraq, not engaging civil society forces early on, and not blocking Jihadists traveling to Syria, Washington passively allowed the military and political landscape inside Syria to dramatically transform the country's geopolitical realities.

During the last quarter of 2012, the tense presidential election campaign in the United States kept the president from launching any military action in Syria for fear of losing votes both on the left and in the center, allowing the Syrian terrain to be irreversibly transformed. Civil demonstrations in Syria practically disappeared, and the street fighting was taken over by ferocious players. On one hand, the regime deployed forceful suppression, not only with air strikes and heavy tanks and artillery but also with Hezbollah militias operating out of Lebanon and supported by the Iranian Revolutionary Guard, the Pasdaran, and by supplies coming through open Iranian-Iraqi-Syrian borders—open because of the U.S. pullout. The military capacity of the regime multiplied, and its brutality deepened. On the other hand, the Free Syria Army made up of offshoots from the regular army had formed. In parallel, Jihadi militias, including the al Qaeda–linked Nusra Front, had emerged and spread through the various zones of rebellion. The secular and Islamist components of the opposition had become very difficult to differentiate. In addition to the evolution of both sides, the regime used chemical weapons, even if in a limited manner, and some components fell into the hands of the Jihadists.[18]

By summer 2013, the Obama administration seemed to have a much weightier but unavoidable decision to make, graver and riskier than those before. It had to act, but at a level equal to the challenges emerging from the many mutations of the conflict. There was a crucial battle in Qussair in central Syria in May. Thanks to the participation of Hezbollah, well-trained special forces, and Iranian military advisers, Assad troops had overrun the rebels' positions in the strategic city, and the regime moved to the offensive on several fronts. Washington had been hoping, before the Qussair battle, that Russia would persuade the regime to make dramatic concessions in Geneva. But Assad's forces leaped forward to crush their opponents as a way to use Geneva's negotiations to their advantage. This at last prompted the Obama administration to approach the battle by a different path: to openly arm the insurgents and possibly set up a no-fly zone over Syria.

The administration moved in the right direction, but late and slowly. Its plans needed to be strategically and comprehensively developed. And engagement plans needed to incorporate vital substrategies to address the ramifications of a Syria intervention, regardless of its scope and size.

The challenges now are many: Who will be the strategic partner inside Syria militarily and politically from beginning to end? Who will seize ministries in Damascus and impose security and stability once change occurs? It must be clarified before, not during or after, the campaign begins. How will the Arabs participate in the projected U.S. effort? How far will the Gulf countries, Jordan, and Turkey go in support of the campaign, especially if Iran counters these efforts? What is the strategic plan of engagement if Hezbollah and Iran respond to U.S. involvement? Is there a Washington global response to an Iranian counteraction in Syria or in the region? Last and not least, how will Syria look after the Assad regime is gone? Will it be a democracy, an Islamist regime, or a military government?

These questions were among the many I raised in congressional briefings, particularly with Representatives Jeffrey Duncan, the new U.S. co-chair of the Transatlantic Legislative Group on Counter Terrorism (TAG); Congressman Robert Aderholt, with whom I worked to set up a Congressional Middle East Democracy Group; Representative Trent Franks; and the Committee on Foreign Affairs of the House headed by Representative Ed Royce. My briefings also reached many European lawmakers visiting Washington, including British member of Parliament Julian Lewis and a multitude of members of the European Parliament attending the TAG's summit in July 2013. Earlier that year, I discussed the Syria choices with U.N. officials in charge of the Middle East. The center of all discussions was, up until the end of summer 2013, the conundrum regarding what force could adequately replace the regime and put a stop to the increasingly sectarian fighting. The fear was that it soon would engulf the entire region. I stressed the need to understand and evaluate the strategic choices of the United States and Europe before the engagement begins so that all actors would be aware of the process and of its consequences.[19]

My position and argument were not created in a vacuum. I had met many leaders and activists of the Syrian revolution before and after the Arab Spring. In Washington, I met many members of the Syrian National Council, including Muslims, Christians, and Kurds such as George Kilo (president of the Syrian National Council), Radwan Ziade, Farid Ghadri, and Sherkoh Abbas. In London, I had long exchanges with Wael al Ejji, a political activist close to the FSA. And in Paris, I met with several leaders including Louai al Muqdad and former vice president Abdel Halim Khaddam. I had several opportunities to listen to the Alawi point of view, including from Bashar Assad's uncle, former vice president of Syria Rifaat Assad, Hafez's brother. I conversed with a broad spectrum of democratic participants, from the most secular and young to the seasoned and former officials of the Baath who broke with Bashar. All Syrian opposition leaders stressed the necessity of backing the Free Syria Army (FSA) and channeling aid to the secular components of the uprising.

Within the political opposition, however, there were severe divisions, including the Syrian National Coalition. These divisions had to do with the cooperation with the Muslim Brotherhood. The more secular elements resented the Ikhwan and accused them of wanting only one thing, the creation of an Islamist state. The conservative Muslim elements argued that the Islamists are not that dangerous in Syria because the civil society is profoundly secular. I personally did not agree with the last assessment, but I accepted the principle that all political forces in society had the right to participate in the building of a new Syria.

Of all those I spoke with, the two most important Syrian personalities were Fahad al Masri (the senior spokesperson of the Free Syria Army, based in Paris), and General Manaf Tlass (an influential commander in the Syrian armed forces and the son of a past minister of defense, Mustafa Tlass). Al Masri, who was at the center of the propaganda battle with the Assad regime, told me the real FSA fight was twofold: "On the one hand we are facing off with the full force of a regime backed by Iran, Iraq, and Hezbollah, but on an unseen level, we are also making sure that the Muslim Brotherhood and the extreme Salafists won't seize the revolution as it moves forward." I was impressed to see that young leaders in the FSA knew how to strategize in the midst of a revolution. "We need swift Western support to the FSA and to the moderates of the Syrian revolution," said Fahad. "Otherwise the Jihadist Salafists would be all over the place, and the post-Assad era would suffer the consequences."[20]

General Tlass, a high-ranking commander of the Syrian Army who defected from the regime, was working on the future stage of the solution. "Beyond who will win on the battlefield, we're talking about the future of a country," Tlass expressed. "The revolt began because people were unsatisfied with the political order, so we need to think of the next political order, not just about who will defeat the other party. How will communities coexist? And will the country remain as one?" He was thinking historically: "The Assad clique will eventually have to go; it can't rule over the country after this revolution. The question now is about the institution that will preserve the country's security and stability and protect citizens. The secular part of the FSA will have to be part of a future Syria; it represents the revolution. But then we need to keep a large part of the regular Syrian army, particularly the Alawi, the Christians, the Druze, and the Sunni moderates in addition to the Kurds. For that purpose, we need to establish a third force made up of all these and to marginalize the influence of the Assads and the al Qaeda-linked groups."[21] Tlass's project was the most logical, for it looked to the future. But reality on the ground was rooted in past hatreds and regional interventions. The Iranian regime and Hezbollah could not afford to have a Syria without Assad. The Muslim Brotherhood would not accept a non-Islamist Syria after Assad. The conflict is destined to continue until the United States and the West assume leadership in partnering with secular military and democracy forces: Help them unite and the battle for a future free and democratic Syria will be won.

This seemed less and less likely by the summer of 2013. Once Assad and Hezbollah forces seized back Qussair, it was clear the advantage of that strategic city would go to Assad, allowing the regime to remain in communication with the northwestern Alawi part of Syria. If it had remained in the hands of the opposition, the "Stalingrad" of Syria would have instead cut the regime's forces in two, giving an advantage to the FSA. With strategic geography once again supporting it, the Syrian-Iranian alliance felt confident it could push back against the opposition and its regional and international backers, particularly as the AKP government of Turkey was facing protests in Istanbul and the Morsi regime in Egypt was in trouble. But the Sunni Arab countries doubled their support of the anti-Assad forces, making it difficult to crush the opposition.[22] By July, Ahmad Jarba, a Syrian opposition leader close to Saudi Arabia, was appointed head of the Syrian Coalition, in hopes that his movement would receive heavy weapons to counterattack the regime.

The projection remained the same: A balance of power would be maintained between the two forces until the United States decides to adopt a new direction in the region.[23]

As the summer ended, the Syrian use of chemical weapons near Damascus was enough to shift Western attitudes and open the way to a change in the confrontation. Once the red line was crossed by Assad, the Obama administration and its European and Arab allies moved to a more offensive position.[24] Many thought an ensuing clash would determine the fate of Syria, and most likely U.S. foreign policy too. But the Obama administration decided otherwise in the fall of 2013. Instead of striking at Syria's chemical weapons, it agreed on a Russian-sponsored political initiative that stopped all U.S. military actions on Syria in return for regime adhesion to a road map that would lead to a meeting with the opposition in Geneva.[25] The dramatic about-face in the American attitude left the opposition divided and emboldened the Assad regime to continue its military offensive on the ground. Moreover, weeks later, Washington announced it was starting a process of political engagement with the Iranian regime. By January 2014, the U.S. confrontational military policy with regard to the Assad regime had been abandoned and the pre-revolution, hands-off status quo had been reaffirmed.[26]

CHAPTER EIGHT

DEMOCRACY AND SECULARISM CAN WIN

AFTER PARLIAMENTARY AND PRESIDENTIAL ELEC-
tions brought Islamists to power in Tunisia and Egypt, legislative as-
semblies gradually prepared to install Islamist states; Libya's "rebels"
announced they would institute Sharia as the law of the land; Jihadists hit the U.S. consulate in Benghazi, killing the ambassador and three
other personnel; al Qaeda penetrated Syria's opposition, unleashing the
Nusra Front to butcher seculars and Christians; and as the top Jihadist
terror organization expanded its operations in Yemen and came back in
force in Iraq, a wave of pessimism engulfed public opinion in the United
States and Europe. This reaction was produced by commentary coming, ironically, from both the right and the left, which asserted that the
Arab Spring, though it may have started positively, had mutated into an
Islamist Winter.

The more conservative side argued that the uprisings were originally planned by the Muslim Brotherhood, which exploited the actions and ideals of a weak liberal youth to help Islamists seize power
all across North Africa and parts of the Levant. The Arab Spring was
never a spring in a Western democratic sense, they argued.[1]

The liberal side of the debate, arguing from a contrary perspective, reached the same conclusion. Many of the academics—those in the media and think tanks who praised the Arab Spring phenomenon in the West, particularly in the United States—theorized that the Arab Spring was a positive movement and was Islamist in nature.[2] Even after millions of Egyptians rose against the Brotherhood, commentators continued to insist that the region was doomed to be dominated by the Islamists.[3]

From a position opposed to both, I had argued in briefings, articles, and interviews since the start of the uprisings that while liberal youth would trigger the revolutions and Islamists would seize them, secular democrats would rise again and struggle against the fundamentalists. I saw their determination in their writings and concluded that deep but silent majorities would side with the nonviolent seculars and shift the ground under the feet of the Muslim Brotherhood and eventually the Khomeinists. My views were shared by a small minority that existed between the conservatives who asserted that the Islamists would face no real challenge and the Western liberals who claimed that the Islamists *are* the true liberals. Both mainstream perspectives were proved wrong by the youth of the region, starting in Egypt, Turkey, and Tunisia.

EGYPT DESCENDS INTO ISLAMISM AND BOUNCES BACK

The Egyptian democratic revolution, which scored its main and only political victory on January 2011 when President Hosni Mubarak abdicated, was rapidly absorbed by the Islamists, who were better organized and financed than the liberals. The Muslim Brotherhood maneuvered efficiently for the next twelve months. As indicated earlier, the Ikhwan were a powerful political organization in Egypt, second only to Mubarak's National Party. The Brotherhood and its allies were strongly backed by the Gulf states on financial and media levels and for decades had gone semi-underground to avoid suppression. As soon as the first waves of protestors opened the path to Tahrir Square, down which the entire political spectrum could deploy, the Ikhwan and the Salafists rushed in. They formed their own square and rapidly developed a strategy of growing within the revolution while steering the popular movement. The first maneuver by the Islamists was launched as early as March, two months after the removal of Mubarak. A constitutional referendum approved by a majority of voters gave advantage to the Muslim Brotherhood and set the stage for a series of elections and referenda, all transferring ultimate power to the Ikhwan.[4]

The chain of political events that elevated the Brotherhood to power in the two years that followed the initial revolt produced an Islamist president, a Brotherhood-led Parliament, and a constitution that prepared Egypt to descend into an authoritarian Islamic state. This outcome was based on three realities: (1) an experienced, well-connected and well-funded Ikhwan, (2) a divided and disorganized liberal leadership, and (3) U.S. backing of the Muslim Brotherhood. The Brotherhood succeeded in seizing power, step by step. The three realities enabled the Islamist force to disperse its secular competitors, push back against the Egyptian military, and project itself internationally under the moral and political protection of the Obama administration.[5]

As early as January 2011, even as their own members were tasked to join the sit-in at Tahrir Square, Brotherhood representatives met with members of the Supreme Command of the Armed Forces of Egypt (SCAF). The Islamists warned the military that with the fall of Mubarak the entire web of political and economic interests would fall into the hands of the "secular revolutionaries." The Brotherhood would be glad to cut a deal with the SCAF over the heads of the youth groups. In March, the Ikhwan asked Washington to limit the influence of its "clients," that is, the military, and asked the SCAF to collaborate to interdict the power of the liberals. In short, the Brotherhood, which had used the secular youth to bring down Mubarak, then used the military to curb the energy of the youth. That subversion made the Brotherhood the ultimate power brokers after the demise of the *Rayess* (chief). The deal between the Ikhwan and the SCAF assured continuity in power of the military headed by Field Marshal Hussein Tantawi. It also meant a careful sharing of influence inside the interim government until elections and a collaboration with Washington. The SCAF would continue to manage strictly military affairs and disburse most of the American financial aid in return for a Brotherhood takeover of the political relationship with the United States. With this understanding, a first referendum on the constitution was won by the Ikhwan, as was the country's first-ever legislative election.[6]

In June 2012, Mohammed Morsi won the presidential election. The election was praised by Washington and the international community as "democratically held." Though questioned, the results were accepted as fact. Morsi was democratically elected inasmuch as the opposition was not able to convince a U.S.-influenced Western coalition that a review of these elections had to be done. This sour reality was a further endorsement by Washington of the Ikhwan (showing a trust in their ability to change for the better), rather than of actual popular representation, for all observers agreed that half of the Morsi voters were not even members of his party, but instead simply were opposed to the other candidate, a survivor of the Mubarak regime.

The march of the Brotherhood to power was aided by both the capacity of the Islamist organization to maneuver and divide and conquer and by implicit U.S. support. According to opposition accounts, the U.S. ambassador to Cairo, Ann Patterson, has played a major role in backing up the Brotherhood leadership with advice and logistical support since the beginning of the Arab Spring. The story of the Ikhwan march to top power is now clear in the mind of historians, particularly since the group's demise in July 2013.

One of the national leaders of the Egyptian opposition, Osama al Ghazaly Harb, told an Egyptian Conference (of which I was coordinator)[7] in Washington in June 2013, shortly before the ouster of Morsi, that "the Brotherhood, a fascist movement by ideology and practice, is usurping power even after it has been elected a year before by a popular suffrage. But being elected alone isn't a guarantee of democracy. It is governing that counts, and the Ikhwan ruled undemocratically."

Morsi used the full twelve months to deconstruct every aspect of the democratic achievements of the initial Egyptian revolution. He issued a presidential "constitutional decree" to modify the basic constitutional

rights of Egyptians, with major setbacks to women, minorities, and seculars, and without consultation from the opposition. On those grounds
alone, Morsi had committed a breach of the constitutional and human
rights of Egyptians. He then attempted to transform the leadership of
the army and security forces into Ikhwan security branches and appointed extremist governors throughout the country, including a member of a terrorist group as governor of the Luxor district, target of the
group's terror strikes in 1997. In parallel, the Brotherhood regime allowed Islamist militias to grow across the country and opened a dialogue with groups in Sinai linked to al Qaeda. In foreign policy, Morsi
stood against a Franco-African campaign against al Qaeda in northern
Mali; consolidated ties with General Omar al Bashir, head of Sudan's
regime (and under indictment by the International Criminal Court);
hosted terror group Hamas in Cairo; aided the Islamist Nahda Party as
they reduced women's rights in Tunisia; and cooperated with the Salafi
militias of Libya, one of which was responsible for the Benghazi attack
on the U.S. consulate in September 2012. In 2013, Morsi presided over
a rally to support the Jihadists in Syria, including the Nusra Front, and
backed suicide fatwas issued by his allies.

On the economic level, the Brotherhood regime mismanaged the
country's finances while at the same time receiving significant funding
from the United States, Europe, and Qatar. The socioeconomic dispari-
ties, already monumental under Mubarak, widened under Morsi.

The Ikhwan regime, though democratically elected, deconstructed
the democratic legitimacy of the one-time election process by becoming an isolated, oppressive elite ruling the country at the expense of all
other citizens. The election made Morsi a legal president, but due to his
antidemocratic actions, his presidency was no longer seen as legitimate.
Egypt had no recall process or impeachment mechanisms. Besides, the
Brotherhood—after being elected to the helms of the legislative and
executive branches (with the financial help of Gulf petrodollars and
their overwhelming organization, which blocked the liberals and seculars from reaching people in the countryside)—had secured as much
power in Egypt as the National Socialists (Nazis) and fascists held in

prewar Europe. The Ikhwan's version of "brown shirts" helped Morsi manipulate the election before becoming his tool to assert power once elected. The Brotherhood's greatest advantage internationally, however, was the lack of interest Western watch groups and governments showed in the validity of this first democratic election. To a point, according to the Egyptian opposition, one wonders if indeed this was a real democratic election. Egypt's democratic forces had no choice but to resort to demonstrations.[8] They staged march after march, but the United States and Europe were silent, hoping Morsi would survive the tremors. The Ikhwan took the silence of the West as yet another endorsement of their policies and used more violence against their opponents. The liberal opposition appealed to the army for months, to no avail. It was only when revolutionary groups such as Tamarod mobilized the masses in the streets against the Brotherhood suppression that Egypt moved closer to its second revolution. Innovating in the Arab Spring, Tamarod called for a national popular demonstration, to vote with their feet for the removal of Morsi on June 30, 2013.

Very few in the West paid serious attention to Tamarod and its bottom-up uprising. Then, on Sunday, June 30, around 33 million Egyptians marched in Cairo and other cities.[9] Statistically, this was the largest demonstration in history, topping the combined masses of the revolutions in Lebanon and Iran. What was morally left of Morsi's regime was shattered by this undeniable referendum. The demonstrators numbered three times as many as had voted for him the year before. Morsi refused the call to resign and ordered his followers to mobilize for "Jihad till death."

The overwhelming majority of Egyptian citizens who took part in the second revolution prompted the country's armed forces to remove the Muslim Brotherhood and contain the Jihadists.[10] The Egyptian army stepped in to prevent a civil war and to end a regime-coup against its own people. The shock of removing Morsi reverberated worldwide, particularly across the petrodollar web that backed the Ikhwan. The goal of the real Arab Spring was accomplished by the people's revolution in Egypt of June 30, 2013, at last.

As soon as the Egyptian military dismantled Morsi's regime, millions of Egyptians celebrated the end of what they felt was a dangerous fascistic regime. But despite the overwhelming popular support for the ousting of the Ikhwan, some U.S. leaders, starting with President Obama (later joined by Republican senator John McCain), argued it was "directed by the Egyptian military against a democratically elected government."[11] Awkwardly, the United States executive branch, with some of its supporters in the legislature, sided with the Muslim Brotherhood, known to be hard-core Islamists, against an obviously wide coalition of democratic and secular forces that had called on the military to help them against what they perceived as a an oppressive regime. How this unbalanced equation could exist has been the question asked by observers both in the Middle East and in the West. Why would Obama and McCain back the Ikhwan while the liberals, seculars, and pro-Western forces of Egypt's civil society rose up against the Islamists? The chaos in Washington has several roots, but one global fact is clear: U.S. foreign policy has lost the Arab Spring. Sadly, the Obama administration resisted the democratic revolt. While arguing that Morsi was democratically elected, it forgot that he governed oppressively. Some international media, such as CNN and the BBC, also endorsed Morsi and his followers, even as armed Islamists roamed through Egypt, killing and maiming citizens.[12] For a long time to come, the second Egyptian revolution will be confronting counterrevolutionary forces, including an unrepentant Ikhwan and a myriad of dangerous Jihadi terrorists.[13] Thanks to its courageous civil society, Egypt has already survived the fundamentalist yoke. Egypt will not be Iran. The millions who took to the streets formed a Nile of democracy that will flood the Jihadists out of Egypt. It will be long and hard, but the Egyptian Spring is now, finally, in progress.[14]

Fortunately for democracy in Egypt, a majority in the U.S. Congress as well as vast popular support among American citizens provided moral and political backing to the second Egyptian revolution during the summer of 2013.[15] The challenge was to the Egyptian military and the interim government to ensure a rapid pace, but not a chaotic migration, toward democratic institutions. Both the Foreign Affairs Committee of the House of Representatives and the European Parliament called on the post-Morsi government in Egypt to be steady and serious in moving through the process.[16] The primary challenge after the second Egyptian revolution was to build a strategic bridge between Egypt's popular democracy and the enlightened leaders and activists in the West, particularly in the United States.

THE SECOND WAVE OF THE SECOND REVOLUTION

Throughout July 2013, the Islamist political machine and the Jihadi networks went on the counteroffensive against the revolution that unseated Morsi. In Cairo, the Muslim Brotherhood organized a permanent rally in the Rabi'a Adawiya public square, countering Tahrir Square and installing their leadership's headquarters in the center. Meanwhile, their militants organized forays into other streets within the capital held by secular democracy activists and launched urban attacks throughout Egypt. The strategy of the Ikhwan was to destabilize the popular move and form a new interim government. The Brotherhood had been invited to join the political process under a pluralist, democratic agenda, but the Islamists rejected the invitation and pressed forward with their urban insurgency efforts. In parallel to the Ikhwan actions across mainland Egypt, including dispersed attacks against Coptic churches, al Qaeda–linked Jihadists waged armed attacks on Egyptian army and security units in the Sinai. The Islamist campaigns against the secular revolution in Egypt aimed at weakening and discrediting the armed forces on the one hand and at terrorizing civil society on the other hand. The Muslim Brotherhood also counted on backing from the region's Islamists, including those in Turkey, Tunisia, Libya, and Yemen. It was clear that the battle for Egypt was the battle for Salafi power worldwide.

In the United States, the Obama administration, under pressure from the Islamist lobby, put a halt to military aid to Egypt, freezing a shipment of F-16 fighters.[17] The move did not have had a real impact on the ground because the Egyptian military at the time did not need additional American weapons to confront the Jihadi terror networks, but the decision had a moral effect as it signaled to the international community that Egypt's popular revolution was a coup and thus it needed to be reversed. Washington, however, stopped short of calling the removal of Morsi a coup. First to take advantage of the U.S. hesitation were the Egyptian Islamists, who unleashed a counterrevolution in Cairo and throughout the country. Mobilizing to defend the June 30 massive revolt and the disbanding of the Islamist government, civil society forces called on the army to protect them from the Ikhwan militias. In response, General Abdel Fattah el Sisi, minister of defense and commander in chief of Egyptian armed forces, called "on the Egyptian people to march on July 26 and mandate Egypt's armed forces to defeat violence and terrorism." On that day, as many Egyptians demonstrated in the capital's public squares and in other provinces as on June 30, some say more, possibly 40 million citizens.[18] The gigantic peaceful marches, which included an overwhelming popular majority of moderate Muslims and Copts, countered any remnant sense of legitimacy regarding Morsi's regime and showed support for both the interim government and the armed forces.[19]

Striking back, Jihadi cells multiplied their attacks in Sinai. The Egyptian forces responded with a wider campaign to deny al Qaeda and its allies an enclave in the Sinai Peninsula. In Cairo, the government and the popular movement representing the 40 million demonstrators braced for the long battle to counter the urban insurgency led by the Muslim Brotherhood. The summer saw a revolution against the Islamists, just as I had projected in 2010, as civil society was forced to bring the country back to the democracy track. The battle to make Egypt a twenty-first-century liberal democracy will be long and difficult, but now its people and its army have given the country a chance at freedom.

In August, as the pressure of public opinion increased, the Muslim Brotherhood militias established two armed encampments inside Cairo (at Rabi'a Adawiya and Gezyia), and armed Islamists attacked dozens of Coptic churches and police stations. The Egyptian army cleared out the militia's enclaves and continued to fight the Jihadists in Sinai.[20] In reaction, President Obama canceled joint military exercises with Egypt's armed forces and instructed the Defense Department to suspend military assistance.[21] In Congress, members led by Senator McCain stood firmly with the Muslim Brotherhood while others, such as Congresswoman Michele Bachmann and Representative Louis Gohmert, stood with the seculars and the Copts against the Islamists. Egyptian democracy movements responded with a renewed commitment to defeat the Jihadists and roll back extremism. Their leaders have affirmed that the real revolution in Egypt is now against the Islamists.[22]

TURKEY'S SPRING 2013

In the early days of June 2013, again to the surprise of most political analysts and observers in the West, demonstrations exploded in Turkey against the Islamist AKP government. As in Tunisia and Egypt, the initial protests were triggered by local residents. In Istanbul, citizens had gathered to reject a government plan to destroy old trees in a public park and to replace the park with a modern mall dedicated to the Ottoman era. The police responded with violence, triggering a flood of demonstrations. From one side to the other of the former Ottoman Empire, demonstrations quickly encompassed dozens of cities and towns, including the capital, Ankara, and the hometown of the prime minister. The AKP government ordered a systematic suppression of the protests, and that action threatened to create a wave of opposition to the very legitimacy of the Turkish government, which was led by a party that had won legislative elections three times since 2003. Prime Minister Recep Tayyip Erdogan refused to accept the notion that a Turkish Spring was under way. Like Mubarak and Assad, he accused "extremists and outside forces" of pushing for the protests. Nonetheless, the marches continued in several cities and were joined over days and weeks by social forces, including labor unions, women's movements, student organizations, and artists and intellectuals. Ethnic minorities, the Kurds being the largest, naturally sided with the protests, demanding greater freedoms. Ironically, most of the mainstream Turkish press and media hesitated to cover the popular explosion for fear of retribution by the AKP government.

From the first days of the anti-Erdogan demonstrations, the Obama administration was quick to comment. It asked that the Turkish government allow freedom of expression without suppression. The AKP criticized Washington's position and dismissed it. That very day I was part of the Turkish-American Council conference in Washington attended by Vice President Joseph Biden and the deputy prime minister of Turkey, Ali Babacan, and I understood the critical position of the administration. Biden was quick to assert that Turkey should not be a "second-class democracy" while Babacan said "laws are made to be obeyed." Former and current U.S. and Turkish officials who attended the event shared with me what was prompting the Obama administration's position in the early stages of the June uprising in Turkey. "The White House, which was facing harsh criticism and hearings on the issue of Benghazi, and was lectured by its opposition on its perceived failures throughout the Arab Spring and vis-à-vis Iran, didn't want to appear as making more mistakes on Turkey," a former U.S. diplomat said to me. "But deep down, President Obama doesn't want to see Erdogan losing ground in Turkey. U.S. officials will stand by the 'principle' of democracy in public to avoid a negative standing similar to the one on Iran's Green Revolution in June 2009, but behind the scenes, the administration will advise Turkey's AKP leaders to handle the situation domestically in a way that will avert a popular uprising." This analysis proved accurate as the Obama administration did not want to lose a political ally in the region, particularly because the AKP government was a major player in the "moderate Islamist" bloc of governments that included Egypt and Tunisia and, to a certain extent, the cabinets of Morocco and Libya.

However, experts on Turkey's politics captured the message of the protests at their roots. Soner Cagaptay, a leading Turkish scholar based in Washington, wrote that something had deeply changed in his country. "Civil society forces have discovered their strength," he argued, "Turks have learned the power of grassroots politics."[23] Cagaptay explained that since the demise of the army as a ruling power and under AKP rule, middle-class Turks have never had a chance to express themselves outside of the traditional political parties, but with social media, mostly Facebook and YouTube, younger Turks have accessed a new space of political expression and organization comparable to the protest movements in the Arab world since 2011. The difference between Turkish civil society and the countries of the Arab Spring, however, is the history of the multiparty system and secular values that Turks have enjoyed for most of the twentieth century, albeit interspersed with periods of military rule. They've had a constant secular culture with sparse periods of democratic change, including the elections that brought the Islamist AKP to power in 2003.

But statements made by the demonstrators and the opposition intellectuals since the spread of the protests indicate that the depth of the confrontation is about their secular lifestyle and how it is being challenged by an advancing Islamization of the country, even if the transformation has been progressing gradually. The initial demonstrations about a small national park in Istanbul raised several social and legal issues but eventually ended up revealing that a significant debate existed in Turkey between the profound secular segment of society and the AKP Islamist Party. In this regard, the Turkish Spring, although with its own unique characteristics, is a popular movement of opposition against a strong Islamist government, elected democratically with a large popular base, but accused by the liberals and seculars of using its power to impose its doctrinal authoritarian agenda.

The evolution of the secular protest movement in Turkey will have a fundamental impact, not just on Turkish politics, but on the region as a whole. Soner Cagaptay had told me three years before the 2013 demonstrations that the expansion of an Islamist political network inside Turkey under the AKP government auspices would eventually clash with the secular core of civil society. "The change in foreign policy may not directly affect seculars in Turkey," he argued. "But once the ideological change would hit the lifestyle of Turks, particularly the Westernized seculars, tensions are projected to grow." Long before the events in

Istanbul, Western-based Turkish experts explained the dual affiliation of politics in Turkey, a duality doomed to clash at some point. Zeno Baran, another leading Washington expert on Turkish affairs, published a book in 2010, *Torn Country: Turkey Between Secularism and Islamism,* which provided its readers with the formula that produced the final intersection of seculars and Islamists in Turkey.[24] Later, she told me that the West has received two separate ideas about Turkey—one, that the country's institutions are very secular and thus nonpenetrable by religious ideas; and two, that Turkey's AKP government is religious but moderate. The accuracy of both ideas would be put to the test in 2013 when the two forces began to settle scores in the streets of Turkish cities. The seculars, attached to the Kemal Ataturk sharp *laïcité,* which bordered on anticlericalism, had given up their suspicion of religious parties and accepted the AKP rule for a decade. The Islamists, who had been governing for ten years, felt it was time to start pushing for cultural Islamization. The frail status quo between the two was about to break. All eyes would be on Turkey to see which direction the country would take after the clashes in the streets. Dr. Burak Kuntay, a Turkish professor of political science specializing in U.S.-Turkish relations, said in a speech at the Turkish-American Council in Washington, D.C., in June 2013, "The events in Turkey are a test of the country's democracy. The world and the West are looking at how government and society are interacting over fundamental issues, including the politics of democracy. The way we as Turks are going to handle this debate will define us in the eyes of the world."

As I observed the continual demonstrations in Istanbul and other Turkish cities, I came to the conclusion that, as in the Arab Spring, something fundamental had changed in this Middle Eastern country. It was not about who would win the next elections or whether the cabinet would resign or not; it was about the political culture of Turkey. The Islamists, through the AKP ascension to power and its reelection three times in a row to a majority in Parliament and its ability to form the government, had been able to end the Ataturk anticlericalism and limit the influence of the army in civilian affairs. However, overreach by the

Islamist government into the freedoms of citizens and the AKP's attempts to Islamize the public space were resisted by the vigorous secular segment of society. This resistance reshaped Turkish politics as a balance between religious traditions on the one hand and unshakable secular culture on the other. Depending on where this new status will come to rest, Turkey's model of coexistence between Islamists and seculars will have a significant and leading impact on similar struggles across the Middle East, from Iran to the Arab world.

CHAPTER NINE

THE ISLAMIST LOBBY WAR ON MIDDLE EAST DEMOCRACY

AFTER THE COLD WAR ENDED, AN INCREASINGLY POW-erful lobby network systematically attempted to shift U.S. foreign policy away from assisting the development of civil society, and thus away from the shaping of liberal democracies in the Middle East.[1] The lobbyists' alternative goal was to create a state of fear among democracy activists to prevent them from engaging the peoples of the region lest they clash with its Islamist militants. This twenty-three-year-long war of attrition against the democracy component of U.S. policy in the Middle East was initially waged by two organized forces acting in one direction with significant influence. The organized networks were the Muslim Brotherhood, on the one hand, and Iranian propaganda on the other. As in the Cold War, anti-American, and in a broader sense antidemocratic, pressure groups within the West employed all the resources at hand to influence Washington's strategic planning, its communications efforts to influence overseas public opinion, and, in the end, its comprehensive global policies. The Islamist lobbies, both Salafi and Khomeinist, burst into activity in the West with the collapse of the Soviet Union. The funding of and high level of activity by these activist networks impacted almost all public and private sectors and exerted influence on Western foreign policy, including the U.S. Middle East agenda.

Only by understanding these post-Soviet lobby wars in Washington can one comprehend American tergiversations regarding the Arab Spring of 2011 and its subsequent spasms. Why were U.S. policies not immediately realigned with the forces of secular democracy at the end of the Cold War? Why would Washington ignore genocide in southern Sudan and Darfur, the continuous Syrian occupation of Lebanon, the brutalization by Saddam of his own people (particularly the Kurds and the Shiites), the repression by Assad in Syria, the persecution of Copts in Egypt, and in general a systematic oppression of civil societies in the Greater Middle East? Why, after the removal of the oppressors of Afghanistan in 2001 and Iraq in 2003 and the forced withdrawal of Syrian forces from Lebanon in 2005—after seven years of U.S. efforts aimed at building freedom and democracy in these societies—would Washington revert to a pre-9/11 mindset and shy away from supporting democratic resistance and instead—as we saw after 2009—partner with Islamists?

THE PETRODOLLARS FACTOR

The central reason the United States, the most powerful liberal democracy in the world, made wrong and unnatural choices for the peoples oppressed by authoritarians in the Arab world and the Middle East was oil.[2] It was all about petrodollars and their influence on the U.S. political system. (This was also true in Europe and other Western societies.) In 1973, the Organization of Petroleum Exporting Countries (OPEC), through its international political arm, showed the United States and Europe that it could use the weapon of oil to create more balance in the West's treatment of the Arab-Israeli conflict. Initially, the oil embargo resulted from a regional conflict, the Yom Kippur War. Arab members of OPEC retaliated against the unilateral support provided by Washington to Israel during the war. The impact of the embargo left Western economic elites shell-shocked.[3] The sight of long lines of cars in front of gas pumps in America, and of European citizens forced to bike to their workplaces, unsettled policymakers, think tank consultants, and corporate officers.

The entire episode created a new reality in world affairs. Non-Western oil producers, particularly Arab oil producers, realized that they had an alternative to building a nuclear arsenal. They could use oil to achieve their goals in international relations. The OPEC club became more influential than ever before, and its economic influence was used to fulfill its political ambitions, or at least to pursue the agendas of some of its more radical or ideological members. But the unified Arab position with regard to forcing the United States to pressure Israel was an exception. There were few other cases in which the oil bloc, by exerting economic pressure, obtained direct political satisfaction. The Arab-Israeli war revealed the weapon of oil, but the leadership of OPEC has failed to use that weapon since. Recognition of the power of deterrence in an embargo, however, changed diplomatic attitudes across the planet. OPEC and its members obtained higher visibility in international circles, and the national interests of its member states were met more quickly. After the 1973 oil shock, the level and sophistication of arms obtained by producers, particularly in the Middle East, rose. The multinational oil companies gained more influence in the West as a result of this demonstration of force. For decades afterward, up until the Arab Spring, the power of petrodollars significantly impacted U.S.–Middle East relations.

With the Iranian Islamic revolution and the rise of other radical regimes and movements in the region—including the Iraqi Baath, Libya's Gaddafi regime, the Salafi Wahabi circles, and the Muslim Brotherhood—the use of oil power for ideological gains became a second reality. At the end of the Cold War, with the vanishing of the Soviet threat and the end of Afghanistan's campaign against the Russians, the international Jihadists—who would become the nucleus of al Qaeda in the 1990s—moved to open new fronts against those whom they called *kuffar*, or "the infidels." The armed Islamist cells of earlier decades designated multiple enemies they wished to defeat. In addition to the continuous obligation to crush Israel, Jihads were declared against India, Black Africa, the Philippines, former Yugoslavia, post-Soviet Russia, and apostate governments in the Muslim world such as Saudi Arabia, Egypt, and Jordan. Battlefields opened in Kashmir, Bosnia, Kosovo,

Chechnya, South Sudan, and the southern Philippines, to name the most prominent locales. The regional and local Jihads were connected to the international Jihad led by al Qaeda in the mid-1990s. All of these battle-fields received petrodollar donations in support.[4] An awkward equation transferred funds from the Gulf to Jihadi fighters around the world. The rulers of the oil-producing regimes did not want these fighters in their countries, but rather engaged elsewhere, fighting "for the good of Mus-lim communities worldwide." But the Jihadists, who had a great appetite for aid, often from private donors as well, were not faithful soldiers to these regimes. In fact, even as the Jihadists exploited the resources, they despised their sources.

Another network also thrived on petrodollars: the Muslim Brother-hood and the Salafi groups. The political Islamists of the 1990s had two main goals. First on their agenda was supporting the worldwide Jihadi battlefields politically, often intertwining with the Jihadists. Second, and no less important, was penetrating the West's foreign policy establish-ment to exert a paralyzing influence on the rise of democracy in the Middle East. The famous petrodollars, the profits from selling oil to the industrial countries, were used by Islamists in the West to prevent secu-lar democracy and liberalism from flourishing in the Arab world and the Greater Middle East. The funding generated from Gulf oil circles, sympathetic to the Jihadists and the Islamists, was the basis of support for what became a powerful lobbying effort on behalf of the Islamist agenda.[5] With the end of the Cold War, oil funding of political influ-ence in America increased swiftly. By the mid-1990s, petrodollars were fueling the rise of both Islamist apologist influences within academia and Islamist lobby groups within the political sphere. Thus, throughout the late 1990s and during the post-9/11 decade, a well-funded "Islamist lobby" had been operating in Washington and several European capitals in order to further the agendas of ideological regimes and movements based in the Middle East.[6]

The Muslim Brotherhood and other Salafi Islamists had their own supporters that included, chiefly, the Council on American-Islamic Re-lations (CAIR) and the Islamic Society of North America (ISNA), as well as other advocacy pressure groups. The Iranian regime had its own defenders, such as the National Iranian American Council (NIAC). But the pressure groups did not end with them; the Arab regimes of Saddam and Assad, among others, had also their pro-Baathist advocates. The sum of all these lobbies formed a Mideast region-wide advocacy bloc in American politics. Initially, as in the 1980s, the central effort of this super-Islamist lobby was to counter pro-Israeli activity within the Beltway and to confront the American Israel Public Affairs Committee (AIPAC), the powerful lobby on matters related to the Arab-Israeli conflict.[7] The prime aim of the so-called Arab lobby, until the early 1990s, was to push back against Israel's influence in Washington.[8] By the middle of the decade, however, the classical Arab pressure group, often represented by the Arab American Institute and other committees, was gradually replaced by a more powerful, savvier, and much more effective Islamist lobby.

ISLAMIST LOBBIES' GOALS FOR U.S. FOREIGN POLICY

The Islamist lobbies operating within the United States at the end of the Cold War represented two networks in the region, the Salafists on the one hand and the Khomeinists on the other. The central goal of this conglomeration was to influence U.S. policy toward the region in a way that would not only minimize an American alliance with Israel, but also pressure Washington to partner with Islamist power centers in Iran and the Arab world. The lobbies thus engaged in joint tracks against pro-Israel pressure groups as well as against secular Middle Eastern dissidents while at the same time pursuing particular causes related to their own national or regional interests. Here is a summary breakdown.

THE PRO-IRANIAN LOBBY

Iranian-American organizations connected to the Iranian regime seek to reduce U.S. enmity to the ayatollahs and to delay any military campaign against Iran or to weaken economic sanctions leveled

by Washington. This lobby guarded the interests of Tehran's elite before Washington's political establishment and served as an advance
shield to the interests of the regime.[9] Also part of the global Iran lobby
were financial interests seeking to establish economic ties with the
regime after the Iranian-U.S. breakdown of 1979. Iran being one of the
most important oil producers in the region, financial interest groups
hoped they could pressure Washington decision-making circles to enter into a dialogue, followed by a rapprochement and eventually a deal
between the two countries. The Iranian lobby disseminated significant research in the United States and Europe about the reality of the
Iranian Islamic Republic and the need for the United States to reach
out to Iran's leaders. This lobby was backed by a pro-Hezbollah lobby
that acted more subtly, since Hezbollah was and remains on the State
Department's list of terror organizations. But the group's supporters,
mainly found among Lebanese Shia, had developed several networks
in the United States.[10] In sum, the Iranian lobby was a state lobby but
acted also as an interest group seeking to influence U.S. policy regarding the Middle East. The well-funded network had a direct and
indirect reach within the various realms of public policy, including access through think tanks, experts, campuses, media, and at times even
official foreign policy circles.[11]

The strategic goals of the Iran lobby, along with its Hezbollah and
Syrian sublobbies, were, by order of importance: to delay the U.S. response to the Iranian nuclear program, to lure Washington into the
policy of engagement, and to attack and delegitimize the Iranian opposition in America. This last goal was by far the most important. Indeed,
in the American political system, public opinion is fundamentally important. When a foreign policy cause gains visibility, Congress and the
executive branch will seize it and address it. The cause of a free Iran,
advanced by Iranian exiles, would thus be the most threatening agenda
to the Iranian regime. For if the American public mobilized around the
idea of liberating Iran from its own ruling elite, U.S. resources would be
directed to support the opposition. It was vital to the Iranian lobby to
eliminate "Iran's democracy cause" in the United States so that the only

remaining option, apart from an improbable military action, was political engagement.[12]

THE ARAB NATIONALIST LOBBIES

As part of the global Arabist-Islamist lobby pressure on U.S. foreign policy, various Arab nationalist interest groups have represented regimes in the region. From Saddam Hussein and Hafez and Bashar Assad to Muammar Gaddafi, each ruler has been backed by support groups operating within the Beltway, starting with but not limited to their embassies. Baathist Iraq and Syria could also count on community organizations formed by émigrés and partisans of these dictators. Gaddafi's followers being rare, his regime counted on professional consulting help. Arab nationalist lobbies, particularly those of Iraq and Syria, did not defend the Islamists—quite the opposite—but they claimed to speak on behalf of Arab Americans in order to influence the U.S. government on issues that Damascus and Baghdad wanted to defend. Syria, until the Cedars Revolution exploded in Lebanon, used its lobby to block any attempt by the Lebanese community to mobilize Washington against Syria's occupation of their country. The supporters of Saddam's regime naturally lobbied hard for Baghdad's Baathist dictator during the Iraq-Iran war of 1980–1987, then against the U.S. campaign during the invasion of Kuwait, and battled George W. Bush's decision to invade Iraq in 2003. Each authoritarian regime had its own narrow agenda: to block access by any opposition to its own regime that might bend the ear of U.S. policymakers. Iraqi Americans, including Assyrians, Chaldeans, Kurds, Shia, and liberal Sunnis, often complained of pressures coming from regime operatives when they raised democracy issues with lawmakers or the State Department. Such was also the case with Syrian Americans of all backgrounds regarding the Assad regime. Systematically, regimes in the Greater Middle East used their clout and influence, as well as interest groups and sometimes consulting companies, to delay, combat, and at times destroy the efforts of exile groups seeking freedom for their homelands. In 1995, as I was participating in a conference on slavery in

South Sudan and Mauritania at Columbia University organized by the American Anti-Slavery Group and coordinated by African American writer and human rights activist Samuel Cotton, I witnessed an attempt by pro-Khartoum regime elements to disrupt the abolitionist event. They were aided by other elements supporting the Mauritanian and, to our surprise, the Egyptian regimes. Uninvited diplomats and local militants interrupted the proceedings by shouting and intimidating participants and guests. Very quickly, however, southern Sudanese, Mauritanian, and other American abolitionists rose against the unwanted guests and forced them to leave. This experience, and many other similar experiences, showed us that regimes in the region were keen to block the causes of freedom that might pique the interest of American public opinion and thus potentially travel to the top of the government's foreign policy agenda. Toward the end of the 1990s and even after 9/11, the Beirut and Damascus regimes used similar methods to suppress Lebanese and Syrian opposition voices within the United States and Europe.

THE ISLAMIST LOBBIES

The most effective and at the same time most dangerous body in the West lobbying against democratic forces in the Greater Middle East were the Islamist networks. In the center of these networks was the oldest militant organization, the Muslim Brotherhood. Within the conglomerate led by the Ikhwan, other Salafi, Wahabi, and Takfiri[13] groups set up bases in the West and in the United States by the end of the Cold War. According to comprehensive research on the Islamist lobby in America, the core of the network was controlled by Brotherhood fronts and significant funding came from the Gulf, principally from Wahabi circles.[14] Research also indicates that a sister network operated in Europe as of the mid-1990s.[15]

The Islamist Salafi lobby has had two fundamental driving forces: financial power and effective organization. The financial power has been the flow of petrodollars into American academia, media, and bureaucratic institutions as a means to developing political influence.

Observers and researchers often cited Wahabi circles as being the main funders of the Islamist network in the United States and the West. These circles were perceived as the main force behind the growth of the global Islamist lobby in America and in the West in general.[16] The argument was that Saudi money and influence was the power behind the Islamist lobby in the United States. It was strongly believed that the Saudis were in command of the Wahabi network, which directs goods and funds to other groups, including the Muslim Brotherhood.[17] While it is true that Saudi funds were invested in education and think tanks and that this created a Wahabi influence, the reality was that it was the Muslim Brotherhood entities that directed the networks and waged the campaigns to influence national security and foreign policy. The initial financing of influence projects may have been Saudi, but Qatari, Libyan, Iraqi, Sudanese, and other Gulf sources also contributed. However, the actual organizations in charge of the activities and of networking were connected to the Muslim Brotherhood. The public, particularly after 9/11, criticized the Wahabi power as deriving from Saudi petrodollars, but the reality was never so simple. The Ikhwan fronts, such as CAIR and its derivatives, had used Gulf funding to build their own political platform in Washington.[18] The diplomats and donors from the Arabian Peninsula opened the doors, but rarely meddled in the actual lobbying campaigns; the Brotherhood network was in charge of striking at political foes and eventually supplanted the donors and backers. Until the Arab Spring of 2011 and the rise of the Brotherhood to power in Egypt (and of their allies in Tunisia, the Nahda, and in Libya, the Salafists), the Ikhwan lobbies in the United States and the West remained under the umbrella of the Gulf donors. In the late 1990s and throughout the post-9/11 years, Qatar's regime partnered with the Muslim Brotherhood, supplanting the Wahabis of Saudi Arabia in leading the Islamist lobby in the West. With al Jazeera leading the war of ideas via its powerful narrative and shows, Qatar's real international influence operation merged with that of the Ikhwan. Doha's elite, with its enormous funding to the Brotherhood, surpassed the Wahabis and moved on to become the epicenter of Salafi Islamist influence in the region and, via lobby groups, within the West. The Brotherhood's peak in the United States came with the victory of candidate Barack Obama in the U.S. presidential election of 2008. The network, via its front groups, supported the campaign, not as a formal entity, but as a prelude to receiving influence within America's bureaucracies and the new administration when Obama took office.[19]

The organizational force of the Islamist lobby, as we have described it, has been rooted in the Muslim Brotherhood since the late 1980s and early 1990s. During the Cold War, the Brotherhood served the interests of both the conservative Saudis and the United States in the worldwide confrontation with the Soviets. Ikhwan cadres migrated to America from Palestine, Egypt, Syria, and other countries in the Middle East. They gradually positioned themselves in academia in Middle East studies departments and related subjects, forming the nucleus of the larger Islamist lobby group. The Muslim Student Association (MSA), the largest network on campuses nationwide, was seen by analysts as the main launch pad for most components of the Islamist Salafi lobby in America.[20] The MSA, founded in 1963, produced cadres to form and launch several generations of Muslim Brotherhood fronts, including the North America Islamic Trust in 1971, the International Institute of Islamic Thought in 1980, the Islamic Society for North America in 1981, and the Holy Land Foundation in 1990, as well as the American Islamic Council and later on the Council on American Islamic Relations (CAIR) in the mid 1990s.[21] As of the late 1990s, a long roster of organizations modeled after human and civil rights groups were launched in the United States, with CAIR, ISNA, and the Muslim Public Affairs Committee (MPAC) in the lead. The group most focused on U.S. national security and foreign policy was CAIR, headed by Nihad Awad, which was linked to the Ikhwan and Hamas.[22]

The national bloc of networks that formed the Islamist lobby was composed of various entities evolved over time. As noted above, the two initial components were Muslim Brotherhood cadres and Wahabi funding. Adding to the latter were petrodollar grants disseminated to impact campuses, NGOs, think tanks, community activities, and media.

Politicians who were supported by this network, bureaucrats who worked with the lobby, and multinational companies profiting from the oil industry added to the power of the pressure group.[23] Taken together, these entities constituted a mega-force with an influence that deeply permeated the American political decision-making system. By the late 1990s it had become exceedingly efficient, so much so that Islamist activists rejected the notion that an Islamist lobby on foreign policy even existed. They argued that "Arab and Islamic groups are too divided to form one corps."[24] The reality was that the larger bloc was in fact as diverse as its basic components when it came to local and national agendas in the region, but the bloc was unified when the issue served the global Islamist agenda.[25] In the final analysis, the Islamist lobby on national security and foreign affairs operating in the United States was essentially made of two main forces having focused strategic goals: the Muslim Brotherhood and the Iranian regime. They were competitive when it came to the specifics of the region but converged when it came to mitigating U.S. influence in the Greater Middle East. Clare Lopez, a former CIA analyst and an expert on Islamist infiltration in the West, wrote: "Should anyone still be laboring under the impression that sectarian differences invariably keep Sunni and Shi'ite jihadis from cooperating, notice what is happening, not in the Middle East, but right here at home."[26]

THE ISLAMIST LOBBY STRATEGIES

The factions within the global lobby had an overarching common interest: to push back against the forces of secular democracy in the Arab world and Iran and thus against their representatives and friends within the United States and Europe, for the real threat to the Islamists in the East was a secular liberal revolution backed by the West. This regional consensus among regimes and organizations opposed to liberal democracies can be called a "brotherhood against democracy."[27] It included the Iranian regime, its allies, Syria's Assad, Hezbollah, and the Salafi networks encompassing the Ikhwan and the other Islamists. The wider Brotherhood comprised the classical authoritarian regimes of the region. Logically, authoritarian regimes and Islamist networks had a joint interest in blocking secular democrats from the region, or their friends in the United States, and keeping them from convincing Washington's decision makers to lend support to freedom movements in the region. But while national authoritarian governments pushed back against their own émigrés or exiles aiming at democratization within their mother countries, the Islamist lobby as a whole systematically attacked voices originating in any country in the Middle East. The Muslim Brotherhood and the Iranian regime have regional ambitions; they resent any rise of liberal democrats on their map, and thus their lobbying efforts since the end of the Soviet Union have been directed at maintaining a gap between regional liberal democrats and the United States government, public, media, and the ensemble of all pressure groups or advocacy organizations seeking liberation anywhere in the Greater Middle East.

When I relocated to the United States in 1990, I had already researched both Islamists and Jihadists and the ultra-radical movements in the Middle East. My earlier experience in the activities of the Middle East diaspora and participation in conferences and seminars in multiple émigré countries in Europe and the Americas enabled me to obtain an understanding of political lobbying on behalf of national and ideological causes. As an American scholar, I researched political interest groups in general and those with Middle East agendas in particular. My academic research and media practice throughout the years has helped me identify the regional forces making efforts to impact American public opinion and those in governmental power. During my travels throughout the West in the 1980s, at community events and in meetings with officials, I noted that most of the efforts deployed by lobbies from the region centered on Palestine and the Arab-Israeli conflict. After Saddam's invasion of Kuwait, Syria's invasion of Lebanon, and the Madrid Peace Conference in 1991, I realized that Middle Eastern lobbying in America took two directions. One pursued all the ethnic, national, and political claims; the other incorporated all campaigns to establish Islamist influence. A keen observer could find Lebanese seeking liberation from Syria, South

Sudanese aiming at self-determination and independence from Khartoum, Assyro-Chaldeans and Copts raising the issues of persecution in Iraq and Egypt, and many Arab and Iranian dissidents and opposition groups. With higher media and political visibility, the respective Israeli and Arab political interests remained the most prominent.

Next to this classical marketplace of region-related interests in Washington, however, another steady, deep, and well-organized network was growing quickly through the use of U.S. lobbying tactics. The omnipresent Islamist lobby became a dominant force in influencing U.S. foreign policy toward the Middle East and the Muslim world. In short, the lobby claimed it was representing both the majority of Muslim Americans as well as the views of the peoples in the Middle East, and the lobby presented itself as an unavoidable associate in American foreign policy. With such a claim of legitimacy, the Islamist lobby essentially demanded its views be included in the creation of U.S. foreign policy and practices in the region. The irony was that Washington's politicians, within and outside of the executive branch, accepted the lobby's claim that it advanced what most American citizens hailing from the Middle East wanted, and so the lobby seemed the best representative for the region. In two decades, the Islamist lobby was able to create political facts chaining U.S. foreign policy not to its national interest or even to what the region's peoples wished for, let alone what a majority of Middle East Americans wanted, but to the goals of the Islamists, such as the Muslim Brotherhood and the Iranian regime.[28] The means by which this monumental achievement was constructed and developed can be seen as a series of long-term, sophisticated, and efficient strategies.

VITAL STAGE: PENETRATING EDUCATION

The first stage in the long-term Islamist lobbying strategy was to penetrate American education. The rationale is simple but powerful. By controlling who and what was taught in Middle East studies in American universities, the Islamist lobby would shape the way Americans read and understand the region's history and politics. These graduates would in time populate newsrooms, courtrooms, war rooms, theaters, and ultimately decision-making circles. With the help of petrodollar grants, members of the Islamist lobby and their allies launched or influenced a web of Middle East studies programs on campuses, and they became the dominant school of thought at the national Middle East Studies Association.[29] The deep influence the Islamist and radical Middle Eastern lobbies obtained in academia led them into all venues of public policy. Once the scholars in charge of teaching or researching the region were aligned with the agendas of the Muslim Brotherhood, Iranian regime, or other radical forces or authoritarian powers in the Middle East, the expert opinion provided by the field was compromised. The reading and understanding of these political and ideological forces of the region (their views, their real intentions) and the ability to construct the appropriate policies in return, before and after 9/11 and particularly before and after the Arab Spring, were compromised. This blurring of vision affected all bureaucracies and higher levels in U.S. administrations from the fall of the Soviet Union until 2014.[30]

FROM THE CLASSROOM TO THE NEWSROOM

The inability of the Western and American media to see Middle Eastern affairs clearly, particularly with regard to the Arab Spring and its aftermath, is traceable to the failure of Middle East studies to provide the right insight. Even the most sophisticated outlets, referred to as "mainstream," with their considerable investigative resources, failed to predict most of the great surges, al Qaeda's war declarations in the 1990s, the road to 9/11, Jihadi radicalization, and, of course, the Arab Spring and its aftermath. This failure cannot be traced to inadequate facts or statistics; the inability to accurately project trends can instead be linked to the reliance on the picture painted by the forces opposed to the United States and the West. In short, communications media failed to understand the Jihadist phenomenon and the civil society resistance to Jihadists mostly because of its vitiated training in Middle East studies. Giants in the field such as the *New York Times,* the *Washington Post,* and

CNN—to name the most prominent—have continued to play a leading role in journalism, but as a perusal of the archives would reveal, they have remained under the influence of the Islamist lobby, either directly or by adopting an apologist attitude toward the political forces opposing the Islamists in the region.[31]

FROM THE NEWSROOM TO THE WAR ROOM

With the academic world producing literature endorsing the Islamist agenda—that is, identifying the Jihadists as "revivalist representatives of the majority's aspirations" and the seculars as "Westernized minorities"—and with a media that corroborates the classroom version of the region, the decision-making centers in foreign policy and national security, otherwise defined as the "war rooms," have also been conditioned by input from these idea-producing industries. Politicians and executive decision makers were forced to rely on advisers from academia, and then measured their decisions by the degree of endorsement from the media. Since academia and the media's Middle East views were deeply shaped by the Islamist lobby, the national security and foreign policy decision centers were conditioned to follow in the same direction.[32]

CHAPTER TEN

THE WEAPONS OF LAWFARE AND ISLAMOPHOBIA

IN THE MID-1990s THE MOST SOPHISTICATED OF IS-lamist pressure groups worked to embed themselves in U.S. domestic politics. They sought to have a legitimate role in defining national security and foreign affairs, and they represented themselves as such to civil rights organizations and community associations. The primary lobby that mutated in this way has been the Council on American Islamic Relations (CAIR), which has claimed to be the "nation's largest Muslim civil liberties and advocacy organization."[1] CAIR, as Evan McCormick of the Center for Security Policy puts it, "works on convincing moderate Muslims that they are being targeted unfairly by the Bush administration's [antiterror] policies, CAIR incites fear in members of that demographic. If innocent Muslims are then convinced that they will be the target of government action, then they have no incentive to reject an extremist ideology that resists the government's anti-terror policies.... This is the essence of CAIR's strategy: shock moderate Muslims about the motivations of the U.S. government, turn them into post-[9/11] victims, and then recruit them as supporters for your political agenda when they are ripe for the taking."[2]

This strategy allowed the Islamist lobby to claim that its foreign affairs agenda represented the aspirations of the majority of Muslim Americans; hence, opposing this Islamist agenda would be an affront to and a diminution of the community's rights domestically. CAIR transformed itself into a superlobby representing, though with no mandate, the ethnic communities hailing from more than fifty-seven countries around the world where Islam is the majority religion or where Muslims are a large minority.

Very few in the U.S. government, academia, or the media questioned the hijacking by CAIR of the representation of millions of Muslim Americans. Shielding its legitimacy in foreign policy agenda-setting under the aegis of civil liberties, CAIR and its allies astutely linked any criticism of the Islamist agenda in the Middle East to domestic politics in the United States. Hence, if Copts exposed the armed attacks by Islamists on their community in Egypt, they were accused of demeaning Muslims in America. Shawki Karas, president of the Coptic American Association, told a conference on Middle East Christian persecution at the U.S. Senate in June 2000: "CAIR and the Islamist network waged a defamation campaign against me and the Coptic Association for daring to raise the issue of Coptic oppression in Egypt."[3] When the South Sudanese demanded self-determination from Khartoum and promoted their cause in Washington, they were blocked by the Islamist lobby. Jimmy Mulla, who has been a representative for the South Sudan cause in the United States since the mid-1990s, provided details to me. "The Muslim Brotherhood's lobbies, particularly CAIR, blocked our efforts at the State Department and across the bureaucracies. They claimed the majority of Muslim Americans were opposed to a southern separation in Sudan. They were making this up, as no one ran a referendum among the millions of Muslims in America, many of whom were opposed to the fundamentalist regime of Khartoum and its allies in the region."[4] Similar obstructive pressures were waged by the CAIR-led lobby against efforts by Syrian, Lebanese, Iraqi, Egyptian, and other nationalities to raise the visibility of their campaigns for democracy within their ancestral civil societies in the region. The lobby also targeted Muslim American leaders, such as Zuhdi Jasser, who stood against the Brotherhood lobby and resisted the Islamist political suppression of dissent in the United States. Jasser, president of the anti-Islamist American Islamic Forum on Democracy (AIFD), led the secular and moderate opposition to the Ikhwan network in the United States. CAIR and its allies attempted to block the AIFD leader from any access to the U.S. government, including his appointment to the Commission on Religious Liberties.[5] Examples of Islamist lobby attacks on Mideast democracy leaders and NGOs are countless. CAIR launched two major campaigns against me in 2011 to block both my testimony in the U.S. Congress in March and my appointment as a national security adviser to presidential candidate Mitt Romney in September of that year.

THE IRANIAN KHOMEINIST LOBBY

For their part, the pro-Iranian networks—such as the National Iranian American Committee (NIAC), the Khomeinist counterpart of the Salafist CAIR—pushed back against Washington's support for the Iranian opposition and delayed an American engagement with Iran's civil society.[6] Two major outcomes of pro-Iranian regime lobbying, according to Iranian opposition figures, were the poor U.S. handling of the Iranian threat and, more important, of the democratic opposition to the ayatollahs' regime. Leaders of the Iranian diaspora rarely agree on uniting their efforts, but their frustration with the Obama administration policy toward Iran is fully unified. During my meetings with various components of the opposition (including the Washington-based son of the late shah and leader of the Iranian Democratic Union, Reza Pahlevi, the Paris-based foreign minister of the Council of the Iranian National Resistance, Farzin Hashemi, and many other dissidents), I learned that they blamed part of the U.S. and European failure on the "pro-Khomeinist lobby" in the West.[7] But unlike the Brotherhood pressure group, the pro-Iranian network did not use the community representation platform, for the public knew all too well that a majority of Western-based Iranians were opposed to the regime. The lobby resorted to a different tactic: It would discredit the opposition to the point where the U.S. government had no "credible" and unified force in exile with which to work or about which to worry, and thus—particularly under the Obama administration—it would ignore any partnership with the secular democratic movement in Iran and instead engage in attempts to break the ice with the ayatollahs.[8]

In addition to the pro-Khomeinist lobby in the United States and the West, apologist media also played a role in discrediting the Green Revolution of Iran and, before 2009, most Iranian dissidents. Media that had been impacted by the lobby's arguments and influence diminished the importance of "dissidents and opposition" and often described them as nonrepresentative. During and after the million men and women march in Tehran, voices in the so-called mainstream media in the United States and Europe claimed the demonstrators were mostly middle-class techies, unrelated to the deeper parts of Iran.[9] During that summer of 2009, I countered these arguments in the international media, particularly on France 24, BBC, Fox News, and U.S. radio, pushing back against an enormous machine portraying the Green Revolution as a failed one. The informational framing of the popular Iranian eruption by the Iranian lobby and its influential followers in the media as a "nonrevolution" allowed the U.S. administration to abandon the uprising, much to the astonishment of the Iranian youth.[10]

ISLAMIST MANIPULATION OF AMERICAN CIVIL RIGHTS

The media and academia's endorsement of the Islamist agenda also impacted socially active entities and broader civil rights coalitions. Posing as representatives of Muslim American, Arab American, and Middle East American communities—without any mandate by these segments of civil society—the organized networks of the Islamist lobby claimed their main task was to defend the civil rights of millions of citizens and residents coming from foreign countries. The lobby lamented the discrimination against Muslims and Arabs in the United States and developed the notion that the community was specifically under duress by bigots, right-wingers, Zionists, Christian extremists, and other far-right elements. The Islamist lobby portrayed itself as a "liberal" front defending the poor and marginalized immigrants from the Arab world and Muslim-majority countries. In a sustained and focused effort, the pro-Islamist lobbying effort situated itself as part of the left while its historical agenda was ingrained in deep fundamentalism. CAIR, ISNA, and the web of Islamist cadres flirted in their narrative with African American, Hispanic, and women's issues (even at one point touching on gay and lesbian issues) with the goal of introducing themselves into the U.S. political debate. The subterfuge worked well; civil liberties groups such as the Southern Poverty Law Center and the ACLU expanded their scope to defend the Islamist network. To them, the new groups truly represented the downtrodden segments of Middle East émigré communities, inasmuch as ethnic communities had also represented the Irish, Italian, and, later, Mexican Americans.[11] The umbrella provided by the traditional U.S. entities to the camouflaged Islamist organizations empowered them and provided them with crucial social and political legitimacy, a cornerstone upon which to build their access to the global and national debate over the U.S. interest.[12]

Once the lobby was integrated inside the broader civil liberties coalition, it was able to strike at its enemies, or at the actors obstructing its influence, with greater force.[13] Its first target included public figures and lawmakers who exposed Islamist influence and Jihadi penetration; its second target proved to be experts and scholars who provided research on the Islamist movement in the region and inside the West; and its third target consisted of the Muslim American and Middle East American NGOs and activists who were opposed to the Islamist agenda.[14] The shield of "civil liberties" provided the Islamist lobby with the support of a much wider coalition and stronger allies who thought they were defending a beleaguered community.

During the March 2011 hearings in Congress organized by the Committee on Homeland Security chaired by Representative Peter King and dedicated to understanding the radicalization threat, the bulk of the Islamist lobby attacked the congressman and the witnesses he invited, including Zuhdi Jasser, an anti-Jihadist Muslim American leader; author Ayan Hirsi Ali, a critic of Islamism; and myself. Nihad Awad, the head of CAIR, led a massive campaign against the hearings, the lawmakers, and the witnesses. Awad claimed he was defending the Muslim community's civil rights. The narrative used by the Islamist operatives was one of "attacks against the Muslims," while the hearings targeted Jihadi indoctrination and radicalization.[15] The Homeland Security Committee was attempting to expose the international Jihadi links to domestic radicalization. It was exposing the expansion of Islamist ideology in the Middle East and its impact on American national security. Most experts vindicated Congress's moves later,[16] but the lobby had demonstrated its capacity to delay national security assessment. More important, during the hearings, a number of lawmakers traditionally outspoken on civil liberties sided with the Islamist obstruction to congressional investigation of radicalization, indicating the success of the lobby's maneuver to brand itself as a defender of civil rights. A few left-wing lawmakers, believing they were opposing bigotry against the Muslim community, kept criticizing the hearings and defending CAIR; they assumed CAIR was an equivalent of the NAACP. Despite the striking facts that the panel included a moderate Muslim leader and the Black Muslim uncle of a Jihadist who committed a terror act, the opposition lawmakers were systematically committed to the arguments of the Islamist lobby. This is only one of dozens of examples on how the network was able to dominate the debate about any matter related to Islamist politics at home and to U.S. foreign policy overseas.

ISLAMIST LAWFARE

The shield provided by the "civil liberties coat" worn by the Islamist lobby was strengthened by what experts have identified as "lawfare." The Islamist lobbies dominated the classroom and the newsroom and influenced the war room, but their ultimate political weapon was the courtroom. They used it to deter their foes and thus obliterate criticism of the Islamist agenda altogether. The Muslim Brotherhood and pro-Iranian entities in the United States, and their sisters in Europe and the West, took to the courts the voices and pens they suspected of "defaming" Islam, the Muslim community, or their symbols—all, of course, as perceived by a specific ideological movement, the Islamists. The lobby's lawyers launched lawsuits against an endless number of bloggers, writers, scholars, and public servants.[17] While the sky may be the limit when it comes to defending one's image and dignity, Islamist lobbies in the United States and the West crossed many red lines, often unseen by the public or judges. Lawfare had successful debuts precisely because of the public's ignorance of Islamist politics and tactics. When academia removes basic information about the very existence of a Jihadist or Islamist movement, and when the media replicate academia's camouflage, those in the court system are at the mercy of what they know or don't know and of what they hear and don't hear. A criticism of the actions of Islamist regimes abroad does not constitute the targeting of entire Muslim communities in the West.[18] A deconstruction of Jihadism as an ideology is not bigotry toward Muslims in the United States and in Europe. But that is precisely what CAIR implied and the argument it often made in its cases against defendants. Often, U.S. analysts and bloggers would blast the ideology of oppressive Islamist regimes or organizations, some of which were listed as terror organizations anyway, only to be legally harassed by Islamist lobbies in the West using academic and media endorsements. Ironically, the Islamist ideology was ripped to pieces by Muslim liberals and seculars and by moderate clerics, particularly during the second year of the Arab Spring. That divergence of opinion should have proven that the Muslim Brotherhood's reading of these ideological agendas was not representative of all Muslims or all views of their religion. Egypt's revolt in June 2013 showed the Ikhwan as a small minority within the Muslims of Egypt.

Unfortunately, U.S. and European political cultures were hijacked by the apologists for the extremists. The definition of what is ideological and what is not in Islamic politics and in the Middle East was left to these extremists, not to the moderates. Lawfare was the most aggressive weapon used by these lobbies to impose a legal silence on critics and thus leave to themselves a free hand in influencing national security and foreign policy.[19] Over the past few years, however, the anti-Jihadist activists and think tanks in the United States have organized a legal counter-campaign against CAIR and its cohorts, forcing them to disclose documents that would have harmed the plaintiffs rather than the defendants in this warfare by law. This defense brought a reduction in the number of court cases, if not something of a retreat.

The Islamist lawfare tactics in fact backfired as many groups of American citizens launched a nationwide movement to ban Sharia laws in state courts. While only a few states, mostly in the South and Midwest, voted for such bans, the powerful pushback by the Islamist lobby led by CAIR and ISNA generated even more resistance from certain segments of public opinion. Michael Kirkland wrote in UPI: "Does Islamic law, Sharia, have a place in American courts? A lot of state legislatures don't think so, and there is a large movement to ban its application in the domestic courts, state and federal."[20] The movement aiming at the ban is led by counter-Jihadist activists. The principal goal is not theological, but political. They assert that by banning the use of Sharia in U.S. courts, the Islamists would not be able to use tribunals to harass their foes and exert control over Muslim communities. The battle over Sharia in the United States is yet another form of lobby war over the control of the national debate.[21]

THE "ISLAMOPHOBIA" ACCUSATION

One of the most redoubtable political weapons used by the Islamist lobby against opponents has been the charge of Islamophobia. It has been said particularly of Americans who warned about the rise of Jihadism, of Christian Middle Easterners who exposed persecution at the hands of Islamists in the region, and of Arab and Middle Eastern liberals who called for secular democratic governments in the Middle East. This accusation, intended to emulate the notion of xenophobia or anti-Semitism, is leveled by Islamist operatives and their Western apologist allies against their opponents and is in reality aimed at demonizing those who question the Islamist agenda. Technically, Islamophobia would mean "an irrational fear of Islam," signaling that individuals or groups who do not know the truth and reality of the Islamic religion fear it and develop bigoted positions toward anything Islamic.[22] Any religion or group having a separate identity within a larger society will have legitimate concerns that some people will resent any collective identity different from their own. This is true in all cultures. The Islamophobia charge, however, as used by the Islamists and their allies, targeted a much wider slice of society.

THE TARGETS OF ISLAMOPHOBIA

Ironically, those first targeted by the architects of the Islamophobia doctrine were not the usual xenophobes. Those attacked by the Muslim Brotherhood in the United States and Europe or by Iranian networks were not ignorant of all things Islamic; just the opposite. The first of those accused of bigotry were writers, theologians, and religious and social entities as well as individuals who criticized the theology of Islam. These anti-Islam or Islam-critical actors in society in fact possessed a significant knowledge—from their perspective—of Islamic theology and the early stages of the religious development of Islam. They had no irrational fear of it, but what one could describe as a rational fear or intellectual concern about it. The debate between Islamic theologians and the critics of Islam should have been part of the normal—and often intense—religious debate among and between men and women of faith. Religious disputes are by nature rough, as the faithful are deeply attached to their beliefs. While it is true that throughout thousands of years of history disputes over theology and dogma have led to violence and upheavals, modern public debates are founded on the right to free expression and opinion. By twentieth-century human rights principles, criticizing a religion, though it emotionally affects believers, is not a forbidden act. Abusing that right to religious criticism in a manner that seeks to demonize an entire community of believers can and should be admonished, but it still cannot be banned by positive laws. The limitation to freedom of expression steps in when the criticism becomes a call for violence against other individuals or communities. Then, phobia or not, the root causes are not the issue. Such violence is not permissible, and calls for violence are a corollary to the actual aggression. The Islamist lobbies attacked the critics of Islam on the grounds that religions should never be defamed.[23] If the critics were using defamation to produce harm, laws can protect people of faith, but if the critics were expressing their own rejection or even condemnation of any theology, as distasteful as this criticism might be, laws should protect them.[24] The Islamist lobbies crossed the line when they sought to impede free thought and free speech. Their strategy was not, however, to limit their own assault on free speech in regard to theology. In fact, their attack affirmed the principle of defamation of religions as a basis for the next level of Islamophobia.[25]

Individuals in the second group targeted by the Islamophobia weapon were historians, academics, and researchers who specialized in the history of the Muslim and Arab worlds—precisely those who contradicted the ideologues and propagandists of the Jihadi and Islamist movements. By teaching the truth—that the expansion of the Islamic empires came mostly by military means, that Jews and Christians were considered second-class citizens under Islamic empires, that violence marred most of the Caliphates, that non-Muslim or non-Arab ethnic communities living in the Middle East today predated the Arab Islamic conquests, that Sharia laws have stipulations that do not provide the universally recognized equality for women and for non-Muslims, and that some use Islamic religious texts to discriminate against Muslims with certain sectarian affiliations—those expressing these widely factual findings came under fire for demeaning Islam and Muslims. That was the equivalent of accusing Native Americans of racism if they stated they predated Europeans in America, or the Celts if they asserted they preceded the Germanics and the Slavs in Western and Central Europe. The Islamophobia charge went so far as to denounce basic history lessons; it was similar to the National-Socialist or fascist rewriting of German or Italian histories in the 1930s. Scholars, professors, historians, and analysts were forbidden to even teach the Islamic texts unless blessed by the Islamist lobbies of America or the West.[26] Campuses and government programs were submitted to an inquisition impaneled by the Muslim Brotherhood and Iranian lobbies.

The third target of Islamophobia's attacks was more serious than the intellectual party line imposed gradually on theologians and historians. The most dangerous attack singled out the tactical and strategic analysts of the Jihadi threat to the United States and the West.[27] As of the late 1990s and increasingly after 9/11, a systematic campaign led by the Muslim Brotherhood fronts and pro-Iranian militants targeted and blasted almost every analyst, scholar, and influential adviser to government or to private sector foundations who specialized in Islamist or Jihadist politics, strategies, or military studies. The goal of the Islamophobia charge against the experts on Jihadism was to legally and politically decapitate any intellectual force capable of advising the United States and other democracies in Middle Eastern and Muslim world politics. The accusation of Islamophobia against writers, bloggers, journalists, and politicians was severe.

According to *FrontPage Magazine,* one of the main pieces of Islamophobia's ideological attack on intellectuals based in the United States was launched by Think Progress, an organization created by billionaire George Soros, a top activist from the far-left wing, and John Podesta, the former chief of staff in the Clinton White House.[28] The entity put out a report written by Faiz Shakir and others called *Fear Inc: The Roots of the Islamophobia Network in America.*[29] According to David Major, director of the Centre for Counterintelligence and Security Studies in Washington, "The study is an attempt to create an industry whereby critics of the Jihadists or of the violent Islamists, or of their ideologies, would be branded as morally wrong and would become legally targeted." Major, a former FBI official who has been training national security agencies for decades, went on to say, "The militant Islamist network in America is an integrated, well organized, focused and strategically capable force that is well funded and deeply embedded in this country. Its main goal is to affect U.S. national security and foreign policy."[30] In a pamphlet, *Islamophobia: Thought Crime of the Totalitarian Future,* the editor of *FrontPage Magazine,* David Horowitz, and director of Jihad Watch, Robert Spencer[31] detailed how "the origin of the word 'Islamophobia' is a coinage of the Muslim Brotherhood."[32]

Over the years, the concept of Islamophobia, which was projected by its architects as an emulation of anti-Semitism, was transformed by the Islamist lobbies as a tactic to crush their opposition.[33] The term by itself can be applied theoretically to individuals who have an irrational fear of what they don't know, and to real xenophobes who unjustly stereotype Muslims. But it was used either against intellectuals who debated theology or, in most cases, against the thinkers and politicians who warned about the real-world Jihadi threat. It is the equivalent of the National-Socialists in the 1930s and WWII who accused Jews and other opponents of being Germanophobes simply because they resisted the Nazis.

The Islamist lobby of the United States and generally inside the West has been using the weapon of Islamophobia extensively at all levels of government, in the media, and online to try to politically incapacitate and demolish the nerve center of American strategic thinking and legislating. By achieving this goal, the Islamists could thoroughly hijack the role of advising government on national security and foreign policy, principally affecting American interests and giving victory to their allies in the region. The "Islamophobia industry"—that is, the think tanks, militant associations, and political lobbies that propagate the myth of a bigoted, right-wing, Zionist, Christian, xenophobe network intending harm to average Muslim American citizens—is in fact the very network that indoctrinates and radicalizes citizens against U.S. foreign policy and undermines national security. But just as important is the fact that the industry is also the hub of targeted campaigns against Middle East democracy advocates and anti-Jihadist NGOs. According to open sources and archival surveys, the Islamophobia charge has been leveled pretty much against all public servants and experts who are involved in training, educating, informing, or legislating and who have demonstrated an ability to identify the Jihadi threat or have criticized the antidemocratic nature of the Islamist movements and ideologies. Over the years, several members of Congress were hit hard by the Islamophobia industry,

including senators Joseph Lieberman, Sam Brownback, and Rick Santorum and representatives Frank Wolf, Sue Myrick, Chris Smith, Trent
Franks, and many other lawmakers. Think tanks, NGOs, and research
centers were also singled out as promoting bigotry. Bloggers and media
commentators were also systematically attacked as hatemongers.

The most dangerous move by the Islamophobia industry, however,
was against the Middle East national security experts and advisers.
Over the past five years, and increasingly since the installation of the
Obama administration in 2009, almost all experts on Islamism and Jihadism in the various national security and defense agencies who exposed the ideology and movements generating radicalization or who
exposed the persecution of minorities in the region were marginalized,
sacked, or separated from their jobs.[34] The attacks focused on lecturers at the FBI, Department of Defense, and other agencies. The charge
would be led by an Islamist lobby such as CAIR, and apologist activists
would follow online or in print. For example, an initial attack would be
launched by CAIR against a lecturer at the FBI, and this would be followed by an apologist far-left blogger a few days later.[35] The inquisition
systematically extended its tentacles through the bureaucracy on both
federal and state levels. Experts such as well-known investigative journalist Steve Emerson, Daniel Pipes, former FBI special agent John Gu-
ondolo, and scores of scholars have been targeted, but so have Muslim
public speakers such as Syrian American Zuhdi Jasser, Iranian dissident
Reza Kahlili, and Saudi American Ali al Yammi.[36] In fact, al Yammi was
adamant: "CAIR does not represent the Muslim American community
and is not mandated to speak on behalf of it and should refrain from
attacking respectable experts like Professor Phares and leading Muslim American voices such as Dr. Zuhdi Jasser. We have enough of this
behavior which reminds us of how Islamist regimes suppress dissent in
the region."[37] The relentless nationwide Islamist campaign has generated backlash among columnists and Middle East American scholars.
Jim Curi, a former law enforcement and terrorism expert, has made the
case that Islamist propaganda is well organized and has significant influence within the Obama administration in national security matters.[38]

In a fundamental piece published in Washington and widely circulated since, Dr. Essam Abdallah, an American-based liberal Egyptian scholar, wrote that

> One of the most powerful lobbies in America under the Obama Administration is the Muslim Brotherhood greater lobby which . . . has secured many operatives inside the Administration . . . there is also a pro-Iranian lobby that has been influencing U.S. policy towards Iran and Hezbollah in the region.[39]

According to Abdallah, and also to other experts in Washington, with the conclusion of the "deal" between the Obama administration and the Iranian regime,[40] one should expect the pro-Iranian lobby, or pressure groups, to attempt to increase their influence over foreign policy. Their first goal will most likely be to present a better face for the Iranian ruling elite to the American public, but in a second stage, the Iranian lobby will unleash a major campaign against its opponents in the West and in the United States to block any opposition to the potential partnership between Washington and Tehran.

Abdallah's piece became a basis for a much wider investigation of the Islamist lobby's influence on U.S. policy in the Middle East in general and on the Arab Spring in particular. A liberal scholar who taught at Ain Shams University underlined that

> One of the most important activities of the Islamist lobby in the U.S. is to wage political and media wars on the liberal Arabs and Middle Eastern figures and groups in America. This battlefield is among the most important in influencing Washington's policies in the Arab world. If you strike at the liberal and democratic Middle Eastern groups in Washington who are trying to gain support for civil societies in the region, you actually win a major battle. You will be able to influence the resources of the U.S. Government to support the Islamists in the Middle East and not the weak democrats. This huge war waged by the Islamist lobbies in America started at the end of

the Cold War and continued all the way till the Arab spring. The two main forces of this lobby are the Muslim Brotherhood fronts and the Iranian fronts. According to research available in the U.S., the Ikhwan fronts such as CAIR (Council on American Islamic Relations), led by Hamas supporter Nihad Awad as well as MPAC, ISNA and others, waged their political war to block the representatives of Arab liberals and Muslim moderates from making their case to the American public. The Iranian lobby such as NIAC led by Trita Parsi (National Iranian American Committee) has been hitting at Iranian exiles.[41]

ISLAMOPHOBIA'S HALLUCINATION

Prior to and in the early stages of the Arab Spring, the Islamist lobby's Islamophobia strategy of smearing its opponents—particularly those who would have advised the U.S. government on the region—was efficiently deployed, particularly in the rigorous and credible arguments utilized in political inquisition. But in the aftermath of Egypt's second revolution of June 2013, the U.S.-based Islamist lobby took the Islamophobia charge to such an extreme that it resulted in it being fully discredited. For example, apologist scholars accused the Egyptian government, media, journalists, and even Muslim clerics of being Islamophobes.[42] According to Ahmad Soliman of the June 30 Coalition in Cairo, "America's Islamists have lost their minds." He continued, "How can they accuse the popular majority of the largest Arab Muslim country of being Islamophobe? Who are these American-based elites to attack 33 million moderate Muslims and call them Islamophobes? They may be able to intimidate a couple of bloggers in the United States, but they cannot play this game with us. We know they are part of the Muslim Brotherhood propaganda machine, and soon enough it will be entirely exposed."[43] In Washington, Magdi Khalil, an Egyptian liberal activist, backed up this view: "The Islamist lobby has created an Egypt Islamophobia scandal. At this point they are hallucinating. Once they start accusing Muslims of Islamophobia, their credibility is shattered. Nothing is left."[44]

A MAJOR FACTOR IMPACTING U.S. MIDDLE EAST POLICY

After having thoroughly reviewed the immense role of the Islamist lobby in America and within the West as it affects Middle East policies, readers can begin to appreciate that the struggle over the future of the Greater Middle East, particularly in the aftermath of the Arab Spring, has been and continues to be centered inside the United States, with ramifications throughout the West. The powerful Islamist lobby, despite the many discrediting findings regarding its links to radical forces and in some cases to terror organizations, has managed to survive these snags and mutate into a political force with a veto over foreign policy and public perception. Representative Peter King wanted CAIR to be investigated as terror-linked.[45] King told me during a briefing, "The group obstructed any meaningful congressional work on identifying the Jihadi ideology. It tries to keep lawmakers, and thus the American public, unaware of that threat. Hence when we want to design foreign policies based on our understanding of these movements in the Middle East, CAIR and its allies block the educational process."[46] The New York lawmaker was right in his assessment, for the Arab Spring showed that Washington was unable to distinguish the radical Islamists from the secular youth, and so it failed in partnering with the democratic forces of civil society. Representative Sue Myrick, the co-chair of the Anti-Terrorism Caucus in Congress and the chairwoman of the subcommittee on intelligence, had similar assessments. "CAIR attacked me repetitively, including in my district, for the leadership role I had in exposing the Jihadist ideology, the role of Hamas and of Hezbollah," she affirmed. Myrick also contended, "But more dangerous was the fact that the Islamist lobby was attempting to intimidate members of Congress, as they did with the Bush administration, to stay away from good experts on the region and from dissidents." She argued that "by eliminating the role of democracy activists from the Middle East in Washington they would simply replace them as sole representatives of the region's voices. That's how the Muslim Brotherhood was able to become the main player in Arab Spring politics. Their allied lobbies inside the United States sidelined the representatives of the region's seculars, moderates, and minorities, hence giving a free hand to the Islamists to be the sole players at the State Department, aid agencies, the White House, and to some degree the Department of Defense."[47]

According to reports, the Islamist lobby was successful in influencing not only bureaucracies, but also political parties, government-funded agencies, and the higher echelons of the administration in varying forms and degrees. The main concern at hand now is to learn how much direct influence the lobby has had on the policymakers' decisions in the two administrations in charge since 9/11 and particularly in the Obama administration, which dealt with the Arab Spring. The other significant questions are these: How much influence did the Islamist lobby have on U.S. foreign policy? And how unified was the political agenda with the voices overseas using the same type of political weapon, Islamophobia?[48]

CHAPTER ELEVEN

U.S. POLICY IN THE MIDDLE EAST

GENERAL RETREAT?

AS THE ARAB SPRING IS CULMINATING ACROSS NORTH Africa and the Middle East in 2014—with Islamists and seculars, dictators and liberals vying to determine the future of the region—the U.S. Middle East policy seems to have faltered, despite the promising initial social movements. In Tunisia, the Nahda and Salafists are locked in a deep conflict with the seculars and liberals; the future of the North African country that was home to the first revolt will be determined by the outcome of this confrontation. Libya is also witnessing a clash between its armed Islamists, particularly its Jihadi Salafists, and Libyan reformers and seculars. As in Tunisia, oil-rich Libya must face an arduous challenge and mitigate the conflict between the two camps before reemerging as a pluralist democracy. Egypt is experiencing perhaps the most dramatic crisis in the dual contest between Islamists and seculars in their various groupings. The June-July anti-Islamist revolution reversed the Muslim Brotherhood regime, but Egypt is still struggling to put the country on a liberal and democratic track. Even after its defeat in Egypt, the Ikhwan network remains a formidable force; it is almost a century old and will be capable of urban unrest for decades to come.

The unending upheaval by the Islamists along the Nile Valley and the Jihadi terror operations in Sinai project future troubles.

In Syria, by early 2014, the horrific civil war had taken more than 100,000 lives—not to mention the millions of wounded and refugees. The clash involves Salafi Islamists on the one hand and an alliance of Syrian Baath, the Iranian regime, and Hezbollah on the other. Civil society, partially represented by some commanders of the Free Syria Army and a number of nongovernmental organizations, is practically crushed between the regime and the Jihadists. In Iraq and Lebanon, 2014 is witnessing a widening of terror activities between Sunni and Shia Islamists. Al Qaeda is spreading among the Sunnis in central Iraq and Sunni enclaves in Lebanon. In Arabia, the Iranian threat is growing, as is the Jihadi menace. More important, five years after Obama took office and thirteen years after the assault of 9/11, the Iranian regime is unchecked and expanding its store of strategic weapons. Last but not least, armed Islamist militias are roaming the Sahel region and Nigeria, even after the French campaign against al Qaeda in Mali and the clashes in the Central African Republic.

The situation in the Greater Middle East as it stands in 2014 is dire. The issues arising from U.S. foreign policy weigh more heavily today than ever before. In none of the countries that has undergone an upheaval is there yet a full democratic success. And all countries that tried or are trying to push back against dictators or Islamists are on a collision course with present American policy instead of being direct partners with the United States. The evolution of the Arab Spring, and the endless race between its secular and Islamist forces, compels more questions: One, why did the Obama administration side with the Islamists as they confronted the seculars and liberals? Two, was there an alternative policy? And three, what should the United States do now that the region is going through convulsions as a result of these struggles over its future between the two major contending forces, liberals and Jihadists? To understand the root causes of the administration's strategic choices during the Arab Spring, one needs to examine its doctrine, its vision, and the steps it took before and after the Arab Spring. In that context, I will share my knowledge about what could have been an alternative to the Obama administration policy, an alternative that was being examined and vetted in 2011 and 2012 by presidential candidate Mitt Romney. Only then, judging from the results of the administration's stance on the Arab Spring and the Middle East until 2014 and the missed opportunity to change that direction in 2012, can we delineate the major steps that need to be taken in the next few years to correct U.S. policy management of Middle East issues.

OBAMA'S VISION OF THE MIDDLE EAST

In 2006, the majority in the U.S. Congress changed from Republican to Democrat, and the effects of that change were felt when it came to U.S. foreign policy in the Middle East. While the United States military was still surging in Iraq against al Qaeda and Iranian-backed militias, both the Muslim Brotherhood and the pro-Iran regime Islamist lobbies in Washington exerted influence on the new congressional leadership to counter the War on Terror initiated and led by the Bush administration. A dramatic manifestation of that change in direction occurred at the congressional level when Nancy Pelosi, then Speaker of the House, made a highly publicized visit to Syrian dictator Bashar Assad in Damascus. Pelosi's visibility in her meetings with Assad and his regime dealt a severe blow to Bush's efforts to isolate that regime after Washington and Paris had orchestrated the withdrawal of Syrian troops from Lebanon between 2004 and 2005. The parallel diplomacy led by the Speaker was the first signal of change to hit post-9/11 U.S. foreign policy. It initiated an "engagement with the foes," or, as critics identified it, "appeasement of the enemy." The stature conveyed on Assad by Pelosi in 2007 was reinforced by Senator John Kerry, a leader of the Senate's Foreign Relations Committee, who visited Assad in 2009. A year later, Secretary of State Hillary Clinton described Assad as a "reformer" only a few months before the regime engaged in mass killings of the Syrian demonstrators in the Arab Spring. Even before the election of Barack Obama as president of the United States, the Middle East policy of the opposition to the Bush administration was heavily influenced by the Islamist lobby in the United States, which was consulted by the new majority leaders of Congress in 2006. Two years before the advent of the Obama administration, a change of direction was already operational. As an adviser to the Anti-Terrorism Caucus in the U.S. House of Representatives and to several national security and defense agencies, I felt the change in direction in early 2007. The Obama doctrine on the Middle East was already operational within the opposition before the 2008 election. The Obama presidential victory in 2008 provided that new doctrine with the highest seal—that of presidential approval. The first steps in the new policy of partnership with the Muslim Brotherhood and reengagement with Iran's regime materialized early on in the Cairo speech and in the attitude toward the Green Revolution of Iran, both in the first few months of 2009.

THE CAIRO SPEECH AND THE NEW DIRECTION

Immediately after Obama was inaugurated, his office announced that he would take steps to change America's image in the Arab and Muslim world. The argument, advanced by the Middle East studies elite and supported by the Muslim Brotherhood and the Iranian regime, was that since 9/11, the Bush administration had projected an aggressive image of the United States to the Muslim world, and thus the nation needed to hit the reset button with an entire civilization. During the 2008 election campaign, I detected a tilt toward the agenda of the apologist camp and its Ikhwan and Khomeinist backers. In October, I had projected, during congressional briefings and NGO discussions at the Foundation for Defense of Democracies where I served as a senior fellow, that Obama, if elected, would dismantle the Bush strategies in the region and go beyond what any previous administration had accepted to concede to the Islamists. Not that the Bush administration was so successful strategically—its failure was due to its own bureaucracy's sabotaging of the democracy programs—but Obama was about to execute a shift never before seen in American foreign policy, a shift greater even that that under the Cold War at the height of the retreating Carter administration. The president was planning a massive change in all relationships with Middle East actors, particularly with Islamist regimes and forces. However, during the first months of his term, he clarified that the change in foreign policy would be as slow as a large ship changing direction. A source familiar with the White House told me in the winter of 2009, "This means you wouldn't feel it as it happens, but you would see that direction has changed with time. The Obama administration will implement small steps so that the ship isn't rocking, but all these steps will head toward the new direction." The source added: "You will see several appointments inside the administration that would increase the influence of the Muslim Brotherhood and their allies on Middle East–related issues and symbolic steps to steer the ship of U.S. policy in the direction of partnership with the Islamists and dialogue with the Iranian regime." And several small moves did signal a dramatic change that would be felt during the Arab Spring of early 2011.

Indications of the potential change had been clear, at least to me, in the campaign rhetoric. In 2008, in hopes of influencing the presidential debate and encouraging both camps to work out new strategies for the Greater Middle East, I proposed the exact opposite of what the Obama administration practiced from day one. A radio anchor said jokingly during an interview in 2009: "If you want to know what the Obama administration's policy in the Middle East is, read Walid Phares' book and reverse every analysis and every recommendation he made." During the first year of Obama's presidency, I was very close to writing a book explaining where American policy was headed. But as Washington was racing to end the wars, withdraw from the region, cease countering Jihadi ideology, and invite Islamists and apologists to provide advice to the executive branch, I noted that, in response, counter-Islamist forces in the Greater Middle East were angry and frustrated and deciding to surge at the very moment the United States was quitting the conflict with the Islamists.

THE AL ARABIYA INTERVIEW

On January 29, 2009, soon after entering office, President Obama addressed the Arab and Muslim world through an interview with al

Arabiya TV.[1] The president's goal was to show those in that region that his policies were closer to their feelings and aspirations. But the essence of the move was to acknowledge that there had been American injustice toward Arabs and Muslims. Regrettably, that was also the essence of the Islamist claim: The United States was the aggressor in the region; the Jihadists were not the aggressors against humanity. Following the interview, the administration rushed to assert a change of direction that signaled that previous policies had damaged the relationship between America and the Islamic world.

In 2013, the al Arabiya journalist and media commentator (and friend of mine) who had sat with the president in 2009, Hisham Melhem, who was closer to the left during his days in Beirut, told me in Washington: "The hopes were high among Arab liberals that the Obama administration was rejecting the more neoconservative policies of the Bush administration to replace them with some progressive trends." Unfortunately, added Melhem, who was and continues to be a supporter of the president, "Obama's handling of Iran and Syria and the venture with the Islamists of the region at the expense of the liberals was a disappointment."

ISTANBUL SPEECH

On April 6, 2009, Obama addressed the Turkish Parliament, which is controlled by the Islamist AKP. There he said: "I know there have been difficulties these last few years. I know that the trust that binds the United States and Turkey has been strained, and I know that strain is shared in many places where the Muslim faith is practiced. So let me say this as clearly as I can: The United States is not, and will never be, at war with Islam."[2] Put in context, the statement meant that in previous years there had been "difficulties" that strained the "trust" between the United States and Turkey, and thus the Muslim world, and that had to be corrected. By reaffirming that "the United States is not, and will never be, at war with Islam," the new president in fact validated what the Islamists claimed. The core of the Salafist and Khomeinist political agitation against the United States and the West was that they were waging a war against Islam. The Ankara speech rejected the accusation but hinted that it was America's fault that the Muslim world felt it was targeted by the West. Thus, by mere logic, the new narrative was developing a mea culpa, with tremendous consequences in the following years.

CAIRO UNIVERSITY ADDRESS: THE OBAMA DOCTRINE ON THE MIDDLE EAST

Two months later, on June 4, 2009, Obama addressed a large audience at Cairo University under the title of "A New Beginning."[3] The speech indicated—and perhaps caused—a major shift in U.S. policies in the Middle East. In the past, relations between the United States as a country and the countries in the region had always been bilateral—government with government. Obama's new political philosophy reconstructed the relationship as one between the United States and an entire civilization. He painted the region as one large religious entity identifiable as the "Muslim world," whereas the United States was a nation-state. The premise for the new relationship came out of the books of the Islamists but was massaged by apologists in academia. The president said: "We meet at a time of tension between the United States and Muslims around the world—tension rooted in historical forces that go beyond any current policy debate. The relationship between Islam and the West includes centuries of co-existence and cooperation, but also conflict and religious wars. More recently, tension has been fed by colonialism that denied rights and opportunities to many Muslims, and a Cold War in which Muslim-majority countries were too often treated as proxies without regard to their own aspirations."[4]

The key premise of this statement is the narrowing of international relations to a crisis between America, on the one hand, and the entire Muslim world on the other. As I asked, pointedly, in my congressional briefings: Why would the Obama administration put the United States in the balance with fifty-seven other countries identified as the Muslim world? Why is it America against a worldwide civilization? Why single out one Western nation, even the strongest, and portray its ties to the Muslim majority world as the cause of all ills?

Obama declared in the speech that he had come to Egypt "to seek a new beginning between the United States and Muslims around the world; one based upon mutual interest and mutual respect." The meaning is clear. America has been the aggressor against the Muslim world by waging two campaigns in Afghanistan and Iraq and by establishing the Guantánamo detention center. His central theme, in Ankara and Cairo, was the same as the international Islamist motto: "America is at war against Islam." Obama repeated in his speech: "In Ankara, I made clear that America is not—and never will be—at war with Islam," almost indirectly confirming that the United States had acted negatively under the previous administration and according to stereotypes regarding the region's religion and peoples. Obviously, he suggested that his administration would end this posture. He went on to say: "And I consider it part of my responsibility as President of the United States to fight against negative stereotypes of Islam wherever they appear." This narrative was an indirect adoption of the Islamist charge of Islamophobia. He was claiming that America had been influenced by Islamophobia and thus he must reform this policy. The reality was the opposite: The Islamist lobby accused Americans of Islamophobia in order to exact more concessions and to ensure that no U.S. policy would confront Islamism. Islamophobia was a political weapon of intimidation used by the Islamists and the Jihadists to force the United States to change its policy away from countering Jihadism and toward facilitating the agenda of the Islamists. That was the essence of the major retreat embodied in the Cairo speech.

Another proposition that encouraged the Islamists and the Jihadists was the commitment to unconditional withdrawal from Iraq: "That is why I ordered the removal of our combat brigades by next August and to remove all our troops from Iraq by 2012." Obama later committed to withdraw all troops from Afghanistan by 2014. Such a commitment to pull out of the region, made to an audience composed significantly of the Muslim Brotherhood, signified a pledge to allow the Islamist forces to come in. In that sense, the speech was a version of an undeclared "Yalta agreement"[5] between the administration and the Islamist forces.

The Ikhwan would rule the Sunni lands, and the ayatollahs would dominate the Shia land. The Cairo address also hinted at a forthcoming understanding with Tehran's regime when the president said, "I have made it clear to Iran's leaders and people that my country is prepared to move forward." This declaration of "moving forward" without partnering with the Iranian opposition to the regime was a critique of the previous confrontation with Iran's regime. This statement was in parallel to a letter sent by Obama to Ayatollah Khamenei in May 2009 asking for a dialogue.[6]

The new administration then turned to the issue of democracy and pledged not to impose it from the outside. Obama said: "I know there has been controversy about the promotion of democracy in recent years, and much of this controversy is connected to the war in Iraq. So let me be clear: no system of government can or should be imposed upon one nation by any other." While a legitimate notion on its surface, the narrative showed a new policy of not encouraging democracy; in other words, of leaving the choice between liberal democracy and its antithesis, Islamism, to the forces on the ground. By citing the example of Iraq, the message was akin to leaving it to the best-organized forces in postwar Germany to impose their views, which would have been the remnant Nazis or the Communists. U.S. policy in the Cold War and after 9/11 was to encourage, whenever possible, the rise of secular democracy and thus to side with democracy forces. The Cairo speech shifted Washington's policy to a neutral position between secular democracy and other forces, including radical ones. The message to the Islamists was unambiguous: If the dictators fall, we will not support the secular liberals over you. The refined version of the message was ominous. It claimed—as the academic advisers of the Obama administration have argued for years—that the Islamists are the backbone of the region's accepted ideologies, and thus the United States would not support the region's liberals so as to avoid a collision course with the Islamists and therefore the region.

Aside from being an incorrect premise, this position was disproved by the Arab Spring and by the deep rise of civil societies in Egypt and

Tunisia in 2013, not to mention the seculars in Turkey and the rest of the region including Iran. President Obama's assertion in Cairo that the Islamists were the legitimate representatives of the region's aspirations was inspired by the Middle East studies elite in the United States—itself influenced, if not funded, by petrodollars. The intense intellectual lobbying for years by the Islamist lobby in America came to fruition after 2009. It became an official policy in Washington to partner with the Muslim Brotherhood, which was thought to be the soul of the region. This policy was pushed back in 2013 with the second Egyptian revolution.

The Cairo speech also committed the United States and the West to a new direction on domestic politics. As President Obama asserted: "Likewise, it is important for Western countries to avoid impeding Muslim citizens from practicing religion as they see fit—for instance, by dictating what clothes a Muslim woman should wear." He added: "I do not believe that women must make the same choices as men in order to be equal, and I respect those women who choose to live their lives in traditional roles. But it should be their choice. That is why the United States will partner with any Muslim-majority country to support expanded literacy for girls and to help young women pursue employment through micro-financing that helps people live their dreams."

The talking points of this statement assumed that mainstream Muslim women in the West are persecuted and forbidden to wear their scarves, the hijab. This was an Islamist talking point, not a cultural and political reality in the West. In France, the ban was about the full, uniform-like niqab, which covers the face and hides the identity of those Muslim women who chose or were pressured to wear it on ideological grounds. It was on security grounds that the niqab was banned in public places. In the United States, a person with a fully covered face could not obtain a driver's license. Hence, the Western cases of banning were not anti-Islamic; they were pro-equality before the law and related to public safety. In addition, they were addressed to the public in general and not directed at Muslim communities. It was the organized Islamist movements that claimed that the specific ban of the hijab was a persecution of religious Muslim women, and it was the Obama administration that adopted this talking point. In the first place, a secular government should not be in the business of siding with one theological stipulation against another or choosing between atheist or religious views. Liberal democracies are supposed to be neutral. They can indeed defend religious rights of individuals and communities, but they cannot decide which opinion is the right one. Washington should not determine whether the hijab is or is not a religious right or obligation among Muslims. Al Azhar, the highest authority in Sunni Islam, opined that it was not obligatory anyway,[7] while the Muslim Brotherhood ideologue al Qaradawi and the Salafi clerics posited that it was an obligation. The Obama administration sided with the Islamists over the Muslim moderates and made that choice known in Cairo in 2009.

In the Cairo speech, the issue of women's freedom and of their equality was dismissed. The notion that "women must not necessarily make the same choices as men in order to be equal" can be reversed to become: If women are unequally treated and they accept this notion, we cannot impose equality on them. Meaning, according to the Obama doctrine, the United States has no business promoting gender equality in countries having a Muslim majority because, culturally, such equality is not accepted. But Obama did not admit that the forces in the Muslim world who claim men and women are not equal are the Islamists themselves. In short, the administration's advisers on the Muslim world convinced the president that the United States should not undermine the Islamists' view of Islam and the Muslim world, in essence siding with the Islamists against other views, including the more moderate or the more liberal elements in the region.

The Obama speech dismissed the issue of women's liberation and focused instead on women's economic opportunities as a consolation prize. But without political empowerment and equality, the advancement of women will remain in the hands of the Islamists, which means that whatever the opportunities, such advances will not be granted as true gains. There is only a limited space for maneuvering bequeathed to them by Islamist males acting as benefactors, and thus, because such actions must be approved and permitted by men, they belittle women.

The June 2009 speech in Egypt was a major shift in American policy in the Middle East. It declared an American-Islamist alliance. The first criticism of the new doctrine was that putting one nation, the United States, in a position to face off with the entire Muslim world was unfair, illogical, and counterproductive. If a dialogue of civilizations had to take place, it should place the entire West, including NATO, the European Union, Australia, and New Zealand, as one party and the Organization of the Islamic Conference as the other party; one bloc of Western countries versus another bloc of Islamic countries. But such a concept in international relations would run against what modern international affairs are based upon: nation-states and international organizations. One would even argue that since Obama and the Muslim Brotherhood and Iran have elevated the concept of the Muslim world to that of an integrated player on the international scene, then the party at the dialogue or the debate should not be the United States or even the West; it should thus logically be the Christian world. In this situation, by the logic of the Cairo speech, an appropriate coalition including the entire West should add Russia and its Slavic and Orthodox allies in Eastern Europe and the Balkans, the entire Catholic Latin American continent, and the countries of half of sub-Saharan Africa, as well as countries such as the Philippines and Armenia. Once the concept of a Muslim world was advanced by the Obama administration—a concept initially produced by the Islamists—a domino effect could be generated with a Christian world, a Buddhist world, and more. The long-criticized doctrine of the "clash of civilizations" advanced by the late Samuel Huntington in 1993[8] would then become a basis of international relations. The civilizations would replace the nation-states at the U.N. General Assembly and Security Council, as Muammar Gaddafi once jokingly proposed. Is the United Nations prepared for this new vision of the planet?

The idea of a "Muslim world and the rest" is an old Islamist doctrine that divides the world between Dar al Islam and Dar al Harb.[9] In modern international relations, such an idea would be destructive and reactionary. Only a small segment in the Muslim-majority countries, the Salafi Islamists and the Iranian Khomeinists, promotes the concept of a Muslim umma dealing with international relations. Only Islamist thinking would accept the equation of a world bloc of Muslim countries sanctioning one nation, the United States, because of its alleged aggressive behavior with the entire umma. The Cairo speech's mistake was fundamental, not a narrative snag. The ideas announced were based on premises advanced by the Islamist lobby in the United States and on incorrect interpretations of Middle East realities by American academic circles, particularly by the Middle East studies elite. They influenced White House advisers who eventually produced Obama's strategic speech. The audience targeted by the new discourse was the Salafi and Muslim Brotherhood camp. The audience marginalized by the speech included the youth, seculars, and minorities.

This address encouraged the Islamists, discouraged the seculars, and made women and minorities nervous. Along with a developing apologist approach to Iran's regime, the Cairo speech and the general new attitude of the administration sent two messages to the region, messages that resonated deeper than the diplomatic cosmetic dressing offered by the traditional discourse of the State Department and the related foreign aid agencies. One message was understood by the Islamists as a push toward becoming the next partner of the United States when the appropriate time came. The other message, to the secular democrats, was that America had changed course and was no longer interested in backing liberal democracy in the region. The significant presence of the Muslim Brotherhood in the audience foretold the events to come and spoke to the forthcoming alliance between Washington and the Islamists in North Africa and the Levant.[10] It would be those who were absent from the audience, whose claims were not mentioned in the speech, who would later make history: the liberals, seculars, women, and Copts.

CHAPTER TWELVE

ABANDONING MIDDLE EAST DEMOCRATS

WASHINGTON'S NEW POLICIES OF ENGAGEMENT WITH the Islamists in the Greater Middle East led to major setbacks to democracy movements there. In short, Iran's regime was left alone to crush the Green Revolution, Hezbollah's domination of Lebanon was not strongly questioned, the Muslim Brotherhood was partnered with as a potential alternative to Arab regimes, the Assad regime was presented as willing to reform, and the genocidal regime of Khartoum was allowed to continue its oppression unchecked. In addition, the persecution of minorities in the region apparently failed to make it onto a list of priorities. The suppression of Copts, Middle Eastern Christians, Berbers, African ethnic groups, Kurds, and other groups was not considered an urgent matter. At the onset of the Arab Spring, U.S. foreign policy seemed to have placed itself at the farthest possible remove from the real revolutionaries: that is, the secular democrats, the reformers, and the minorities.

IRAN'S REVOLUTION ABANDONED

As noted earlier, in May 2009, shortly after his inauguration, Obama sent a letter to the Islamic Republic of Iran's Supreme Leader, Ayatollah

Ali Khamenei, seeking rapprochement and cooperation.[1] The move
came in the wake of the new administration's major shift on strategies
for dealing with Iran. Under the Bush administration, Iran's regime was
identified as a sponsor of terror and recognized as actively involved in
attacks on the United States and allied forces in Iraq. In addition, Iran
supported Hezbollah, itself a terror organization responsible for killing military personnel and taking civilian hostages. Under the Obama
policy, Iran's Pasdaran (Revolutionary Guard) and its ally Hezbollah remained on terror lists and were subjected to economic sanctions, but the
long-term goal mutated from regime change by way of supporting democratic uprisings (as was the case under the Bush administration) to a
management of the American-Iranian relationship with hopes of ending
the crisis through political engagement. The letter to Khamenei came as
a prelude to what was projected to be a new era in the American-Iranian
relationship, one of pragmatic understanding of mutual interests.

Critics asserted that the new Iran policy of the Obama presidency
was the result of influence by a pro-Iranian lobby in the United States.
The lobby had operated for years, but with the new administration in
2009, it was able to convince decision makers of the benefits of a change
in policy toward Tehran's regime.[2] The Iranian lobby, as I have said earlier, is funded by the petrodollar power of the ayatollahs. According to
researchers dedicated to this field, the pressure group was able to move
deeper into the sphere of influence within the Obama administration
thanks to former officials, multinational corporations, and consulting
companies.[3] The author of the report, former CIA analyst Clare Lopez,
told me, "Iranian-American front groups, including think tanks and academics, have developed a great deal of influence across bureaucracies
inasmuch as the Muslim Brotherhood have." David Major is the director
of the Centre for Counterintelligence where he trains law enforcement
and defense agencies in how to detect terror activities. He told me, "The
Iranian penetration's main goal in the U.S. is not just about spying or
preparing cells for possible terror attacks; it is also about exerting influence on the country's foreign policy. And on top of these goals, ensuring
Washington will not use its power and resources to strike at Tehran's

military power, help an Iranian resistance or simply stand by an Iranian peaceful opposition to the regime."[4] By the first months of the new administration, Tehran's ayatollahs understood that the tough years of Bush had passed. Informed by their lobbies about the opening in Washington, Iranian policies in the region strengthened. After the letter to Khamenei, the regime took for granted that it was not fundamentally threatened by the Obama administration. This perception helped Tehran's elite opt for a crushing oppression in June of that same year.

When millions of young men and women hit the streets of Tehran in mid-June 2009, they initially protested voter corruption and the forced reelection of Mahmoud Ahmedinijad as president. Later, they pushed against the regime as a whole. It was a defining event in the Middle East. The world witnessed a moment in which the regime in Iran was very close to crumbling. The Green Revolution threatened the very foundation of the Khomeinist regime for the first time since it was established in 1979. It came four years after the first popular nonviolent uprising in the region, the Cedars Revolution of 2005, and it preceded the titanic revolution against the Muslim Brotherhood in Egypt in 2013. As the Iranian demonstrations reached a peak in Tehran, there came an opening for a speech by Obama similar to Ronald Reagan's "Mr. Gorbachev, tear down this wall." But instead of calling on the regime to step down and asking the international community to support the Green Revolution, Obama asserted, limply: "It is not productive, given the history of U.S. and Iranian relations to be seen as meddling in Iranian elections."[5]

The statement was perceived as a green light by the mullahs, according to the Iranian Democratic Union in exile and other opposition groups. Days after the apex of demonstrations, the Pasdaran led a harsh campaign to crush the demonstrations, killing, wounding, and torturing hundreds if not thousands of protesters. The would-be Iranian Spring was then dismantled as the world watched and the White House delayed. Iranian youth chanted in the streets of their capital: "Obama, Obama, are you with them [the regime] or with us?" Iranian revolutionaries were disheartened by the American inaction. They had been waiting for this moment for decades, and firmly since 9/11. A leader of the Green Revolution whom I met in Paris told me, "Your president abandoned us; he allowed the regime to crush the revolution." I asked him why his companions had believed that Washington would assist them in their uprising. He replied, "President Obama spoke of change, of assisting the weak, during his campaign. But we now understand the change was in the other direction—to cut a deal with the regime."[6] The presidential statement prompted a seemingly undeniable understanding of the grand strategy of the new administration. It was profound in design, and there was a solid commitment to it. The era of American support for the Iranian opposition was over, and the era of pragmatic engagement had come. However, when a tidal wave of Iranian videos showing the depth of that revolution and the criticism against Washington were posted on YouTube and Facebook, the administration rushed into damage-control mode. On June 20, after the young protesters were subdued and dispersed, Obama declared:

> The Iranian government must understand that the world is watching. We mourn each and every innocent life that is lost. We call on the Iranian government to stop all violent and unjust actions against its own people. The universal rights to assembly and free speech must be respected, and the United States stands with all who seek to exercise those rights.... As I said in Cairo, suppressing ideas never succeeds in making them go away. The Iranian people will ultimately judge the actions of their own government. If the Iranian government seeks the respect of the international community, it must respect the dignity of its own people and govern through consent, not coercion.[7]

It was too late. The statement was too general and had no impact in Iran. The revolt was crushed, and the region missed a tremendous opportunity to defeat terror forces and the regimes in four countries: Iran, Iraq, Syria, and Lebanon.

The abandoning of the Iranian revolution, which in my view was cataclysmic, convinced many youths in the region that the time for self-reliance had come.

THE "MODERATE HEZBOLLAH AND IKHWAN"

The new direction of the Obama administration favored the Islamists in the region. It encompassed Salafists and Khomeinists who aimed at a gradual political engagement as a prelude to an ending to the conflict between the United States and these forces. As framed in the Cairo speech and the letters to Khamenei, the new goal was to "regret and apologize" for the wrongdoing of America and to seek reconciliation with the Islamists. The implications for national security were enormous. Washington had been in a strategic countering position to Iran and its allies, including Hezbollah, while also fighting al Qaeda, the Taliban, and their Jihadist allies, and, in principle, countering the extremist ideologies of the Salafists, including the Muslim Brotherhood. The strategic posture against the foe— either the enemy on the ground or hostile ideologies—that had been in place since September 11, 2001, had expanded widely and was backed by American public opinion. It was natural in the minds of most Americans that Iran was a foe, al Qaeda and its Jihadist allies were enemies, and the Islamists who aimed at establishing narrow Sharia-based regimes were not U.S. allies. Thus, the first effort of the Obama administration's advisers and counterterrorism officials was to mollify the public opposition to the change of label.

To do this, several steps had to be taken. The first was to tranquilize the most influential pressure group involved in the Arab-Israeli conflict: the friends of the state of Israel in Washington and their extended constituencies. Obama never missed an opportunity, including speeches at the influential AIPAC conferences, to reassure the Jewish American community and the friends of Israel that the administration "will have Israel's back" if attacked.[8] The equation promoted by the administration was that as long as Iran's regime and its allies, Hezbollah and Hamas, threatened Israel, Washington would back Israel. The unspoken variable in the equation was that the United States would not allow Israel to strike at Iran or at Hezbollah unilaterally. The "if attacked" became the center of the new strategic relationship. The difference between the two sides was noted by the Israelis.[9] The narrower guarantee to Israel gave the administration sole decision-making power. The motto became "Washington will decide when to strike Iran, not Israel." This posture, however, encompassed another principle: The Obama administration would decide whether the Iranian regime was to be targeted or whether it would be "politically engaged." The decision to engage the Iranians and the Muslim Brotherhood, once separated from the Arab-Israeli peace process, was now only for Washington to decide.

Once the Arab-Israeli conflict was disconnected from other regional issues, three more steps had to be implemented in order to launch the engagement policy with the Islamists. The next step was to remove the anti-Jihadi literature from the American narrative. A constant effort had been under way, within the Bush bureaucracy and much more strongly within the Obama administration, to eliminate any research, policies, and plans that countered the ideology of Jihadism and supported the framework that kept the Islamists from partnering with the United States.[10] Once Jihadist ideology was removed as a subject of public debate, Americans were prevented from seeing the reality of Jihadist movements and regimes. With such a void in the public perception of the threat, the administration, aided by the academic and media elite, could present the Iranian regime, Hezbollah, and the Muslim Brotherhood as manageable entities. Unlike Nazism, fascism, and Bolshevism, they could be handled and eventually trusted. With such new parameters becoming official policy, the cleaning up of the image of Jihadist movements began.

The top counterterrorism official in the administration, CIA Director John Brennan, declared that a moderate branch inside Hezbollah could be reached.[11] The statement was a debut of what could have been a dialogue with Hezbollah had the Arab Spring never occurred. The British, following the lead of the United States, said they might engage in a dialogue with Hezbollah's political wing.[12] Later, James Clapper, the director of national intelligence, declared at a congressional hearing that the Muslim Brotherhood consists of a "loose coalition of secular groups."[13] Both attempts to legitimize Hezbollah and the Muslim Brotherhood were later debunked by experts and, more important, by the region's developments. The Iranian-funded, Lebanon-based organization was declared terrorist, not just by the United States, but also by a number of Arab states, including the UAE and Bahrain, and the European Union.[14] As for the Muslim Brotherhood, while not yet identified as a terrorist group by the West, it was accused by Egypt, the country of its origin, then by the UAE, Kuwait, Jordan, and Saudi Arabia, of promoting extremism and violence. The Obama administration's strategy of seeking a dialogue with the two brands of Islamism, while a winner in 2009, was floundering.

SURRENDERING IRAQ TO IRAN AND AFGHANISTAN TO THE TALIBAN

The next goals were to offer up Iraq, after the U.S. pullout, to Iranian influence as a price for rehabilitation of Iran's regime in the club of nations and to concede Afghanistan to the Taliban in return for peace with the Jihadists. The two strategies to be followed after U.S. withdrawal were mixed with military surges in both countries, which signaled to the American public that the evacuations were not retreats but victories. It was argued in Washington that the military would deliver enough pressure to weaken the foes before legitimate negotiations could occur. In reality, despite the successful military surges, the Taliban came back, knowing that the United States would soon be leaving. The mistake of the administration was to announce its 2014 withdrawal while still conducting military action in 2012. All the Taliban had to do was wait for the pullout and then advance. In Iraq, the Obama administration launched a military surge, the last campaign before the withdrawal. It was an odd move, essentially telling the foes, both Iran and the Jihadists, "We are attacking you for the last time so that we retain credibility with our public as we pull out from the country, but de facto, you have taken it away from us." At least this is how the anti-American forces perceived the moves at the time, according to many international experts on Iranian and Islamist strategies, including Paulo Casaca, a former member of the European Parliament and the European Socialist Party:

It was clear that the Obama Administration was executing a retreat from Iraq, remitting the central government to Shia politicians, many among whom were Islamists and allies to Tehran. This was as part of an indirect deal with Iran's regime while Washington was sanctioning the latter economically.... The same has been happening in Afghanistan. Washington continues the fight on the ground but is negotiating with the Taliban politically; it doesn't make sense.[15]

Indeed, as of 2010, the Obama administration had moved to engage the Taliban even though U.S. and NATO forces were clashing with Jihadi militias. Over the following three years, contacts and meetings took place, either directly or via Qatar.[16]

The Cairo speech and the letters to Khamenei, as previously argued, aimed at provoking a "coup" in U.S. policies in the Middle East, not a reform. The terror groups were to be upgraded to factions that the country needs to deal with in order to withdraw from the region and end the global state of War on Terror. Following the intellectual line of Middle East studies, itself influenced by petrodollars, the circle was complete. Ending the wars meant the United States could engage the forces it was fighting without any reform by them. In other words, the United States was ceding terrain to the radicals and surrendering populations to the Iranian regime in Iraq and the Salafi Islamists in Afghanistan in deals that would bring a return to a pre-9/11 mindset. Iran would rule most of Iraq, the Muslim Brotherhood–type of Islamists would dominate the politics of the Sunni Triangle, and the Taliban would take back Afghanistan—or at least the largest part of it. Throughout the presidential campaign of 2012, Obama praised his pullout from Iraq "on time" at the end of 2011 and committed his administration to executing a withdrawal from Afghanistan by the end of 2014.[17]

In addition, the United States has disengaged itself from the global War on Terror *and* from the war of ideas. During the fall of 2008, I projected that the new administration would modify the narrative on counterterrorism. It would eliminate references to Jihadist ideology and to the antidemocratic nature of the Muslim Brotherhood and its allies as a way to convince the American public of the credibility of the new partnership. The general retreat from real battlefields and from the battle of ideas was in full swing from 2009 to 2013. But the Arab Spring's second explosion in 2013 disoriented the Obama policies. With the Egyptian anti-Islamist revolution; the rise of secular oppositions in Tunisia, Libya, and Turkey; and the surge of two oppositions in Syria—one Jihadist and the other secular—the grand partnership between Washington and a regional Islamist force is now in trouble. One question at hand as one reviews possible alternative policies toward the Middle East is this: Was there an alternative, potentially more successful set of ideas that could have led to a different American policy in the Middle East after 2009? For some who attempted to work on an alternative, there *was* a different policy approach, one advanced by the Mitt Romney campaign in 2011–2012. It would have departed from the current policies and could possibly have brought different outcomes for the Arab Spring, Iran, and the Jihadists.

Some may believe, others hope, that we can still change policies in time to save the region from a global meltdown. A pessimistic view might be that it is actually too late because the current policies continue to take us in a counter-productive direction. An optimistic view suggests that, despite the unfolding disasters, a massive change in U.S. policies toward the Middle East, at any time, even by the current administration, could still save the day (yet at a higher cost). In my historical view, any strategic change to the current policies can produce results—under the current or a future administration. The most important matter is to generate a change, the faster and the deeper the better. If this happens under the incumbent, theoretically speaking, it could still help stop the greater disasters from unfolding. If it happens under the next administration, it would need gigantic efforts, greater than any we've witnessed in past decades. To borrow President Obama's own words, foreign policy is comparable to a huge ship, and to change course requires time and focus—which is what already happened between 2009 and 2014. To change course again will require a greater sacrifice and more time. Can the Middle East wait so long for such a journey to materialize?

And in the end, is there an alternative policy, a short cut to save the day, and the world? Unless the region's civil societies rise higher, coordinate tighter, and consent to greater sacrifices to reach freedom on their own, the United States will continue to find itself as a major actor in shaping the future of the region. At this point, what American foreign policy is minimally urged to accomplish is at least not to obstruct the natural aspirations of freedom and democracy of the peoples of the Arab world and the Middle East. A better moral position would be to side with these civil societies against oppression, as America eventually did with Eastern Europe and Latin America. An equal treatment of all nations seeking liberty is a moral obligation embedded in America's historical fabric.

CHAPTER THIRTEEN

ROMNEY'S ALTERNATIVE VIEW

IN SEPTEMBER 2011, PRESIDENTIAL CANDIDATE MITT Romney appointed me as one of his nine senior national security and foreign policy advisers as well as one of the three co-chairs for his Greater Middle East and North Africa working groups. The appointment, which came under heavy fire from the Islamist and far-left lobbies, not to mention Obama campaign allies, was part of a much larger shift in policies proposed by the challenger to the sitting president. Many of the appointees in Romney's quasi shadow cabinet were officials who served in the George W. Bush administration. Others were sharp critics of policies implemented since 2009.

Any alternative to Barack Obama's perception and handling of the Greater Middle East had to take into account the first four years of his presidency. In 2008, candidate John McCain represented a continuation of Bush's eight years, and it was candidate Obama who promised a radical change in international politics. During that first campaign, the Obama team was not clear on the significance of the changes in terms of strategic choices in the region. On the surface, withdrawing from Iraq, fighting al Qaeda, and denying Iran the nuclear bomb were almost a match for the McCain defense agenda, but they were better articulated, with a note of hope—a trademark of the Obama candidacy. However, four years after the election, the American people were able to see for themselves the practical results of the Obama administration's handling of the region and the growing influence of the Islamist lobby in Washington, D.C. This is why Romney's view of policy overseas, particularly in the Middle East, became a viable alternative. It allowed Americans to choose between vastly divergent perspectives. Mitt Romney's view of how to address the national security threat, Iran, al Qaeda, and homegrown Jihadists was diametrically opposed to the incumbent's policies. The choice was titanic and dramatic and would have incalculable consequences, many of which are already apparent in 2014. Since I was part of the Romney team, I will share my view on how and why the alternative to Obama's Middle East was present and ready to engage in a different direction. Other members of the team may have their own views of that stark difference and how Americans and the world could have seen a different evolution of history had Romney been in office.

ROMNEY'S STRATEGIC VIEWS

First, let me share what I believe is fundamental in understanding why a Romney administration would have been different, not just from the Obama administration in terms of strategic choices in the region, but also from the Bush *and* other previous administrations, at least since Reagan. Romney understood the threat and was willing to move strategically and decisively on a global scale to defeat this menace. I detected this perception of the Jihadist threat during my interactions with Mitt Romney between 2006 and 2012. In 2006, ABC News, interviewing Romney, wrote:

> "They are terrorists, yes, but more directly Jihadists." Romney wants the public to know that Jihadists are not an "armed group of crazed maniacs in the hills of Afghanistan." Rather, Romney says the United States is facing a "far more sinister and broad-based extremist faction" with a "very 8th century view of the world."[1]

In 2007, Romney ran an ad titled "Jihad," stating that "violent, radical Islamist fundamentalism" is "this century's nightmare." ABC said:

"Romney highlights his regular stump claims to 'increase the military by 100,000 troops,' and in a carefully worded phrase, 'monitor the calls al Qaeda makes into America.'" ABC added Romney also tried to tie the threat of Jihad to Iran, saying that "we can and will stop Iran from acquiring nuclear weapons."[2] That year, the Islamist lobbies, particularly CAIR (Muslim Brotherhood) and NIAC (Iran's regime), noticed the serious narrative of Mitt Romney when it came to the Jihadists and to Iran's Khomeinist regime. I issued an endorsement of the governor, because I felt that Romney had his finger on the strategic pulse.

In 2008, while I noted that most Republican candidates identified the threat in the same way as the Bush administration did—that is, as "radical Islam" or "the Islamic Fundamentalists"—candidate Romney's narrative underlined the existence of an actual global movement known as "the Jihadists" and moved by a specific ideology, "Jihadism." Having monitored and analyzed the U.S. political debates on the war of ideas since 9/11, I also realized that the Republican candidates, particularly John McCain, described the threat as much broader than the narrow concept of the al Qaeda organization, while the Democratic candidates, including Barack Obama and Hillary Clinton, focused on the organization of al Qaeda, dismissing the ideological factor. But that year I noted that Mitt Romney presented something different: he advanced a link between al Qaeda and an ideology, calling for as much effort in the war of ideas as in the kinetic confrontation with the Jihadists. Physically fighting al Qaeda is not enough, and endlessly confronting the terrorists was not the solution. For Romney, particularly during his campaign of 2012, it was a global, ideologically driven movement that constituted the threat, and a democratic response via supporting civil societies was the long-term counter strategy.

A noted analyst in national security told me in December 2007 that the Islamist headquarters in Washington had already opted for Senator Barack Hussein Obama as the candidate closer to their views than Hillary Clinton. In early February 2008, the same analyst told me, the Islamist lobby had read my endorsement and circulated it. The analyst went on to say that the lobby understood that Romney would be a major challenge to their post-Bush agenda and because of that they were vying to block him as a candidate in the primaries and even as a possible vice presidential running mate if he were not the nominee.

This portended ill for Romney's presidential bid that year and introduced my name modestly into the national conversation.

After the presidential election gave victory to Obama, U.S. Middle East policy gradually—some argue quickly—shifted toward attempts to engage with the Iranian regime and advance the notion that Hezbollah has a moderate wing, as noted earlier in the book. But the most troubling and marked change in policy direction was Washington opening its arms to the Muslim Brotherhood. The year 2009 provided early evidence of the new track with Iran while partnership with the Ikhwan became a growing and noticeable phenomenon within the Beltway.

During the years leading up to his second bid for the presidency, I met several times with Romney. We discussed foreign policy, national security, and, of course, the Middle East. By this time a major change had already occurred in the political landscape. It would have been one thing to have a Romney administration immediately after George W. Bush, but it was another thing to envision a Romney administration after four years of Obama's Middle East policies. Four years of diverting attention away from the War on Terror and away from supporting secular democracy forces, as well as four years of backing the Islamists, would leave tremendous challenges for any post-Obama administration if Obama lasted for one term, but the consequences would be incalculable after two terms. The governor and I reviewed these assessments at a long meeting in 2008. It was then that I shared with him my view that strong winds of change might soon be coming to the Middle East and that the United States had to be ready for these events. I predicted the rapid rise of the Islamists, the explosion of civil societies, the Jihadi forces spreading out way beyond Afghanistan, and the democracy forces thirsty for Western support. To my surprise, Governor Romney shared with me his vision of a reorganized U.S. outreach overseas and particularly in the Middle East:

We should reorganize the resources of the U.S. government in a way to engage civil societies in the Middle East and help those folks who want to move forward toward real democracy and pluralism and build strong bridges to them. Our foreign aid, and all forms of assistance that we already have, including also media, economic, and other realms, should be tasked with a specific mission that is to strengthen and empower those with whom we are in agreement over the future. I am thinking of regional hubs with plenipotentiary directors working with local communities throughout the Middle East. We would have the right structure and a good ability to partner with the region's population, against the seditious work of the Jihadists. I can see how Hezbollah and Hamas win hearts and minds. We need to be in that battle and win it ideologically.

I was delighted that a potential presidential candidate for 2012 had this vision as an alternative to the "engagement." Over the following years, Obama's actual policies and the Romney alternatives became antitheses of one another. It was imperative to offer Americans a real alternative at the presidential election while also preparing for the deep changes to come in the region through a broad engagement with the youth, women, minorities, and moderates—not with the extremists in hopes that they would change.

Toward the end of 2009 and into early 2010, I reviewed the chapter on Middle Eastern issues in Mitt Romney's book *No Apology*.[3] The content of the book was signaling the governor's readiness for a second attempt to win the White House. I supported the idea and informed his team that I was ready to help, as much as I could, to ensure there would be a real alternative to the U.S. policy at play in the region at the time. In fact, as of summer 2009, especially after the June abandonment of Iran's Green Revolution and the increase of influence of the Muslim Brotherhood on both sides of the Atlantic, I decided to join the Romney pre-campaign discussions on foreign policy. Since I saw the future presidential candidate drawing lines and connecting many of the dots, I understood he was thinking strategically. He absorbed information quickly and grasped instantly the complex equations of geopolitics in the region. Though he had many advisers specialized in different fields, in the end, after he consulted with them, he clearly developed his own synthesis. He counted on advisers to understand, but his analysis was his own as he factored in economics and other social factors. I respected the man tremendously, but my certitude that America could have a chance to break through the powerful blockades installed by the lobbies and the international powers behind them was based on the way he processed input. His brother-in-law, Dr. Jim Davies, once told me, "Mitt is a learning machine: he reads tremendously and processes orderly." That was impetus that compelled me to work on his presidential campaign as an adviser on the Middle East and national security. Romney selected his advisers on foreign policy carefully, gathering many who had served in the Bush administration and some who had never served in the executive branch, like myself. I needed to trust a future leader who understood the strategic challenge personally, not just based on his advisers' suggestions and reporting. Governor Romney was that leader who would have taken the appropriate decisions regarding the Middle East.

STRATEGIC CONSENSUS AMONG MAIN CANDIDATES

The alternative to the Obama administration's policy on the Greater Middle East was not confined only to Governor Romney's platform, though it did become the official Republican position in opposition to that of the incumbent in August 2012. Having worked closely on several projects, including books, film documentaries, and briefings with several other Republican candidates, I knew there was a consensus among them on the perception of the national security threat, though with differences in narratives. I had met with Senator Rick Santorum several times and worked with his team on foreign policy awareness projects. The senator had a crystal clear understanding of the Jihadist and Iranian regimes' menaces on the strategic level. I also met with former Speaker of the House Newt Gingrich and his team and contributed to *America at Risk,* a film he produced with his wife, Callista, also showing high awareness of the dangers facing the world and the United States. In addition, I worked closely with defense and national security advisers to candidates Herman Cain and Michele Bachmann. My assessment was that a strong consensus existed among all of the above experts on the general dangers facing the United States since 9/11 and the necessity of confronting these challenges, should it be the ideology of al Qaeda or the Iranian regime.

Throughout these Republican presidential campaigns, particularly among the advisers in charge of the Middle East, there was a convergence of vision: Afghanistan should not be offered to the Taliban, Iraq should not be left to Iran, Lebanon should not be abandoned to Hezbollah, and Jihadism as an ideology should not be ignored. Moreover, as the Arab Spring exploded, Romney and his Republican competitors had a unified concern about the rapid rise of the Islamists across North Africa while at the same time recognizing with nervousness the violence directed against Christian minorities in the region as one of the Arab Spring byproducts.

However, the Romney vision of a possible alternative to the Islamists and Jihadists within the Arab Spring uprisings was more optimistic than the other candidates. After gaining the nomination, Romney argued that the Arab Spring provided an opportunity to the United States to work directly with the forces of civil society in the region. Romney believed in the deep forces of good in each society and wanted to reach out to them. During our conversations in 2008 and 2009, I had drawn a model representing Arab and Middle Eastern societies in the region and shared with him what I believed was unavoidable. There were very well-organized Islamists and Jihadists on one edge of these societies and vibrant secular and liberal segments on the other. I posited, however, that existing in the center of these more visible elements was a large, untapped silent majority. I pointed out to the governor that this silent majority would be the final partner, the one that could carry out the change in the region. To my surprise, and unlike other leaders I spoke with, Mitt Romney had a basic trust in the capacity of the people, particularly the silent majorities in the Middle East: "We need to reach out to the folks; they can make the change. We can do it with the resources that we already have, but we need to direct them in the right direction." In 2007, Romney had said, "By working with moderate Muslims to break down and defeat terror organizations like Hezbollah militarily, we can then turn to a new 'Marshall Plan' approach that strengthens the foundations of freedom and prosperity in burgeoning Middle East democracies."[4]

Newt Gingrich also trusted the deep will of the people of the Middle East and wished to reach out to them by bypassing the Islamists. Rick Santorum wanted to focus first on the persecuted minorities as a prelude to widening cooperation with all other communities. Later on, in 2013, during my meetings with Congresswoman Michele Bachmann in preparation for her visit to Egypt in support of its revolution against the Muslim Brotherhood, she told me about her intention to support anti-Jihadist forces in Egypt. In short, in addition to the strategic commitment of presidential candidate Mitt Romney to a renaissance among people of good will in the region as a strategy to push back against the radicals, there was a consensus among most other Republican candidates regarding the central challenge in the Middle East: People there were suffering from the Islamists, and a massive change had to take place. However, not all candidates agreed on trusting civil societies to start uprisings that would result in happy democratic endings.

Most criticisms of the Obama policies toward the Arab Spring, except for those by Romney and to some degree by Gingrich, centered on the bad decisions to abandon Mubarak, Ben Ali, and even Gaddafi. I heard this same opinion within the foreign policy circles at the Romney campaign as well, but the majority of advisers—as well as the presidential candidate himself—supported the departure of the dictators and hoped for the arrival of the democrats. Very few were able to see the three-stage sequence: Civil society rises to push dictators out, Islamists seize power, and civil society pushes the Islamists out. By mid-2012, almost no one in Washington or Brussels had a full grasp of the dynamics of the real Arab Spring. Perhaps even the leaders of the various movements of the upheavals did not know what the future held for them.

CHAPTER FOURTEEN

ALTERNATIVE POLICIES REGARDING THE MIDDLE EAST

IRAN

IN AN ARTICLE PUBLISHED BY THE *WALL STREET JOUR-NAL* on November 10, 2011, Mitt Romney committed to stopping the Iranian nuclear weapons program by any or all means, not excluding any scenario. He wrote: "Barack Obama is leading us toward a cascade of [nuclear] proliferation in the Middle East."[1] The Romney shadow cabinet on national security and foreign policy discussed several plans and strategies for dealing with Iran. In Washington, the Romney team went into depth to establish an alternative to Obama's policy. It confirmed three approaches: (1) to coordinate strategically with Israel and the Gulf countries, addressing each one independently to avoid Iranian political manipulations; (2) to increase the deployment of U.S. assets, naval and air forces, in the Persian Gulf facing Iran but also at a strategic distance from Hezbollah in Lebanon; and (3) to provide support to the Iranian popular revolution, particularly the secular democrats and the ethnic minorities.

It was evident in the article that Romney understood the opportunity missed by the United States when Iran's Green Revolution emerged from the 2009 stolen election. He pointed out Obama's plan to "not meddle" in Iran's affairs as the theocratic regime violently cracked down on civil society there. Romney mourned the lost opportunity: "A proper American policy might or might not have altered the outcome; we will never know. But thanks to this shameful abdication of moral authority, any hope of toppling a vicious regime was lost, perhaps for generations."[2] Understanding that Iran is a regime that supports global terrorism and the killing of American soldiers, in addition to being a destabilizing force in the Middle East, Romney recognized what was and is at stake in the region. The differences between the Romney and Obama agendas were immense and irreconcilable.

Obama sought to reach an agreement with the ayatollahs in which Washington would recognize Iran's interests in the region and refrain from meddling in its domestic affairs (hence the June 2009 abandonment of the Green Revolution), and, in return, Tehran would recognize the economic interests of the United States in Arabia and other places on the Arabian peninsula. This vision, conceived in 2009, became official policy in September 2013 when Obama declared that his administration would begin officially engaging the government of Iranian president Hassan Rouhani.[3]

The Romney policy was diametrically opposed to this approach. Instead, he advocated increasing pressure on Tehran and significant support to the opposition. In short, the Khomeinist regime, supporter of Hezbollah and other terrorists, would not be considered a partner by a Romney administration. When Republican candidates criticized the administration's position on Iran, they were systematically attacked by Iranian regime apologists based in the United States, such as *Mother Jones*'s charge against Senator Santorum of misleading the public and *Daily Beast*'s criticism of Romney, declaring him unequivocally wrong in his criticism during the campaign.[4] The Obama administration, in its second term, was still looking toward a possible realpolitik approach.[5]

The opportunity for engagement with the ayatollah's regime came, ironically, during the summer of 2013, when the Assad regime used chemical weapons in limited attacks against opposition areas, killing up to a thousand civilians. The U.S. president ordered American battleships to the coast of Syria, warning the Iranian ally to dismantle its systems or face surgical strikes. At one point, the world was close to a new U.S. war in the region, which would have spilled over to Lebanon and Iraq, but most importantly would have generated a confrontation with Iran's regime. During these weeks of hesitation, I strongly made the case that the administration would have to fight Iran over Syria but there were no indications the Obama administration was contemplating such an endeavor. I argued on al Arabiya and the BBC several times that the U.S. threat of action against Syria—if not carried out—would lead the White House to a dramatic reversal of foreign policy positions, including those on Iran. I had noted that the pressure groups in favor of engaging Iran were still very active and confident in Washington despite the Syria situation, which indicated that discrete talks had continued between Washington and Tehran. On the other hand, the fall of the Muslim Brotherhood of Egypt in June 2013 took out one of the administration's partners in the region. Logically, the White House had to wage war in Syria, and thus clash with Iran, or cut a deal to lead to a cessation of hostilities to end a conflict it could not and did not want to be part of.

Obama chose the road of the deal. In two moves, Washington ended two crises, or thought it did. Using a Russian mediation proposed by President Vladimir Putin, Obama demobilized the ships and accepted a deal with Syria that called for negotiations between Assad and his opposition regarding Syria's acceptance of dismantling the chemical weapons. Taking advantage of the momentum, the administration reached a quick deal with the Iranian regime on their nuclear program.[6] On November 23, the world woke up to a U.S.-Iranian agreement adopted by six leading powers. The deal granted Iran's regime the right to enrich uranium for peaceful goals and lifted economic sanctions against the country. The Grand Ayatollah Khamenei endorsed the accord negotiated by Iran's newly elected President Rouhani. Khamenei made sure to affirm that the deal did not stop the Islamic Republic from obtaining a legitimate nuclear weapon at its will.[7] Inside the United States, the U.S. Congress threatened more sanctions and refused to lift the existing ones.[8] A large segment of the foreign policy establishment criticized the accord,[9] but the mainstream media backed the president.

Israel's prime minister Benjamin Netanyahu called it a "historical error" while President Obama termed it a "historical achievement."[10] In the Arab world, Saudi Arabia, Jordan, Bahrain, and Kuwait displayed dissatisfaction with Washington's outreach to a common adversary. The map of alliances started to change. After the mishaps in Egypt and Libya followed by indecision on Syria, the U.S. administration leaped into the unknown through an agreement with a regime bent on regional expansion.

My main argument against the Obama administration's option in this case is the lack of evidence that the Iranian regime has actually changed strategic direction. Unlike Gorbachev, who launched his Perestroika and Glasnost policies in 1986 to deeply reform the Soviet Union, President Rouhani of Iran had acted more like Nikita Khrushchev, displaying only a façade of change to obtain relaxation from his foes in the international scene. After thirty years of monitoring and analyzing the regime, I believe the Khomeinists of Iran were maneuvering to delay domestic social upheavals; consolidate power in Iraq, Syria, and Lebanon; and gain time to complete their strategic missile fleet. The interim nuclear agreement of November 2013 was a delaying strategy to cover up for a massive leap forward by the regime.[11] The United States fell into the trap, but the immediate victims of the maneuver were the Iranian opposition and the country's democracy forces, followed by the opposition movements to Iran's allies in Iraq, Syria, and Lebanon. The deal did not stop Tehran's strategic buildup, but it was a setback to the Levant's civil societies. Such a policy was what we warned about in 2012 at the foreign policy discussions in the Romney shadow cabinet.

HEZBOLLAH

The Obama administration's position on Hezbollah did not change in form from what it had been in the days of Bill Clinton and George W. Bush. It kept the Iranian-backed organization on the U.S. terrorist list. It did, however, continue to engage the Lebanese cabinet, which has included Hezbollah since 2009, and failed to take a more strategic posture in support of the internal opposition to Hezbollah and the Syrian regime in Lebanon. As noted earlier, the administration's advisers in the early years of the Obama presidency advocated engagement with the so-called moderate wing of Hezbollah. And when the international tribunal set up to investigate the assassination of Prime Minister Rafik Hariri in 2005 accused members of Lebanese Hezbollah of being responsible for it, the administration failed to follow up with an international campaign for their arrest and for the disarming of the organization under United Nations Security Council Resolution 1559. Until months into the Arab Spring, the Obama administration continued to consider dialogue and an eventual political settlement with Hezbollah.[12] It was only when Hezbollah decided to fight openly inside Syria that Washington escalated politically, making stronger statements against the Iranian-backed organization.[13] Even now, in 2014, the United States has not taken a lead in disarming the terror group, or even in supporting the Lebanese groups that are confronting Hezbollah. This reality leads me to believe that Washington is still contemplating a dialogue with the militia despite the sanctions in place. As with Hezbollah, so with Iran: the advisory body of the Obama administration believes it is not yet a lost cause.[14]

On Hezbollah, again, Romney was clear: Hezbollah is a terrorist organization. It must be disarmed and its Iranian backing must be cut off. He argued in 2007:

> Bloodthirsty terrorist organizations like Hezbollah and Hamas have smothered the progress of the people and nations where they have built their networks, Lebanon serving as an example. These terror organizations cannot and should not be allowed to gain an advantage with the citizenry in Muslim nations just because they mask their terror agenda with an offering of some vital service.[15]

During the deliberations of Romney's national security shadow cabinet in 2012, a solid consensus emerged on the identification of Hezbollah and on future U.S. policy toward the terrorist group. The organization was seen as a cancer devouring the body of a small nation, Lebanon. This term was later used by Lebanese American congressman Darrell Issa at an annual conference. Obama's seemingly neutral and practical attitude toward Hezbollah was really a pro-active policy. As one of the advisers working on Lebanon and the Middle East for the campaign, I suggested that the United States should first cut off support coming from Iran to Hezbollah (via Syria) by establishing international control of the Lebanese-Syrian border, particularly since a revolution had already exploded inside Syria in March 2011. Second, the United States should engage deeply and efficiently with the liberal Shia opposition to Hezbollah, one that has existed for years but has been royally ignored by the Obama administration. These suggestions still needed strategic and detailed crafting. But for that we needed to assess the available U.S. government capacities, resources, and tactical intelligence on these matters.

THE TALIBAN

The Obama administration did not hide its intention to engage the Taliban and eventually settle the war in Afghanistan by an agreement with the Jihadist militia. The rationale advanced by its supporters, as early as 2009, was that the Taliban has a moderate branch. Many liberal groups in Afghanistan, however, pushed back, arguing that all Taliban are Jihadists and that a U.S. deal with the Taliban would endanger women and civil society.[16] From the first day of the Obama administration, engagement with the Taliban through third parties was pursued as an implementation of the doctrine advanced in Obama's Cairo speech: America was at fault in its clash with the Islamists and thus had to cease its intervention in Muslim lands. Even as a U.S. military surge was launched against the Taliban in 2010 and 2011, the more distant aim of the policy was to settle politically with the Jihadi network to allow a withdrawal of America's military units in 2014.

The Romney position on Afghanistan stood diametrically opposed to that of the Obama administration. Romney understood the Taliban were the enemy to defeat and the Afghan people were the ally to empower, particularly using the strength of civil society, women, minorities, and youth. He argued that the United States should not cut deals with the Taliban, but instead train Afghan forces and, above all, enable the Afghans to resist the Jihadists.[17] In Afghanistan, as in Egypt and the rest of the Middle East, Romney's bet was on the forces of civil society to resist the terror forces. "Only the Afghanis can win Afghanistan's independence from the Taliban," he asserted.[18] The difference between the Obama policy on Afghanistan and the Romney alternative was stark. President Obama banked on an eventual partnership with the Taliban, or with a moderate version of it, a version that did not exist.[19] Romney wanted to invest in the Afghani people's will to move their country away from the Jihadists.

During meetings on foreign policy during the campaign, Obama's plan to announce a withdrawal by 2014 was criticized as immature for communicating a pullout date to the foes, an appropriate criticism. But no alternatives were prescribed, I must admit. Romney opposed Obama's Afghanistan policies and knew what he wanted to see and often announced it—an Afghan national mobilization against the Jihadists—but as far as I know, his experts didn't produce a detailed strategic plan as an alternative. Several times, in conference calls and at the comprehensive strategic seminar of winter 2012, I attempted to advance the project of an Afghan Spring. The idea was adopted by Romney, but it was not hammered out by the team tasked with Afghanistan and Pakistan. The anti-Taliban Spring I believed in and advocated for never became a U.S. policy, of course, for Romney was defeated in the November elections.

Shortly after his second inauguration in 2013, Obama strongly committed to ending the U.S. and NATO presence in Afghanistan. The plan to engage the Taliban came back in force.[20] Criticism of Washington's policy regarding the Jihadists, however, was also mounting again. Analysts projected that the Taliban were manipulating the administration in order to obtain a victory in Afghanistan after 2015.[21] But the Obama decision to let go of Afghanistan is unchanged and has its roots in the genesis of this administration's policy in the region. It is about retreating from an imagined space, described by the Islamists as theirs to dispose of: the Muslim world. The original conceptual sin perpetrated in the Cairo speech reverberates throughout the administration's agenda despite the mistakes, the results, and the clear trends in the Arab Spring. In 2013, the Taliban opened an office in Qatar, the home of the regime that funds al Jazeera, as a way to engage in negotiations with the United States in preparation for the upcoming withdrawal.[22] There may be snags on the road, but the Obama administration will eventually offer Afghanistan back to the Taliban. The policy is definitively set. While an alternative exists theoretically, it has no chance of being carried out before 2017, at which point it will be too late.

IRAQ

The Iraq campaign generated a deep political division inside the United States after the initial military operations on the ground came to an end in 2003. That division exploded during the Kerry-Bush presidential duel in 2004 as it became apparent that the advertised quick victory was an illusion. Though the Bush war in Iraq can be severely criticized for strategic mistakes in terms of time, prosecution, and regional consequences, the political opposition to the war was mostly based on arguments made by regional opponents of the United States. The Iranian regime and the vast network of the Muslim Brotherhood regimes and movements were behind the global attack on the intervention in Iraq. "The Brotherhood against Democracy" included all forces and interests in the region that opposed popular democracy, particularly secular and liberal cultures. Senator Obama was among those in the United States who opposed the Iraq war altogether and voted against it and against the 2007 surge, but as president he approved a military campaign known as the Second Surge, led by General David Petraeus, to weaken al Qaeda. This move, however, was made to prepare for an eventual withdrawal.

The debate in Washington is no longer about the decision to invade Iraq, topple Saddam, and attempt to create a pluralist and democratic state. How that decision will be perceived is now in the hands of historians, but more so in the hands of future Iraqi generations. Was Iraq better off under a strong but bloody, genocidal non-Islamist, or better off freed from him? The question leveled by the apologists in America was to compare a stable Iraq under Saddam and a chaotic country after Saddam. The real comparison should have been with the level of oppression under the Baathist regime in Baghdad and the massacres of Kurds, Shia, and liberal Sunnis in what came after. The immediate post-Saddam state is, of course, better without the horrors committed by his regime before its demise.[23] But the postliberation management of Iraq's new freedom was targeted by forces that took advantage of the fall of Saddam only to establish another authoritarian regime, one allied with Iran in the Shia areas and a Jihadi emirate in the Sunni areas.

In my own briefings to Congress between 2006 and 2011, I strongly argued that Iraq is better off without the Saddam regime but that it should also be freed from Iranian and al Qaeda influences. The choice is not between Saddam, Iran, and al Qaeda. The choice should be made to pursue a pluralist, moderate, and democratic Iraq.

President Obama aimed at pulling U.S. and coalition troops from Iraq regardless of the initial mission of the Bush war planners. He was against that war and wished to end it, on the grounds that there should be no U.S. interventions in the domestic affairs of Muslim nations, a reflection of the Cairo speech doctrine. Obama's military surge was not aimed at defeating the two forces confronting the United States and fostering a future democratic Iraq. Rather, the last military effort was to allow a faster pullout, scheduled for the end of 2012. The Obama administration had one goal on its Iraqi agenda: pulling out. There was no goal to defeat Iranian influence and Jihadi penetration.

The Romney agenda envisioned a different Iraq. As of 2008, the governor perceived Iraq as a project that could produce a strong democratic ally, even though it might take years to emerge. Romney saw legitimate internal forces pushing back against terrorism. The problem in the stated alternative to Obama's clear strategy on Iraq was the absence of a future strategy among the opposition. As a national leader of the opposition in 2012, Romney rightly criticized Obama on his almost unilateral withdrawal from Iraq.[24] The hasty retreat opened the path for Iran to rush through, but Romney's foreign policy team did not develop a full vision of an Iraq free from Tehran and al Qaeda influences. Between 2008 and 2011, I heard the governor speaking about his grand design for partnership with the peoples of the region, but I did not see that vision translated into detailed policy papers or even talking points within the shadow cabinet. Yet in a comparison between Obama's clear move toward surrendering Iraq to Iran—following the grand architecture of the Cairo speech—and Romney's vision of resisting Iran's and al Qaeda's influence and of working with a pro-Western partner in Iraq before pulling out, the choice was clear. It is evident that the alternative to the Obama administration's strategy, the Romney alternative (though not extensively developed), was headed in a better direction. The Obama choice was to offer the governance of Iraq to Iran, with all the inevitable consequences for Syria and the Gulf states. Romney would have chosen to stay longer in Iraq, until it was enabled to stop Iran, or until democracy forces were in government. Yet his road map toward that end was not clear.

SUDAN

The Bush administration was very effective—or at least active—in helping South Sudan become an independent country. Senior leaders in the Sudan People's Liberation Movement (SPLM) told me in Washington in 2007 and again in 2011after the referendum that freed them, that without the support of the Bush administration and congressional leaders, "We would have been still a guerrilla force in the jungle and our people in bondage under a Jihadi regime." The Obama administration accepted the terms of the referendum obtained from the agreement between the Islamist regime of Bashir in Khartoum and the SPLM in the south, but it tried to delay the vote in the southern areas, under pressure from the Islamist lobby in Washington. South Sudan leaders asked the United States to explain why it had demanded that postponement in the first place.[25] The Muslim Brotherhood, significantly influential within the Beltway, was attempting to buy time for its ally, the

Khartoum regime, in hopes that the latter would create facts on the ground that would stop the referendum and postpone independence for the nascent African republic. But as the Arab Spring blossomed in Tunisia and youth calls for uprisings spread, the attention of the Obama administration shifted to North Africa, where greater events were to happen. In a way, I would argue, this diversion of U.S. attention saved the South Sudanese from political maneuvers by the Islamists that could have barricaded the road to independence.

In 2011, ministers and lawmakers from Juba (the capital of South Sudan) visiting Washington shared with me their concerns that the administration was not doing enough to support the new country and instead was doing more to reinstate Bashir in the community of nations, despite his indictment by the International Criminal Court (ICC). The rationale behind such suspicions was again the grand architecture of the Cairo speech. Bashir's regime had roots in the Ikhwan movement when the Brotherhood was seizing power in Tunisia, Libya, and Egypt and pushing forward in Gaza, Jordan, and Syria. Undermining the Bashir regime in Sudan would have weakened the regional rise of the Pan-Islamists, potential partners of Washington. This analytical equation was repeated to me by leaders of the North Sudan ethnic opposition. Mohammed Yahiya of the Darfur movement, Ibrahim Ahmad of the Beja Congress, and Khalid Jerais of the Nubian group, all based now in the United States, shared their concerns about Washington's tacit neutrality toward Khartoum. "The administration may not like al Bashir personally, for all the mistakes he committed, but the wider alliance with the Muslim Brotherhood, the international umbrella under which Khartoum regime was protected, [was prioritized] over removing an entire regime on the grounds of human rights abuse," a Sudanese opposition leader relayed. "The administration didn't apply on the Khartoum dictator what it applied on Gaddafi, Ben Ali, and Mubarak. The man indicted by the ICC has led massacres of genocidal proportions on Africans in his own country. We never heard Washington asking him to step down. We wonder what and who protects Bashir in America?"

The Romney team issued strong statements on Sudan. They affirmed the independence of South Sudan and the necessity of supporting the young republic, but also strongly condemned the Bashir Islamist
regime. Act for Sudan, an independent coalition of NGOs, received a
letter from the Romney presidential campaign: "Mitt Romney recognizes that for too long far too many Sudanese have been victims of war
crimes and other atrocities committed by the government in Khartoum
and its proxies." According to the letter, Romney also recognized that
in Darfur, non-Arab populations have been and continue to be victims
of a slow-motion genocide, and he described the current situation in
the border regions of Sudan as "so dire that at least a quarter of a million people in South Kordofan will be pushed to the edge of famine
by March this year." In the letter, Romney stressed that he was "committed to protecting innocents from war crimes and other atrocities,
ensuring that humanitarian aid reaches those desperately in need, hold-
ing accountable those leaders who perpetrate atrocities, and achieving
a sustainable peace for all who live in Sudan and the Republic of South
Sudan."[26]

The differences in approach to the Sudan question between the incumbent administration and the Romney campaign could reasonably be
considered the product of the influence of the Islamist lobby in Washington. For the Obama administration, the optimal outcome would be
to produce reconciliation between the regime in the north and Juba's
government in order to save the northern government from collapsing under the international pressure of the ICC genocide charge and
the rising ethnic opposition. Good relations between President Omar
al Bashir and South Sudan president Silva Kir would in fact reinstate
Bashir as a partner of the southern republic. The former bully's political
future and the fate of his Islamist regime would be saved by his former
victims, who would confirm the new "good behavior" of Khartoum's Jihadists. This architecture angered the African minorities in the north.
"Because the south won't receive U.S. support unless it cooperates with
the Islamist north, we, the minorities marginalized and oppressed by
Bashir, will suffer," Ibrahim Ahmed and Khalid Jerais from the Beja

and Nubian leaderships told me. Had the Romney administration been elected, a strong policy of support for Juba would have been established with the goal of considering South Sudan as a direct strategic ally to the United States. A more involved United States with South Sudan would have deterred factions from fighting a civil war in 2014. In addition, the democratic secular opposition of the north and the four main minorities there would have received recognition and validation. Bashir would have been isolated, not reinstated.

ARAB SPRING

As outlined here, the Obama administration's approach to the Arab Spring was based on its global Middle East approach. It may not have always been spelled out formally, but it could be clearly seen when it came to political decisions and actions, such as in Iraq, Afghanistan, and Iran before the explosions and upheavals.[27] The final goal was—and continues to be—to reach an understanding with two major forces (the Muslim Brotherhood and the Iranian regime) over the future of the region and maintain traditional relations with other regional actors such as Israel and the monarchies. The previous chapters dealing with the explosion of the Arab Spring have demonstrated that throughout North Africa, Yemen, and Syria one consistent approach was to shepherd the Islamists to power while attempting to moderate them in their relationship with the United States. The other consistent approach was to reach out to Iran's leadership, first under Ahmedinijad and, since the summer of 2013, under Rouhani, to find an accommodation. Syria seemed to be the only arena where neither approach was practicable, forcing Washington to play tough with Assad while still seeking a political solution between the two competing (warring) parties at Geneva. Practically, this means that the Assad regime, though not necessarily the dictator, would partially survive and be maintained according to Washington's diplomatic architecture.

Romney's program for the Arab Spring was again diametrically opposed to that of the Obama administration. During October 2012, the

Romney campaign issued a clear statement on the global direction of a Romney administration. Romney did not mince words about the threats in the region.

The Council on Foreign Relations wrote: "Mitt Romney hailed the Arab Spring as an 'opportunity for profoundly positive change,'" but also warned of a potential opening for U.S. adversaries—namely Iran and Jihadist groups—to push for greater sway in the region. "A Romney administration will pursue a strategy of supporting groups and governments across the Middle East to advance the values of representative government, economic opportunity, and human rights, and opposing any extension of Iranian or jihadist influence."[28]

The language was clear, as were its policy projections: The menace is Jihadism and Iranian Khomeinism, and America's allies are governments and groups that advance the values of human rights. The Muslim Brotherhood and the Tehran regime, including Hezbollah and all other Jihadists, were not part of a Romney alternative, neither for partnership nor for outreach. Those partners sought by a Romney administration would be civil societies, representing the silent majorities. I was not surprised by the governor's crystal clear reading of the Arab Spring, for by the early summer of 2010, Mitt Romney had already absorbed the notion that a revolution was coming, that it would be an opportunity for a positive democratic change, and that the Islamists and the Iranian regime would try to hijack it when it came. Romney was concentrating on engaging communities to work against the Islamists while the incumbent administration had been working with the Islamists since day one.

The conflicting aspirations of the Arab Spring, blurred by an anti-Romney and pro-Obama media, affected the policies of the two U.S. parties differently. On Egypt, Obama made no distinction between the Muslim Brotherhood and the secular youth when he described the protesters. But in practice, his administration walked hand in hand with the Ikhwan, parading them around Washington and granting them full support.[29] Years before the contest of 2012 Romney considered the Muslim Brotherhood a threat to the United States and to the region. In 2007 he warned, "The nation must be mindful of all militant Islamic groups, including the Muslim Brotherhoods, who are seeking the destruction of the West."[30] When Mohammed Morsi was elected president of Egypt in June 2012 and his regime began persecuting seculars, liberals, and Copts, Romney condemned the oppression and blamed the Obama administration for partnering with them. Within the Romney foreign policy team, there was a solid consensus on the Ikhwan double game, and discussions had begun on how to reach out to the secular forces. I had prepared a program to connect with the seculars, liberals, youth, women, and Copts whom had Romney won over. That program was partially implemented by NGOs during the winter and spring of 2013, along with media and political activities that accompanied the democratic revolution of Egypt in June of that year. Basically, what happened in Egypt after the defeat of Romney was a tribute to what could have happened throughout the region had he won.

On Tunisia, the Obama administration first backed the Islamist Nahda Party, then the regime established by the Islamists. Romney would have encouraged the forces of civil society in Tunisia. In 2012, as an adviser on foreign affairs and the Middle East, I invited representatives of the secular democracy movements of Tunisia to Madrid to meet under the aegis of the Foundation for Analysis and Social Studies (FAES), a think tank presided over by former prime minister José María Aznar. Mahmoud May, then deputy secretary general of the Social Democratic Party and a lawmaker, argued, "We need a U.S. administration that would identify the logical partners in the Arab Spring, particularly in Tunisia." He agreed with a Romney vision of partnering with secular democrats in Tunisia and North Africa.

On Libya, the sides in the Benghazi debate in the fall of 2012 were very clear. The Obama administration practically, even wholly, sided with the Islamists, even to the point of contracting Salafi militias in East Libya to secure positions. Romney warned about the Jihadists seizing the momentum. During our debates at the Foreign Policy Board of the campaign during early 2012, the advisers identified the Jihadi militias as a direct threat while some experts were warning about the balance of power given to the Islamists after the demise of Gaddafi.

Last but not least among the crises of the Arab Spring was Syria's. The Obama administration could have moved on the issue in 2011, when the revolt was peaceful, the demonstrations were unarmed, and the groups within civil society were in charge. More important, U.S. troops were still in Iraq and the Assad regime was isolated geopolitically from Iran. Washington tergiversated in 2012 because of the presidential elections, and by 2013 the situation had changed. The administration had pulled U.S. forces out of Iraq, opening the path for Iran to connect with the Assad regime; al Qaeda had penetrated the Syrian opposition; and Russia had hardened its position after seeing the results of NATO's intervention in Libya. Going into 2014, Syria's crisis has mutated, and the Obama administration has been locked into several international equations that have paralyzed action. In contrast, since the spring of 2011 Romney had been calling for giving support to the opposition before it was penetrated by the Jihadists. In our early conference calls, the initiatives centered on pressing all candidates to focus on bringing down Assad while reaching out to minorities. I made significant efforts to underline the issue of ethnic and religious minorities in Syria as an important factor. Romney's reading of Syria was more detailed than Obama's. He spoke of securing the Alawites as a price of removing Assad, a condition sine qua non for success in a multiethnic pluralist society after the Iranian and Hezbollah-backed regime is removed. And he was very consistent on wanting to push back against the Jihadists before they became a major problem. In short, there could have been another path for Syria had action with the right partners been taken earlier—before Iran penetrated Iraq and al Qaeda penetrated the opposition—but that path was not allowed to materialize. There should have been a track for working with all minorities, seculars, reformers, and, more important, the regular Syrian army. In 2012, many high-ranking commanders in the Syrian army were looking for U.S. leadership before making a move. Not all Syrian generals would trust the Islamist militias to defect to the opposition. The right plan would have been to work with a third force, not to mention civil society. The Obama administration failed to do so because its Islamist partners had no interest in seeing the seculars win the day in Syria.

AL QAEDA

The difference between the administration's assessment of al Qaeda and the alternative assessment was wide. The Obama perception, advanced by his advisers, was that al Qaeda was on its path to decline after bin Laden and al Awlaki were killed. Romney's team was clear on the matter. They emphasized that the organization was expanding. Furthermore, Romney gave serious warnings regarding Mali, the Sahel, and the weapons gathered by the Salafi militias upon the fall of Gaddafi. He was vindicated months later, after the election, when the French took the lead in confronting and defeating the Ansar al Din in Mali before they spread out across the Sahara.

Perhaps the most striking difference between the two views in dealing with al Qaeda and the Jihadists was the perception of the Jihadist ideology. The administration openly rejected the very existence of an ideological factor. It eliminated all use of terms indicating the existence of Jihadism and replaced them with a neutral narrative that focused on the criminality of the perpetrators. Obama spoke of a war against al Qaeda instead of against the Jihadists, and mentioned at times the "criminal ideology" of bin Laden. But interestingly enough, his administration never explained what the substance of this ideology was. Romney stressed the ideological factor constantly. He often explained the principles of this doctrine and called for a counter-radicalization program based on responding to this ideology. There was a valley of differences between the two perspectives, which had consequences in the real world.

THE ALTERNATIVE, IMPERFECT, EXISTS

A comparison of agendas shows clearly that there was and still exists a clear, strategic, and global alternative to Washington's current policy for the Greater Middle East. It existed before the presidential contests of 2008 and 2012; it even existed under George W. Bush. During the 2008 campaign, Senator McCain's proposed strategy for the Middle East was weak; what Senator Obama proposed was unclear. Four years later, the Obama administration's policies and attitudes toward Iran, the Jihadi ideology, and the Arab Spring were clear for all to see. Romney's agenda on the Middle East contrasted dramatically with Obama's. The choice was there, and Americans had an opportunity to take it into consideration. But the outcome of the November election doomed the alternative.

THE HOT SUMMER OF THE ARAB SPRING

DURING THE SUMMER AND FALL OF 2013, THE ARAB Spring experienced its deepest transformation. As all the masks hiding their intentions fell away, the players could no longer engage in secret games unknown to the public. Every force surged, and every world power moved. Some failed in their attempts and others succeeded, but no one was neutral in the game once the true faces of the players were revealed. The heat of Middle Eastern revolutions set the Arab Spring ablaze in preparation for its rebirth from the flames.

As I have relentlessly demonstrated throughout this book, the Islamists in the region are now rushing to secure what power they can in North Africa and the Levant after the crumbling of the Muslim Brotherhood government in Egypt and the challenges in Tunisia and Libya. The pro-Iranian radicals are also determined to retain their territories, from Beirut to Tehran (passing through Syria and Iraq), by using the "deal" obtained from the West during the fall of 2013 to enhance their position. Strongman regimes—from Syria to Algeria, Sudan, Yemen, and other countries in the region—are maneuvering between the secular liberals and the Islamists to assert their own dominance. The moderate monarchies of the Arab world struggle to survive the pounding by the Islamists and the Iranian menace. Meanwhile, al Qaeda's Jihadists and their affiliates are seizing opportunities wherever they appear. From Mali to Benghazi, from Iraq to Yemen, from Somalia to Syria, Jihadi combat networks are upping their activities and extending their reach.

The last players in the upheavals are the secular democracy forces, who are also determined to push back against three obstructionist powers: the nonreforming dictators, the Iranian-Syrian alliance, and the Islamists. Events in the summer and the fall of 2013 enflamed already volatile civil unrest and brought the region to an unparalleled state of chaos. Of all the players vying for victory or survival, however, the Islamists and the liberals are the only two that have been making progress. Monarchies and dictatorships have been attempting to maintain their stability and political unity, but Islamist forces and the secular democrats went on the offensive in early 2014.

EGYPT'S SPRING STRETCHES

In Egypt, the Muslim Brotherhood was removed by a massive popular uprising. The first move was to organize a popular petition to recall Mohammed Morsi. It obtained 22 million signatures, 10 million more than the vote that brought the Islamist president to power.[1] It was followed by a massive demonstration that began on June 30, joined later on by the military, and culminated with a second popular explosion on July 26. The Ikhwan responded with ongoing urban violence that paralleled the Jihadi terror campaign in Sinai. The forces of civil society, cautiously closing ranks with the army, have been resisting the violent Islamist militias and moving toward enacting a deeper ideological and political revolution. Having learned about the real goals of the Muslim Brotherhood when they came to power in June 2012, most Egyptians are now engaged in what could become a cultural revolution, a revolution directed against the very foundations of Jihadism and its corollary, the political Islamist agenda. Members of U.S. Congress who paid a visit to Egypt and met with its civilian and military leaders as well as the Coptic pope came back very encouraged. "We stand by you," they said in a press conference in Cairo, speaking to the Egyptian public. Louie Gohmert, Steven King, and Michele Bachmann affirmed their belief. "The Muslim Brotherhood has attempted to suppress Egyptians' liberties, but non-violent citizens rose and gave an example of democratic revolution to the entire region." The delegation also argued that "the U.S. must change its policies towards Egypt. Under the Islamist regime, we need to stand with the opposition. Under the democracy government, we will stand with the wishes of civil society."[2] By the end of January 2014, Egypt had voted yes on its referendum and a new leadership was emerging to confront the Jihadists and the large armed Ikhwan counter revolution.[3] Egypt is moving forward, having put the Muslim Brotherhood on its terror list, dismantling the Ikhwan financial empire, and mobilizing other Arabs to move in the same direction.[4] The challenge is to move from a post-Ikhwan era to the early stages of a liberal and pluralist democracy.

My latest discussions with Egyptian politicians and democracy leaders, both in Egypt and in the West, as well as with U.S. lawmakers, have confirmed to me that the race between seculars and Islamists in Egypt is competitive and dynamic. The Brotherhood will wage a long struggle against the secular state; the liberals must undergo a deep ideological revolution to cut off the Jihadi ideology at its roots. The Egyptian Spring has now become a protracted struggle between the two camps, but hopes are higher than ever before that a true civil society will emerge.

The question, as I am closing my thoughts on the "lost spring," is: What can be done to help Egypt rise as a free society and a pluralist democracy? A defense and military experts' delegation I was advising, who went to Egypt in the fall of 2013 to meet civilian, military, and spiritual leaders, told me that the country's deeper yearning was to defeat Jihadism as an ideology and gradually move forward toward a working democracy. K. T. McFarland, a former official with the Reagan administration and a Fox News national security expert, told me that the Muslim Brotherhood "sent an electroshock into Egyptian society. The non-democratic practices and the forcing of a fundamentalist constitution broke the back of the camel." Indeed, the Morsi Islamist rule showed the country's majority a glimpse of a Taliban-like future. Having tasted freedom after 2011, Egyptian youth, women, and minorities would not tolerate an Ikhwan rule for decades to come. Egypt was, significantly, saved not by outsiders or by a foreign army, but by its own people who, while at the cliff's edge, had an opportunity to look into the abyss. Rick Francona, a CNN military expert in the delegation and part of the meetings with General el Sisi and the spiritual leaders Sheikh Azhar and Pope Tawadros, told me that the Brotherhood "are still around and strong, they can derail democracy efforts, and they can submit Egypt to a rough Jihadi campaign." There is also the question of how Washington will handle Egypt now that a massive majority of Egyptians has rejected the Muslim Brotherhood and are in the process of rebuilding a secular democracy. In my briefings to members of Congress in October and to the European Parliament in November 2013, I argued in favor of a simultaneous policy shift from Washington and Brussels toward Egypt. Instead of cutting down aid as punishment for removing the Islamist regime via a popular nonviolent uprising (as the Eastern Europeans removed pro-Soviet regimes in 1989–1990, without punishment), the United States and Europe should muster a joint democracy-aid fund for Egypt's renaissance.[5] If the United States and the West help Egypt now against the Jihadi terror and Brotherhood violence, the international community will witness the rise of a powerful Arab democracy along the Nile with the potential to lead the struggle against al Qaeda and its Jihadi ilk across North Africa and the Arab world. Moreover, if Egypt moves forward, even gradually, toward a pluralist democracy with growing rights for the Copts and for women, civil societies in the region will emulate and follow. If the U.S. administration stubbornly continues to side with the Ikhwan against Egyptian democrats, the Egyptian revolution may nevertheless win, but only after a longer period of struggle and with a high and bloody price for the country, the region, and international stability. Washington can make a positive difference, but does it want to?

NORTH AFRICA'S FATE

Tunisia is somehow following an Egyptian path, but with its own national characteristics. The Islamists of the Nahda government are attempting to delay the rise of a massive secular movement (backed by labor, students, and liberal parties) that is attempting to crumble the Islamist regime and bring about a secular democratic government instead. The U.S. administration and the European bureaucracy in Brussels are still clinging to the Tunisian Islamists, despite growing popular opposition calling for a true secular and democratic Tunisia. Here again, the rationale of a desperate Western attachment to the Nahda and its Islamist agenda—which the U.S. administration continues to describe as "moderate" even though a majority of Tunisians sees it as a force aiming at the establishment of a Caliphate—is incomprehensible. Just as in Egypt, the Obama administration and European bureaucrats are still held hostage in their policies toward Tunisia and Libya by the Western-based Islamist lobby's view of the region. It will take a change of policy direction in Washington to advance the cause of liberal democracy in Tunisia and Libya. Short of that change, both North African countries face a long phase of struggle between Islamism, paired with its Jihadi ally, and secularism, with its liberal forces.

While Tunisia still has a national army that could maintain security as the political scenery evolves, its neighbor Libya lacks the central security institutions to defend its civil society from the Jihadi militias. Washington assisted in bringing down the Gaddafi dictatorship, but it willfully permitted the Salafists to assert their power in its place. That decision continues to hurt Libya's democrats and reformers and must be changed. As should be done in Egypt and Tunisia, the U.S. administration should change direction and partner with the youth and those in society who wish to create stable, liberal democracies.

SYRIA'S SPRING: TERROR ON BOTH SIDES

By winter 2014, the Syrian civil war became the worst and bloodiest conflict in the region. The United States had failed to address it. George

Sabra, president of the Syrian National Council whom I met in Washington, D.C., in 2013, confirmed to me that until the end of 2011 Syria's civil society groups could have partnered with the international community and triggered a multi-sectarian unified uprising. "The Obama administration didn't seem to be interested in a secular opposition but in the Islamist opposition," he told me.

By the end of August 2013, chemical weapons had apparently been used by the Assad regime against its opposition in the suburbs of Damascus.[6] At the same time, the Jihadists inside the opposition had grown in number and had expanded their influence, committing human rights abuses and targeting Christians.[7] The Obama administration at that point decided to make a limited strike against these forbidden weapons—but deferred to Congress for authorization. Russia promised to seize the chemical arms, but meanwhile the destructive war between the Iranian-backed regime and the opposition (within which al Qaeda–linked groups continued to rise) remained active and unstoppable. In the United States, the debate about what to do in Syria has become very complicated and divisive. One party does not want to intervene, preferring that the two main factions fight each other till the end. Another party would like to send weapons to the "rebels." And a third party, the Obama administration, hopes to make a limited strike and then push the two fighting camps toward Geneva talks.

I objected to these three views in my briefings and in the media. Simply allowing the two radical sides, the regime and the Jihadists, to bleed each other will not lead to a good outcome. Eventually, they will end their conflict—once Syria is divided—and two radical states will emerge, both heavily armed. In such a case, the true losers in Syria would be the democrats and the minorities. Arming the opposition without distinction would end up arming the Jihadists, a significant menace to the region. Unfortunately, a limited strike aiming at forcing a peace process will not work either. At the end of summer 2013, I suggested that the West take the initiative to support the gradual rise of a "smaller free Syria," based initially in the northeastern part of the country, where the Kurds and Christians are the main players, with Arab

Sunni seculars and moderates working with them. In that free Syria, opposition factions could be vetted and the liberation of the country could
move forward. But the Obama administration ran in the other direction,
away from partnering with the secular and moderate segments of the
opposition, giving more time to the Assad regime and even inviting the
Iranian regime to be part of the Geneva talks process. The Jihadi militias multiplied, soaring in several areas of Syria with al Qaeda–linked
al Nusra and Daesh (Islamic State of Iraq and Shamm) taking the lead.
Meanwhile, Hezbollah and the Iranian-backed Iraqi Shia militias increased their numbers and established permanent bases in Syria. By the
end of January 2014, units of the Free Syria Army pushed back against
the Jihadi militias while at the same time resisting Assad's forces. Syrian civilians were dying in the thousands. U.S. policy in Syria has led to
near catastrophe and must be reshaped. In addition to revising the whole
approach to Iran's regime and people, Washington must redesign strategies to help Syrians free themselves from both the Assad regime and the
al Qaeda–backed Jihadists.

IRAN'S PEOPLE, ABANDONED AGAIN

The Obama administration, fully engaged in outreach to the Iranian
regime in 2014 and firmly convinced that Tehran's ayatollahs will come
along and respond in kind, has abandoned the Iranian people and a viable opposition to the Khomeinist regime for the second time since 2009.
More ominous is the release by the United States of close to eight billion
dollars in cash to the Iranian leaders. As part of the "deal," this transfer
of funds won't solve Iran's economic crisis or be used by the ayatollahs to
ease the pressures on their citizens. With sanctions gradually lifting and
pressures easing, the Pasdaran-controlled Islamist regime's first prior-
ity will be to ensure that no future sanctions will be leveled and that no
support will be extended by the West to a forthcoming new revolution.
They will use the freed-up resources to pay for a war of ideas—a massive international propaganda operation designed to discredit, cripple,
and isolate the Iranian opposition worldwide, particularly in the United

States. Thus, the "2013 deal" will provide Iran's regime with a financial weapon to disarm Western actions in the future, particularly when Tehran's mullahs decide to unveil their atomic arms. For, although the regime has allegedly committed to freezing its uranium production under a certain level, it has not stopped taking other steps toward building its strategic weaponry system. Conventional missiles are being produced, ramps are being deployed, and advanced anti-aircraft missiles are being sought. This assessment of the regime's intentions is agreed upon by a wide array of Iranian opposition leaders, from the shah's heir, Reza Pahlavi, in exile in Washington, to Mariam Rajavi, leader of the Paris-based National Council of Iranian Resistance.[8]

This new abandonment of the Iranian people, masked as a diplomatic success, is being felt by the country's civil society, women, ethnic minorities, and youth (who have expressed their views in countless online postings).[9] Moreover, moderates in the region—in Gulf countries such as Kuwait, the UAE, Jordan, and Saudi Arabia, as well as the civil society forces in Lebanon, Syria, and Iraq—are also feeling the impact of Washington's empowerment of Iran's regime. The next round of confrontation within the Iranian-dominated part of the Middle East will be between democracy resistance movements and the Khomeinist regime and its allies in four countries. Two factors will affect the outcome: One is the capacity of the Iranian opposition to surge against the regime despite U.S. abandonment, and two is the possibility of a change in Washington's foreign policy. The interaction between the domestic opposition and U.S. policies will either hasten the rise of the opposition in Iran or hamper it, opening the path for a nuclear-armed Iran and the consequences that would follow.

LEBANON'S CEDARS REVOLUTION SHOULD COME BACK

In Lebanon, Hezbollah backs Assad's regime, and the Salafists support the Islamist fighters in Syria. The situation is deadlocked, partially because Hezbollah paralyzes the government and the army, but also partially because the politicians of the March 14 Alliance have yet to adopt a proactive strategy. They have remained cramped in a waiting posture for years, praying for Syria's outcome to affect Lebanon, hoping a collapse of the Assad regime will weaken Hezbollah. The reality is that only a popular movement in Lebanon, reigniting the Cedars Revolution, can move the country toward liberation. Lebanese member of parliament Nadim Gemayel (the son of Bashir Gemayel, the president-elect of Lebanon killed by the Syrians in 1982), told me that "the Christians of Lebanon are smashed between Hezbollah and the Jihadists, and so are all Lebanese supporters of the Cedars Revolution, Sunnis, Druzes, and Shia. We feel abandoned by the U.S. administration and left under the menaces of the two most dangerous terror organizations in the world." Another rising activist in the Shia community, Mustafa Geha II, now in exile in Stockholm and the son of the assassinated writer Mustafa Geha, told me that "the U.S. and the Europeans could have backed us, liberals of the Shia community, to rise en masse and oppose Hezbollah on its own turf." Geha, who was targeted for assassination in 2013, continued: "Instead, the West wants to accommodate Hezbollah and fantasize about a moderation process of a highly ideological movement, as they've attempted with the Muslim Brotherhood and failed."

MIDDLE EAST REVOLUTIONS ARE STILL BREWING

The Obama administration, after having trusted Russia's initiative to solve the Syrian conflict by resolving the chemical weapons issue, also attempted to resolve the confrontation with Tehran, Hezbollah, and their allies, Assad and Iraqi politicians, by cutting a deal with the Iranian regime in the fall of 2013. But across the region, the revolts have not died out. In Iraq, reformers are active inside their respective communities. Only a coalition of all moderates—Sunnis, Shia, Kurds, and Christians—can simultaneously oppose the dominant pro-Iranian forces and the armed Salafi opposition. In Sudan, four revolts are brewing against Khartoum: the Beja in the east, the Nubians in the

North, Darfur in the west, and the African tribes in the Nuba Mountains in the south. In Tunisia, the secular democrats are determined to unsettle the Islamist Nahda regime. Ironically, as secular Tunisians are rising against the Islamist Nahda politically, the Tunisian army is in full confrontation with the Jihadists, who espouse the same ideology as the Islamists in power.[10] By mid-January 2014, Nahda had accepted the formation of an interim government and new elections, fearing a repeat of Egypt's events.

In Algeria and Morocco, civil society forces are emboldened by the events in Egypt and Tunisia. Across North Africa, Kabyles and other Berber communities are also looking ahead for a renewal of their spring, as part of a second Arab Spring that could result in democratic allies. In the Arabian Peninsula, freedom activists are restless. In Turkey, the secular demonstrators are back to the streets. Last but not least, Iran's youth, women, and minorities have not vanished, despite the setback of June 2009. Their moment will arrive in the future. The Islamist Winter is chilling, but the Arab and Middle East Spring is still blooming. Two seasons are hovering over the Middle East at the same time. The warmer one will eventually win. The question is, however, at what price?

Between 2009 and 2014, the United States had a historic opportunity to defeat the Jihadi Salafist and the Khomeinist totalitarian movements by opting for a partnership with the peoples of the region and democracy forces. Sadly it chose instead to stand by the Islamists of the Arab world and the ayatollahs of Iran. The first Arab Spring was lost. Now a second Arab Spring, part of a global Middle East democratic revolution, is on the way. It will be a current made of many majority and minority movements, rising against medieval ideologies and seeking progress, freedom, and prosperity. The U.S. partnership with the suppressors of this new spring cannot last indefinitely. No deals or accommodations that ignore the longing of youth for a better future can last. Hence, Washington must change its ideas to be ready for the change that is coming from the Levant.

I finished this last chapter on the day Nelson Mandela left this world. There is no better symbolic moment to urge America and the West to respond to the appeal of a large segment of humanity still suffering from a lack of freedom in the birthplace of civilizations and religions, east and south of the Mediterranean.

Washington, D.C., December 5, 2013

NOTES

INTRODUCTION

1. Mahdi militias, launched in Iraq after the U.S. invasion in 2003 under the leadership of radical Shia leader Muqtada al Sadr and backed by the Iranian regime, conducted attacks against coalition forces and Iraqi Sunni groups.
2. The Muslim Brotherhood of Egypt and the Nahda of Tunisia are main Islamist movements who succeeded via parliamentary elections, and because of their healthy, old and organized networks, they were able to seize the governments in Cairo and Tunis after the first wave of the Arab Spring.
3. "Kerry Says Well-Organized Muslim Brotherhood 'Stole' Egyptian Revolution," *Washington Post* and *Associated Press,* November 20, 2014.
4. *Ikhwan* is an abbreviation of the translation of the term "Muslim Brotherhood." *Ikhwan* translates to "brotherhood." Thus we will use *Ikhwan* and *Muslim Brotherhood* interchangeably.
5. Hizb al Nahda al Islamiyya (translates to "Party of the Islamic Renaissance") is a Tunisian Islamist Party that opposed President Ben Ali and won enough seats in the postrevolution legislative elections to enable it to form the government in 2012.
6. "Shabab al Jihad" (translates to "the youth of Jihad"), commonly known as "Shabab," is a Jihadi militia operating in Somalia over the past five years. It is affiliated with al Qaeda and classified as a terrorist group by the United States. It is responsible for attacks in Somalia and Kenya, and some of its members are U.S. citizens.
7. "Boko Haram" (translates to "Western culture is forbidden") is a Jihadi militia operating in Northern Nigeria over the past few years and is affiliated with al Qaeda. Boko Haram is on the U.S. terror list and has been engaging in violent attacks in several provinces of the country and in neighboring states.

CHAPTER I

1. Soeren Kern, "Qatar Financing Wahabi Islam in France, Italy, Ireland and Spain," *Gatestone Institute: International Policy Council,* February 9, 2012.
2. Lorenzo Vidino, "The Muslim Brotherhood's Conquest of Europe," *Middle East Quarterly,* winter 2005, 25-34.
3. Ken Dilanian, "U.S. Intelligence Official Acknowledges Missed Arab Spring Signs," *Los Angeles Times,* July 19, 2012.
4. On the absence of a Western analytical vision of the real root causes of the Arab Spring, see Gaïdz Minassian, "Debat sur les Printemps arabes, indignés, les

sociétés s'attaquent à la légitimité du politique," *Le Monde,* November 26, 2011. On the intellectual frustration regarding the Arab Spring, see Alain Frachon, "Printemps arabe: 'Tout ça pour ça !'" *Le Monde,* April 18, 2013. The author also published an article on the failure of academia in predicting the movement: Walid Phares, "Scholars Failed to Predict the Arab Spring," *Newsmax Magazine,* December 6, 2011.

5. Other academic articles in the United States discussing the intellectual failure in the prediction of a movement as vast as the Arab Spring include F. Gregory Gause III, "Why Middle East Studies Missed the Arab Spring: The Myth of Authoritarian Stability," *Foreign Affairs* 90, no. 4 (July/August 2011).

6. Tony Karon, "Tunisia Domino? No, but a U.S. Democracy Dilemma," *Time,* January 18, 2011; see also Mark LeVine, "Tunisia: How the US Got It Wrong," *Al Jazeera English,* January 16, 2011.

7. Joby Warrick and Perry Bacon Jr., "Obama Urges Egypt to Heed Protests, Pursue Reforms," *Washington Post,* January 29, 2011; see also Linda Feldmann, "At Last, Obama Addresses Egypt Protests . . . on YouTube," *Christian Science Monitor,* January 27, 2011; see also Jennifer Rubin, "On Egypt, Obama Offers 'Too Little, Too Late,'" *Washington Post,* January 30, 2011.

8. Bradley Klapper, "US Unsure on Military Options for Libya," Associated Press, March 1, 2011.

9. David Stringer, "Assange: Obama Exploiting Arab Spring in Campaign," Associated Press, September 26, 2012.

10. Awr Hawkins, "Welcome to Obama's Arab Spring," *Breitbart News,* June 24, 2012.

CHAPTER 2

1. Rania Abouzeid Friday, "Bouazizi: The Man Who Set Himself and Tunisia on Fire," *Time,* January 21, 2011.

2. Jake Hess, "Iran Awaits 'Kurdish Spring,'" *Al Jazeera,* June 29, 2013.

3. See Matthew Arnold and Matthew LeRiche, *South Sudan: From Revolution to Independence* (New York: Oxford University Press), 2012.

4. A leader of the South Sudan People's Movement, Pagan Amun as well as commanders of the Sudan Popular Liberation Army, founded by Colonel John Garang, whom I met in Washington, told me that "achieving self-determination for their people was practically a miracle, but after September 11, history changed its course in the region, and we were ready." Interviews by Walid Phares, Washington, D.C., February-March 2011.

5. Lemonde.fr, Agence France-Presse, and Reuters, "Référendum du Sud-Soudan: Omar Hassan Al-Bachir s'engage à reconnaître le résultat" [Referendum of Southern Sudan: Omar al Bashir getting ready to recognize Southern Sudan, editorial], *Le Monde,* February 7, 2011.

6. "South Sudan to Begin Rebel Peace Talks, Renewed Fighting," AFP, January 2, 2014.

7. Alec Castonguay, "Le printemps arabe," *Le Devoir* (Canada), January 29, 2011.

8. We have debated with Tunisian politicians, including leaders of the Joumhouri Party and members of the Foreign Affairs Committee of the U.S. House of Representatives, the reasons that incited the international community to quickly support the Tunisian revolution; see also Agence France-Presse, "L'armée se porte 'garante de la révolution' en Tunisie" [The army guarantees the revolution in Tunisia], *Le Point,* January 24, 2011.

9. Hizbul Tahrir is a global Islamist movement, launched in the late 1950s early 1960s, with branches across the Arab and Muslim world, promoting the unification of all Muslim countries and the reestablishment of the defunct Caliphate.

CHAPTER 3

1. Based on discussions with leaders and cadres of the first Egyptian revolution in 2011, including Cynthia Farahat, leader of the Liberal Democratic Party and an exile in the United States as of 2012; Professor Essam Abdallah of Ain Shams University in Cairo, June 2012; and Ahmed Sleiman, one of the spokespersons for the liberal coalition of June 30, 2013.
2. Zakarya Moukine Billah, "La bataille pour l'Egypte se joue aussi sur Facebook" [The battle for Egypt is being fought also on Facebook], *Le Monde,* February 4, 2011.
3. Ahmad Tarri, *al Watan,* Cairo, June 27, 2013.
4. Ambassador Randolph Bell et al., *Minority Religious Communities at Risk,* Freedom First Center, 2013 Report (March 2013).
5. U.S. democracy agencies such as the International Republican Institute and the Democratic National Institute, which were training a number of Egyptian youth, told us then that the push from Washington was to organize Egyptian students and NGOs to demand civic and political reforms, not for a complete collapse of the Mubarak regime.
6. The Pasdaran, or the Iranian Revolutionary Guard, are a powerfully armed central militia operating under the supreme guide of the Islamic Republic to ensure its defense against its enemies. The Bassij are a popular militia, lightly armed and mostly located in neighborhoods to serve as the eyes and the arms of the regime and execute its orders, particularly against opposition elements. It operates under the Pasdaran.
7. Jose Antonio Vargas, "Spring Awakening: How an Egyptian Revolution Began on Facebook," *New York Times,* February 17, 2012; see also Billah, "La bataille."
8. Congressmen Robert Aderholt and Louie Gohmert told me in July 2013 during Congressional briefings on Egypt that they and many of their colleagues were concerned about the role of the Obama administration in supporting the Muslim Brotherhood against moderates in Egypt; also see Jerry Philipson, "Obama Angry and Upset about Muslim Brotherhood Getting Tossed Out in Egypt," *Canada Free Press,* July 7, 2013.
9. Ahmed Douma to Egyptian Dream 2 TV and al Qahira wal Nas TV at several occasions during February 2013.

CHAPTER 4

1. Mohamed Eljarh, "Marking Two Years of Libya's Revolution," *Foreign Policy,* February 13, 2013.
2. Catherine O'Donnell, "New Study Quantifies Use of Social Media in Arab Spring," *University of Washington,* September 12, 2011.
3. Hugh MacCleod, "How Schoolboys Began the Syrian Revolution," *Global Post,* reprinted by CBS News, April 25, 2011; see also Rania Abouzaid, "Syria's Revolt: How Graffiti Stirred an Uprising," *Time,* March 22, 2013; see also Benjamin Barthe, "Les enfants de Deraa, l'étincelle de l'insurrection syrienne," *Le Monde,* March 8, 2013.

4. They could be compared to the Tonton Macoutes of Haiti, but on much larger and bloodier scales.

5. Jonathan Spyer, "Defying a Dictator: Meet the Free Syrian Army," *World Affairs,* May/June 2012.

6. Interviews with representatives of the Free Syria Army (FSA) in Europe in June 2012 and their spokesperson, Fahd al Masri, in Paris in June 2013.

CHAPTER 5

1. J. Dana Stuster, "How Does Yemen's Revolution End?" *Foreign Policy,* April 26, 2013 ; see also Hélène Thiollet, "L'autre 'place Tahrir' que faire de la révolution yéménite?" *Le Monde,* November 22, 2011.

2. Christian Caryl, "The Strange Revolution in Bahrain, One Year On," *Foreign Policy,* February 14, 2012; see also Armin Arefi, "Bahreïn: La révolution que l'on ne veut pas voir," *Le Point,* February 15, 2012.

3. The Khomeinists are the supporters of the Iranian regime founded by Ayatollah Khomeini.

4. Michael Stephens, "The Kingdom of No Surprises," *Foreign Policy,* February 19, 2013; see also Kevin Sullivan, "Saudi Arabia's Secret Arab Spring," *Washington Post,* October 23, 2012; see also Mehdi Lazar, "Une révolution est-elle possible en Arabie Saoudite?" *Atlantico,* February 11, 2013.

5. Mohamed al Thani, *The Arab Spring and the Gulf States: Time to Embrace Change* (London: Profile Books, 2012); see also Laurence Louër, "Les monarchies du Golfe face au printemps arabe," CERI Records, September 2011, http://www.ceri-sciences-po.org; see also Elisabeth Vandenheede and Elisabeth Dubois, "Les monarchies pétrolières du Golfe à l'épreuve du printemps arabe," December 17, 2012, http://www.medea.be/2012/12/les-monarchies-petrolieres-du-golfe-a-lepreuve-du-printemps-arabe-2/.

6. Vince Coglianese, "Yusuf al-Qaradawi, the Muslim Brotherhood's Spiritual Leader, Returns to Cairo," *Daily Caller,* February 18, 2011; see also Ahmad Azem, "The Extent and Limits of Qatar-Hamas Ties," *Al Monitor,* May 16, 2013; see also Agence France-Presse, "Morsi Ouster in Egypt 'Invalid': Qaradawi Fatwa," July 6, 2013.

7. Elizabeth Dickinson, "Tiny Qatar Played Outsized Role as Arab League President. Will It Last?" *Christian Science Monitor,* March 28, 2012; see also Colin Freeman, "Qatar 'Playing with Fire' as It Funds Syrian Islamists in Quest for Global Influence," *The Telegraph,* April 27, 2013.

CHAPTER 6

1. Fouad Ajami, "The Arab Spring at One: A Year of Living Dangerously," *Foreign Affairs,* March/April 2012; see also Bichara Khader, "Le printemps arabe: un premier bilan," *El Kalam,* March 2013.

2. "Text of Obama's Speech in Cairo," *New York Times,* June 4, 2009; see also "Obama in Egypt Reaches Out to Muslim World," CNN, June 4, 2009.

3. "Analyst: Obama Has Formed Strategic Alliance with Muslim Brotherhood," interview with Barry Rubin, *World Tribune,* June 30, 2013; see also Ted Belman, "Why Is Obama in Bed with the Muslim Brotherhood?" *American Thinker,* February 26, 2012.

4. Letta Tayler, "Yemen's Hijacked Revolution," *Foreign Affairs,* September 26, 2011.

5. Simon Henderson, "Bahrain Boiling," *Foreign Policy,* September 23, 2011; see also Ali Alfoneh, "Between Reform and Revolution: Sheikh Qassim, the Bahraini Shi'a, and Iran," *American Enterprise Institute,* July 12, 2012.

6. James Lewis, "Dangerous Times: Obama's Arab Spring Logic," *American Thinker,* July 6, 2013.

7. Michael Emerson et al., eds., "Political Islam and European Foreign Policy: Perspectives from Muslim Democrats of the Mediterranean," *Centre for European Policy Studies,* December 2007.

8. Nick Witney, "Europe's Role in the Arab Spring," *European Council on Foreign Relations,* September 26, 2012; see also Ferhat Mehanni, "L'Europe et les printemps arabes," seminar at FAES in Madrid, *Tamurt Info,* March 25, 2012.

CHAPTER 7

1. Jackson Diehl, "Is Obama to Blame for the Arab Spring's Failures?" *Washington Post,* June 24, 2012; see also Sharif Nashashibi, "Arab Spring 2013: Revolutionary Wave Enters a Third Year," *Al Arabiya,* December 31, 2012; see also Nonie Darwish, "Egyptian-American Writer Analyzes Failure of Arab Revolutions," interview in *Al Arabiya,* May 25, 2012.

2. David French, "The Profound Moral Failure of Benghazi," *National Review,* May 7, 2013; see also Committee on Oversight and Government Reform, "Benghazi: Exposing Failure and Recognizing Courage," U.S. House of Representatives, May 08, 2013; see also Al Cardenas, "Benghazi Is a Massive Failure of the Obama Administration," *US News and World Report,* May 9, 2013; see also "Benghazi: les "ratés" du Département d'Etat pointés du doigt," *Liberation,* December 19, 2012.

3. David Kirkpatrick, "A Deadly Mix in Benghazi," *New York Times,* December 2013, also Howard Kurtz, "Benghazi, the Pundits Take on the New York Times," Fox News, December 31, 2013.

4. Report by the Libya Benghazi Study Group submitted to members of Congress, January 4, 2014 (Arabic).

5. Chris Stephen, "Libya: Tensions between Government and Militias Come to a Head," *The Guardian,* June 13, 2013; see also Agence France-Presse, "Libye: attaque contre un QG d'anciens rebelles à Benghazi," *Le Monde,* June 8, 2013.

6. Borzou Daragahi, "Libyan Activist Shot Dead in Benghazi," *Financial Times,* July 25, 2013.

7. Barry Rubin, "Tunisia: Goodbye Democracy? Islamists Start to Take Over Media," *Middle East Review of International Affairs,* July 5, 2012; see also R.N., "Tunisie: face à l'inquisition islamiste, la naïveté des intellectuels?" *Le Matin* DZ, August 21, 2012.

8. Yasmine Ryan, "Tunisia's Vocal Salafist Minority," *Al Jazeera English,* October 11, 2011.

9. Andrew Lebovich, "Confronting Tunisia's Jihadists," *Foreign Policy,* May 16, 2013; see also Fethi Belaid, "Jihadists Hunted in Tunisia 'Former Mali Fighters,'" Agence France-Presse, May 8, 2013.

10. Martin Jay, "Tunisian Girls Head to Syria to Offer Themselves to Islamic Fighters as Part of Sexual Jihad," *Daily Mail,* April 4, 2013.

11. Agence France-Presse, "Tunisians Mark Political Killing of Chokri Belaid," German DW, March 16, 2013.

12. Serge Halimi, "Tunisia's Revolution Annexed," *Le Monde Diplomatique,* March 2013.

13. Salah Horchani, "A propos du crime de Tataouine: Les Islamistes tunisiens sont passés de l'appel au meurtre à l'assassinat de leurs opposants," *Le Grand Soir,* October 19, 2012.

14. Reuters, Agence France-Presse, "Tunisia's Tamarod Movement Launched," July 3, 2013; see also Associated Press, "Thousands in Tunisia Protest Islamist Extremism," *CBS News,* January 28, 2012.

15. Agence France-Presse, "Tunisie: l'opposant Mohamed Brahmi tué par balles," *Le Figaro,* July 25, 2013; see also Hamid Saïdani, "Le député Mohamed Brahmi tué jeudi par les salafistes" [Lawmaker Mohammed Ibrahimi was killed by Salafists], July 27, 2013; see also Bouazza Ben Bouazza and Paul Schemm, "Thousands Protest Government at Tunisia Funeral," Associated Press, July 27, 2013.

16. Scott Wilson, "Obama Move to Arm Syrian Rebels Comes as Assad Gains Upper Hand," *Washington Post,* June 14, 2013; see also Yves-Michel Riols, "La France envisage d'armer les rebelles syriens," *Le Monde,* June 14, 2013.

17. Patrick J. McDonnell and Nabih Bulos, "Syrian Government Holds Victory Celebration in Battered Qusair," *Los Angeles Times,* June 9, 2013; see also Jean-Pierre Filiu, "La Syrie passe sous contrôle de l'Iran et du Hezbollah," *Le Monde,* June 7, 2013.

18. Carol J. Williams, "U.N. Team to Probe Sites of Reported Syrian Chemical Weapons Use," *Los Angeles Times,* July 31, 2013.

19. Phil Sands, "Syrian Rebel Fighters Blast Muslim Brotherhood for 'Delaying Victory,'" *The National,* April 1, 2013.

20. Ibid.

21. Conversation with General Manaf Tlass on June 5, 2013.

22. Karl Vick, "The Fall of al-Qusayr: Capture of Strategic Syrian Town Marks a New Phase in the War," *Time,* June 5, 2013.

23. Khaled Yacoub Oweis, "Syrian Opposition Head Expects Advanced Weapons to Reach Rebels," Reuters, July 7, 2013; see also Elizabeth O'Bagy, "Jihad in Syria," *Middle East Security Report 6,* Institute for the Study of War, September 2012.

24. Editorial, "Has Syria Crossed Obama's 'Red Line'?" *San Francisco Chronicle,* August 26, 2013; see also David Shenker, "Forget the Red Line and Engage in Syria: There Are Strategic Reasons to Intervene," *New York Daily News,* August 25, 2013; see also Mark Landler, Mark Mazzetti, and Alissa Rubin, "Obama Officials Weigh Response to Syria Assault," *New York Times,* August 22, 2013.

25. "Syria Accepts Russian Chemical Weapons Plan," *Al Jazeera,* September 10, 2013.

26. Mark Landler, "Obama Defends U.S. Engagement in the Middle East," *New York Times,* September 24, 2013.

CHAPTER 8

1. Khaled Abu Toameh, "From an Arab Spring to an Islamist Winter," *Gatestone Institute,* October 28, 2011; see also David Horowitz Restoration Weekend Panel, "Arab Spring, Muslim Winter," *FrontPage Magazine,* December 2, 2011; see also Michael Totten, "Arab Spring or Islamist Winter?" *World Affairs,* January/February 2012.

2. See Peter Beaumont, "Political Islam Poised to Dominate the New World Bequeathed by Arab Spring," *The Observer,* December 3, 2011.

3. Amir Taheri, "Opinion: Arab Spring, Islamic Winter, Military Summer," *Al Sharq al Awsat,* July 5, 2013.

4. Neil MacFarquhar, "Egyptian Voters Approve Constitutional Changes," *New York Times,* March 20, 2011.

5. Monica Crowley and Karl Rove, "Obama Administration Recognizes Egypt's Dangerous Muslim Brotherhood," *Hannity,* Fox News, June 30, 2011.

6. Richard Engel, "Egyptians Fear Decades of Muslim Brotherhood Rule," NBC, December 1, 2012; see also Zvi Mazel, "Analysis: Brotherhood Taking Total Control of Egypt," *Jerusalem Post,* August 23, 2013.

7. Coptic Solidarity Conference, June 2013, US Congress.

8. Paul Bonicelli, "Muslim Brotherhood Spokesman Confirms Democracy and Group's Ideology Don't Mix," *Foreign Policy,* July 21, 2013.

9. "The Lead with Jake Tepper," CNN, July 3, 2013.

10. Reuters, "Tamarod Urges Egyptians to Support Army on Friday," *Egypt Independent,* July 24, 2013.

11. "Obama Concerned about Egypt," *Huffington Post,* July 3, 2013; see also Sean Sullivan, "McCain Calls for Suspension of U.S. Military Aid to Egypt, Others Disagree," *Washington Post,* July 7, 2013.

12. In August 2013, Amnesty International published a document accusing the Muslim Brotherhood "of using torture against the population." See Hassiba Hadj Sahraoui, deputy director for the Middle East and North Africa at Amnesty International, "Egypt: Evidence Points to Torture Carried Out by Morsi Supporters," Amnesty International, August 2, 2013.

13. Mohamed Soliman, "Why What Happened in Cairo Isn't a Coup," *Cutting Edge News,* July 5, 2013.

14. Mohammed Hawary, spokesperson of the June 30 Coalition, "Mr. Obama, I Really Don't Want to Be a Terrorist," *Canada Free Press,* July 6, 2013.

15. Ahmad Taheri, "Congress Asks Obama to Remove Morsi," *Al Watan,* July 3, 2013.

16. "Statement by EU HR Ashton on Developments in Egypt," European Union @ United Nations, July 3, 2013; see also "Chairman Royce and Ranking Member Engel Release Joint Statement on Ongoing Events in Egypt," House Committee on Foreign Affairs, July 5, 2013.

17. Faith McDonnell, "Rep. Louie Gohmert's Challenge to America on Egypt," *FrontPage Magazine,* July 23, 2013; see also Brian Jones, "Obama's Delays F-16 Delivery, Takes First Step to Distance from Military Rule in Egypt," *Business Insider,* July 25, 2013.

18. "Millions Rally in Egypt, Responding to Army Call," CBS, July 26, 2013.

19. See "Tamarod Urges Egyptians to Support Army on Friday," *Egypt Independent,* July 24, 2013, Reuters; also "Christians Join Protests in Egypt," Radio Vatican, July 1, 2013.

20. Abigail Hauslohner and Michael Birnbaum, "Egypt's Government Tells Police to Break Up Pro-Morsi Protests," *Washington Post,* July 31, 2013; see also James Rosen, "Persecution of Coptic Christians Grows Worse in Egypt," Fox News, August 21, 2013.

21. Mark Landler and Peter Baker, "Obama Rebukes Egypt's Leaders," *New York Times,* August 15, 2013.

22. Mutaz Nadi, "Al Thwara al haqiqiya sa tqum dida al ikhwan al muslimeen" [The real revolution will rise against the Muslim Brotherhood], *Al Misri al Yom Daily,* July 26, 2012.

23. Soner Cagaptay, "Turks Have Learned the Power of Grassroots Politics," *Atlantic,* June 4, 2013.

24. Zeno Baran, *Torn Country: Turkey Between Secularism and Islamism* (Stanford: Hoover Institution Press, 2010).

CHAPTER 9

1. Walid Phares, *Future Jihad: Terrorist Strategies Against America* (New York: Palgrave, 2005); see also Walid Phares, *Future Jihad: Terrorist Strategies Against the West* (New York: Palgrave, 2006).

2. I discussed this in *The Coming Revolution: Struggle for Freedom in the Middle East* and earlier writings.

3. Chaim Herzog and Shlomo Gazit, *The Arab-Israeli Wars: War and Peace in the Middle East* (New York: Vintage Press, 2005); see also U.S. Department of State, Office of the Historian, *OPEC Oil Embargo, 1973-1974;* see also Walter Pincus, "1973 U.S. Cable on Mideast Mirrors Current Events," *Washington Post,* November 29, 2007.

4. David E. Kaplan, "The Saudi Connection: How Billions in Oil Money Spawned a Global Terror Network," *U.S. News & World Report,* December 7, 2003.

5. Walid Phares, *The War of Ideas: Jihadism Against Democracy* (New York: Palgrave Macmillan, 2007).

6. Admiral James Lyons, "The Muslim Brotherhood's Long Reach," *Washington Times,* July 9, 2013.

7. Raphael Israeli, "The Muslim Lobby as an Impediment to the US-Israel Relationship," *New English Review,* July 2010.

8. Mitchell Bard, *The Arab Lobby: The Invisible Alliance That Undermines America's Interests in the Middle East* (New York: Broadside Books, 2011).

9. Clare Lopez, "Rise of the 'Iran Lobby': Tehran's Front Groups Move On—and Into—the Obama Administration," *Center for Security Policy,* Washington, D.C., February 2009.

10. Sylvia Longmire, "Hezbollah Presence in the United States Is No Surprise," *Homeland Security Today,* January 10, 2012; see also Suzanne Kelly, "Experts: Hezbollah Positioned for Attack in U.S.," CNN, March 21, 2012.

11. Stephen Schwartz, "The Iran Lobby Buys a Friendly Face for Despotism," *American Thinker,* March 10, 2013; see also Adam Kredo, "Congressman Ed Royce Slams Iran Lobby: NIAC Intern Pushes Pro-Tehran Propaganda at Presser, Congressman Says," *Washington Free Beacon,* July 30, 2013.

12. Hassan Dai, "Iranian Appeasement Lobby," *Iranians Forum,* November 2012. According to former CIA expert on Iran Clare Lopez, "the Iran lobby in the US is backed by a major financial interest group which is seeking to make immense gains as a result of a US Iranian deal. When billions will be transferred from Washington to Tehran, the lobby will be receiving huge amounts of money to increase its influence." (Clare Lopez, "The Iran Lobby Power," US Senate Briefing, January 7, 2014).

13. Takfiris are Salafi Jihadists who focus on the process of casting the identification of "infidels and apostates" on non-Muslims and Muslims who oppose the Islamists. *Takfir* is the verb of rendering the opponents as *Kafir* (infidel), thus targeted for attacks or punishments.

14. Paul Sperry, *Infiltration: How Muslim Spies and Subversives Have Penetrated Washington* (Nelson Current, 2005).

15. Soeren Kern, "Europe's Muslim Lobby," *Gladstone Institute,* January 20, 2011.

16. Winfield Myers, "The National Prayer Service and the Wahhabi Lobby," *American Thinker,* January 17, 2009; see also Frank Gaffney, Jr., "The Wahhabi Lobby Loses," *Fox News,* August 21, 2002; see also Patrick Poole, "Georgetown University's Islamic Wahhabi Front," *FrontPage Magazine,* February 29, 2008.

17. Stephen Schwartz, "CAIR vs. the NYPD: The Wahhabi Lobby Attacks," *Weekly Standard,* April 11, 2008.

18. Investigative Project on Terrorism (IPT), "CAIR Identified by the FBI as Part of the Muslim Brotherhood's Palestine Committee," *Counter Terrorism Blog,* August 8, 2007; see also Stephen Schwartz, "CAIR vs. the NYPD."

19. Martin Barillas "American Muslim Group Applauds Defeat of Republican Candidates," Spero News, November 7, 2012; "CAIR Poll: More Than 85% of American Muslims Picked Obama," CNS News, November 9, 2012.

20. Erik Stackelbeck, "Muslim Student Group a Gateway to Jihad?" *CBN,* August 29, 2011; see also John Guandolo, "The Muslim Brotherhood in America: Part III—'The Settlement Process,'" *Human Events,* March 29, 2011; see also Rory Cohen, "Tracking Muslim Brotherhood's 'Grand Deception,'" *Orange County Register,* December 3, 2012.

21. Magdi Khalil, "Amrika wal Ikhwan al Muslimeen" [America and the Muslim Brotherhood], *Muntada al Hiwar,* December 29, 2012, Washington D.C.

22. IPT News, "Federal Judge Agrees: CAIR Tied to Hamas," *The Investigative Project on Terrorism,* November 22, 2010; see also Neil Munroe, "Hamas-Associated CAIR Applauded by White House," *Daily Caller,* March 18, 2011.

23. Steven Rosen review of Mitchell Bard, *The Arab Lobby: The Invisible Alliance That Undermines America's Interests in the Middle East* (New York: Harper, 2010), in *Middle East Quarterly* (Spring 2012).

24. Alexander Gainem, "Is There a Muslim Lobby in the US?" *On Islam,* July 16, 2012.

25. Clare M. Lopez, "History of the Muslim Brotherhood Penetration of the U.S. Government," *Gatestone Institute,* April 15, 2013.

26. Clare Lopez, "U.S. Iran Lobby Rallies to Muslim Brotherhood," *Clarion Project,* August 5, 2012.

27. *The Coming Revolution: Struggle for Freedom in the Middle East.*

28. Daniel Pipes and Sharon Chadha, "CAIR: Islamists Fooling the Establishment," *Middle East Quarterly* (Spring 2006): 3-20.

29. Check Martin Kramer, "MESA Culpa," *Middle East Quarterly,* Fall 2002, 81-90.

30. Cinnamon Stillwell, "Obama's Middle East Studies Mentors," *American Thinker,* November 2, 2008.

31. Phyllis Chesler, "Why Is the NY Times Islamist Terrorism's Apologist?," *Arutz Sheva,* November 27, 2012; see also Bob Taylor, "Further Evidence of Islamic Influence in the U.S.," *Washington Times,* January 10, 2013.

32. Kerry Picket, "Muslim Advocacy Groups Influence Heavily on U.S. National Security Protocol and Lexicon," *Washington Times,* September 24, 2012; see also Magdi Khalil, "How Close Is the U.S. to the Muslim Brotherhood?" *FrontPage Magazine,* August 23, 2013.

CHAPTER 10

1. CAIR's website at www.cair.org.

2. Evan McCormick, quoted in "Discover the Networks," August 24, 2013.

3. Dr. Shawki Karas, address to the Middle East Christian Committee Conference at the U.S. Senate, under the chairmanship of Senator Sam Brownback, June 30, 2000.

4. Interview with Jimmy Mulla, Washington, D.C., October 4, 2004.

5. Billy Hallowee, "CAIR Protests Muslim's Appointment to Religious Freedom Watchdog: 'Sock Puppet for Islam Haters,'" *The Blaze,* March 30, 2012; see also

Lauren Markoe, "Muslims Call New Religious Freedom Appointee a 'Puppet' for Islam Foes," *Washington Post,* March 27, 2012.

6. Eli Lake, "Iran Advocacy Group Said to Skirt Lobby Rules," *Washington Times,* November 13, 2009; see also Richard Schoeberl, "Iranian Spies in Our Midst: It Is Time for the United States to Fight Back in the Iranian Information Wars against Tehran's Dissidents," UPI, March 7, 2013.

7. Personal interviews by Walid Phares and Iranian leaders in exile, 2004-2013, in several cities around the world.

8. Christiane Amanpour, "Obama Sent Letter to Iran Leader Before Election, Sources Say," CNN, June 24, 2009.

9. See, for example, Robert Mackey, "A Green Revolution for Iran?" *New York Times,* June 10, 2009.

10. "Obama to Iran Green Revolution Dissidents: Drop Dead," *Investor's Business Daily,* February 28, 2012; see also Michael Ledeen, "Setting the Record Straight on the Green Movement, Washington Can Do More to Help Iranian Democrats," *Foreign Affairs,* September 4, 2012.

11. Lee Stranahan, "Southern Poverty Law Center Provides Cover for Jihad Apologists," *Breitbart News,* April 27, 2013.

12. Byron Tau, "ACLU, CAIR Call for Probe into W.H. Funding for Muslim Surveillance," *Politico,* February 27, 2012; see also Jim Koury, "CAIR and ACLU: Court Blocks Anti-Sharia Law in Oklahoma," *Family Security Matters,* January 16, 2012.

13. For example, see ACLU defense of the Islamist lobby in Heather L. Weaver, "The Anti-Muslim Movement's Manufactured 'Sharia Threat' to Our Judicial System," *ACLU Program on Freedom of Religion and Belief,* May 17, 2013.

14. Billy Hallowell, "Muslim Group Seeks to Ban Sharia Law in America," *The Blaze,* September 13, 2011.

15. Nihad Awad, "King's Attack on U.S. Muslims: Head of CAIR Says Terrorism Hearings Will Stoke Fears," *New York Daily News,* February 28, 2011.

16. Crystal Wright, "Rep. Peter King Was Right, America Has a Homegrown Muslim Terrorist Problem," *Townhall,* April 22, 2013.

17. Aaron Eitan Meyer, "Islamist Lawfare," *American Spectator,* September 15, 2009.

18. Ken Timmerman, "Victims of Islamist 'Lawfare' Fight Back," *Newsmax Magazine,* March 12, 2010.

19. Brooke M. Goldstein and Aaron Eitan Meyer, "How Islamist Lawfare Tactics Target Free Speech," *Middle East Quarterly,* April 29, 2009.

20. Michael Kirkland, "Islamic Law in U.S. Courts," UPI, May 19, 2013.

21. Omar Sacirbey, "Anti-Shariah Movement Gains Success," *Huffington Post,* May 17, 2013.

22. For a discussion of the definition, see Fernando Bravo López, "Towards a Definition of Islamophobia: Approximations of the Early Twentieth Century," *Ethnic and Racial Studies* 34, no. 4 (2011): 556-573.

23. Jackson Doughart and Faisal Saeed al-Muta, "Opinion: Stop Calling Criticism of Islam 'Islamophobia,'" *National Post,* September 25, 2012.

24. David Suissa, "Criticism Is Not Islamophobia," *Jewish Journal,* April 22, 2013.

25. Cinnamon Stillwell and Rima Greene, "Berkeley Profs: 'Islamophobia' Greater Threat than Islamic Terrorism," *FrontPage Magazine,* May 27, 2013.

26. Polly Curtis, "Ofsted Head Accused of Islamophobia Over Attack," *Guardian,* January 17, 2005.

27. For an example of a full-fledged attack against what the apologist lobby calls Islamophobes, see Steve Rendall and Isabel Macdonald, "Making Islamophobia

Mainstream: How Muslim-Bashers Broadcast Their Bigotry," *Fairness and Accuracy in Reporting* (FAIR), November 1, 2008.

28. David Horowitz, "Think Progress Witch Hunt," *FrontPage Magazine*, August 26, 2011.

29. Wajahat Ali et al., *Fear Inc: The Roots of the Islamaphobia Network in America* (Washington, D.C.: Center for American Progress, August 2011).

30. Conversation with David Major, CI Center, March 27, 2011.

31. David Horowitz is the founder of the David Horowitz Freedom Center and author, most recently, of *A Point in Time: The Search for Redemption in This Life and the Next.* Robert Spencer is the director of Jihad Watch and the author of the *New York Times* bestsellers *The Politically Incorrect Guide to Islam (and the Crusades)* and *The Truth about Muhammad.*

32. Robert Spencer and David Horowitz, "Islamophobia: Thought Crime of the Totalitarian Future," *FrontPage Magazine,* September 7, 2011.

33. See "Politics of Islamophobia," in "Discover the Networks," adapted from "Hyping Hate Crimes vs. Muslims," *Investor's Business Daily,* December 7, 2007.

34. Niraj Warikoo, "FBI Ditches Training Materials Criticized as Anti-Muslim," *Detroit Free Press,* February 20, 2012; see also "FBI Makes Changes to Not Offend Muslims," CBN News, June 10, 2013; see also Catherine Herridge, "FBI Removes Hundreds of Training Documents after Probe on Treatment of Islam," Fox News, February 21, 2012; see also Glenn Kessler, "Is the FBI Unable to 'Talk About Jihad'?" *Washington Post,* May 3, 2013.

35. "CAIR Seeks 'Swift' FBI Action on Revelations of Anti-Muslim Training," *PR Newswire,* September 15, 2011; there followed a response by far-left Adam Serwer, "FBI: Okay, Fine, We'll Do Something about That Anti-Muslim Training," *Mother Jones,* September 21, 2011.

36. Adam Kredo, "Smearing Zuhdi Jasser," *Washington Beacon,* April 10, 2012; see also Billy Hallowell, "CAIR Protests Muslim's Appointment to Religious Freedom Watchdog: 'Sock Puppet for Islam Haters,'" *The Blaze,* March 30, 2012; see also Caroline May, "CAIR Pushes DoD to Drop Ex-CIA Operative Lecturer, Claims Anti-Islam," *Daily Caller,* July 24, 2012.

37. W. Thomas Smith, "Congressman King Rejects Pressure to Drop Notable Scholar of Islam from Congressional Testimony," *Cutting Edge News,* March 4, 2011.

38. Jim Curi, "FBI Implements Obama's Politically Correct Counterterrorism Training," *The Examiner,* April 21, 2013.

39. Essam Abdallah, "Islamist Lobbies' Washington War on Arab and Muslim Liberals," *Cutting Edge News,* February 16, 2012.

40. Jennifer Rubin, "Iran Reminds Us: Obama's Deal Is a Fraud," *Washington Post,* January 16, 2014; also Reuters, "Barack Obama Hails Iran Deal, Argues against New Sanctions," January 13, 2014; also Leigh Ann Caldwell, "Iran Deal May Define Barack Obama's Legacy, for Better or Worse," CNN, November 24, 2013; also Alan Caruba, "Obama's Disastrous Iranian Deal," *Western Journalism,* November 14, 2013; also "Obama Defends Iran Nuclear Deal from Chorus of Critics," Fox News, November 26, 2013.

41. Abdallah, "Islamist Lobbies Washington War."

42. Daniel Greenfield, "Hatem Bazian and Al Jazeera Accuse Egyptian Government of Islamophobia," *FrontPage Magazine,* August 23, 2013.

43. Ahmad Soliman phone interview with Walid Phares, August 25, 2013.

44. Magdi Khalil interview with Walid Phares, Washington, D.C., August 27, 2013.

45. Brad Knickerbocker, "Why Did Peter King Take on CAIR at Radicalization Hearings?" *Christian Science Monitor,* March 10, 2011.

46. During a briefing in Congress, office of Representative Pete King, Washington, D.C., February 2011.

47. Conversation with Congresswoman Sue Myrick in Congress, Washington, D.C., April 2012.

48. Deborah Weiss, "OIC Ramps Up 'Islamophobia' Campaign," *FrontPage Magazine*, February 28, 2013.

CHAPTER 11

1. Courtney C. Radsch, "Obama Reaches Arabs, Muslims via Al Arabiya," *Al Arabiya*, January 29, 2009.

2. President Barack Obama, "Remarks to the Turkish Parliament," Turkish Grand National Assembly Complex, Ankara, Turkey, April 6, 2009, http://www.white house.gov/the_press_office/Remarks-By-President-Obama-To-The-Turkish -Parliament.

3. Jesse Lee, "The President's Speech in Cairo: A New Beginning," White House, June 4, 2012, accessed: http://www.whitehouse.gov/blog/NewBeginning/.

4. "Text: Obama's Speech in Cairo," The text of President Obama's prepared remarks to the Muslim world, delivered on June 4, 2009, as released by the White House, in *New York Times*, June 4, 2009.

5. Allied leaders at the Yalta Conference knew that an Allied victory in Europe was inevitable but recognized that a victory in the Pacific theater might require a protracted fight—and even then, they might not win. Soviet participation would provide the Allies a strategic advantage in the region. At Yalta, Roosevelt and Churchill came to an agreement with Stalin outlining the conditions for Soviet involvement in the war against Japan: influence over the southern portion of Sakhalin and the Kurlie Islands, a lease at Port Arthur, and a share in the operation of the Manchurian railroads. This agreement was the major concrete accomplishment of the Yalta Conference (see U.S. State Department for full details of the agreement).

6. Ewen MacAskill, "Obama Sent Letter to Khamenei Before the Election, Report Says," *Guardian*, June 24, 2009.

7. "Al Azhar Confirms Hijab Is Not a Part of the Religion," *World Muslim Congress*, May 23, 2012.

8. Samuel Huntington, "The Clash of Civilization," *Foreign Affairs*, Summer 1993; see also Huntington, *The Clash of Civilizations and the Remaking of World Order* (New York: Simon & Schuster, 1997, 2011).

9. "House of Islam and House of War."

10. DPA, "Muslim Brotherhood in Audience for Obama Cairo Speech," Ikhwan Web, June 3, 2009.

CHAPTER 12

1. Christiane Amanpour, "Obama Sent Letter to Iran Leader before Election, Sources Say," CNN.com, June 24, 2009.

2. Jamie Glazov, "Iran's Lobby in the U.S.," *FrontPage Magazine*, May 8, 2008.

3. Clare Lopez, "Rise of the 'Iran Lobby': Teheran's Front Groups Move On—and Into—the Obama Administration," *Center for Security Policy*, February 25, 2009.

4. Conversations with Clare Lopez and David Major during a seminar on Iranian strategies at the Counter Intelligence Center in Virginia during April 2010.

5. "Obama Refuses to 'Meddle' in Iran," BBC, June 19, 2009; see also Ali Frick, "Obama: 'Given the History of U.S.-Iranian Relations,' U.S. Shouldn't 'Be Seen as Meddling' in Iran's Elections," *Think Progress* (Advocacy organization close to the Iranian lobby in the U.S.), June 16, 2009.

6. Conversation with Iranian opposition leader in Paris, June 2011.

7. The White House, "Statement from the President on Iran," June 20, 2009.

8. Brian Montopoli, "Obama: U.S. Will Always Have 'Israel's Back,'" CBS, March 5, 2012; see also Amie Parnes, "Obama Says He Has 'Israel's Back,' Urges Patience to Let Iran Sanctions Work," *The Hill,* March 4, 2012.

9. "As Obama Pledges to Have Israel's Back, Netanyahu Says It Will Be 'Master of Its Fate,'" FoxNews.com, March 05, 2012.

10. Steven Emerson, "Investigative Project Releases Gov't Memos Curtailing Speech in War on Terror," *IPT News,* May 2, 2008; see also Erick Stakelback, "Government to Ban Use of Word 'Jihadist?'" *CBN,* May 2, 2008; see also Robert Spenser, "Obama Administration Bans the Truth about Islam and Jihad," *FrontPage Magazine,* October 24, 2011; see also PJTV, "U.S. Bans 'Islam' and 'Jihad'–PC or Strategic Censorship?" *PR Newswire,* April 12, 2013.

11. Michael Rubin, "Brennan's Quest for a Moderate Hezbollah," *Commentary Magazine,* January 7, 2013; see also Patrick Goodenough, "CIA Nominee John Brennan Has Touted Hezbollah's 'Moderate Elements,'" *CNS News,* January 9, 2013.

12. Ian Black, "UK Ready for Talks with Hezbollah," *Guardian,* March 4, 2009.

13. Steven Nelson, "Muslim Brotherhood a 'Secular' Organization' Says Clapper," *Daily Caller,* February 10, 2011.

14. Associated Press, "EU Declares Hezbollah's Military Wing a Terror Group," *Khaleej Times,* July 23, 2013; see also Agence France-Presse, "GCC Warns of Steps Against Hezbollah," *Gulf News,* June 2, 2013; see also Habib Toumi, "Bahrain to Probe Hezbollah Activities: GCC to Look into Their Activities in the Gulf Region," *Gulf News,* June 5, 2013; see also James Kanter and Jodi Rudoren, "European Union Adds Military Wing of Hezbollah to List of Terrorist Organizations," *New York Times,* July 22, 2013.

15. Conversation with former member of the European Parliament Paulo Casaca in December 2011.

16. Dean Nelson, "Washington Ready to Negotiate with Mullah Omar," *The Telegraph,* October 28, 2011; see also "Karzai: Afghanistan, U.S. Negotiating with Taliban," Associated Press, June 18, 2011; see also "How Qatar Came to Host the Taliban," BBC, June 23, 2013.

17. Editors, "America to Negotiate with Taliban as It Plots Return," *Investors Business Daily,* June 16, 2013; see also Patrick Christy and Evan Moore, "Talking with the Taliban: Obama Is Wrong in Negotiating with the Taliban," *US News and World Report,* July 2, 2013.

CHAPTER 13

1. Teddy Davis, "'Know Thine Enemy,' Romney Says of 'Jihadists,'" *ABC News,* April 30, 2006.

2. Theresa Cook, "Romney's 'Jihad' Threat Ad," *ABC News,* October 12, 2007.

3. Mitt Romney, *No Apology: The Case for American Greatness* (New York: St. Martin's Press, 2010).

4. Kathryn Jean Lopez, "Candidate Romney: We Must Defeat Groups Like Hezbollah," *National Review* (August 3, 2007).

CHAPTER 14

1. Mitt Romney, "I Won't Let Iran Get Nukes," *Wall Street Journal*, November 10, 2011.
2. Ibid.
3. See Mark Landler, "Obama Defends U.S. Engagement in the Middle East," *New York Times*, September 24, 2013; also "Obama Directs Kerry to Pursue Talks with Iran Over Nuclear Weapons Deal," Fox News, September 24, 2013; also "Iran Press Hails Obama's U.N. Speech," Agence France-Presse, September 25, 2013.
4. Andy Kroll, "Rick Santorum Misleads on Obama and Iran's Green Revolution," *Mother Jones*, February 22, 2012; see also Omid Memarian, "Why Obama Is Right and Romney Is Wrong on Iran," *Daily Beast*, October 11, 2012.
5. Benjamin Weinthal, "Is Obama Serious About Isolating Iran?" *National Review*, August 17, 2012; see also "U.S. Says Obama Open to Meeting with Iran's Rouhani," Reuters, September 19, 2013; see also pressure by pro-Iranian writers to convince President Obama to cut a deal with Iran's regime: Fred Kaplan, "Take a Chance on Iran: President Obama Would Be Crazy Not to Seize the Opportunity That Iranian President Hassan Rouhani Has Given Him," Slate.com, September 20, 2013.
6. Anne Gearan and Joby Warrick, "Iran, World Powers Reach Historic Nuclear Deal," *Washington Post*, November 23, 2013.
7. Khamanei: "The Geneva Agreement Is a Basis for More Intelligent Moves," al Arabiya, November 24, 2013; also "Mohamed Zareef, Iranian Foriegn Minister, 'The Resistance won,'" Reuters, November 24, 2013.
8. "Senate to Weigh Six-Month Window on Iran Sanctions: US Senator," Reuters, November 24, 2013.
9. See John Bolton, "Abject Surrender by the United States," *Weekly Standard*, November 24, 2013.
10. Philip Rucker, "Obama Blasts 'Tough Talk and Bluster' of Iran Deal Critics" *Washington Post*, November 25, 2013; David Simpson and Josh Levs, "Israeli PM Netanyahu: Iran Nuclear Deal 'Historic Mistake,'" CNN, November 25, 2013.
11. Audrey Hudson, "Gen. Hayden: Iran Deal 'Worst of All Possible Outcomes,'" *Newsmax Magazine*, November 24, 2013.
12. David Ignatius, "Obama Weighs Dialogue with Taliban, Hezbollah," *Washington Post*, March 18, 2011.
13. "Obama Extends US Sanctions on Hezbollah Linked Assets," *Ya Libnan*, July 30, 2013.
14. Ryan Mauro, "Obama Meets with Pro-Hezbollah Groups Ahead of Mideast Trip," *FrontPage Magazine*, March 12, 2013.
15. Kathryn Jean Lopez, "Candidate Romney: We Must Defeat Groups Like Hezbollah," *National Review*, August 3, 2007.
16. Editors, "Dialogue with Taliban Endangers Women's Rights," *Asia News*, September 9, 2009.
17. Deborah Charles, "Romney Says U.S. Should Not Negotiate with Taliban," Reuters, January 16, 2012.
18. Mitt Romney, "Only the Afghanis Can Win Afghanistan's Independence from the Taliban," Republican Presidential Debate in New Hampshire, Reuters, June 13, 2011.
19. John Boone, "Obama Bid to Turn to Moderate Taliban 'Will Fail,'" *Guardian*, March 8, 2009; see also Saeed Abbasi, "Amrulla Saleh: Moderate Taliban Do Not Exist," *Tribes News*, October 12, 2011.

20. Kathleen Hennessey and Mark Magnier, "Obama Welcomes Taliban Assent to Afghanistan Talks," *Los Angeles Times,* June 18, 2013.

21. Marc A. Thiessen, "The Taliban Is Playing Obama," *Washington Post,* June 24, 2013.

22. "Taliban 'Set to Open Office in Qatar," *Al Jazeera English,* June 18, 2013; see also David Rising and Rahim Faez, "Taliban Office in Qatar Explanation Sought by Afghanistan," Associated Press, June 23, 2013.

23. Kanan Makiya, *Republic of Fear: The Politics of Modern Iraq* (Berkeley: University of California Press, 1998).

24. Steve Holland and Jim Gains, "Romney: Iraq Pullout a "Signature Failure,' for Obama," Reuters, December 22, 2012.

25. Xinhua, "U.S. Envoy Denies Proposal to Delay South Sudan Referendum," *Xinhua,* October 31, 2010.

26. Elizabeth Blackney and Susan Morgan, "Mitt Romney Statement on Sudan," *Act for Sudan,* January 31, 2012.

27. Ian Black, "Barack Obama, the Arab Spring and a Series of Unforeseen Events," *Guardian,* October 21, 2012; see also Ben Shapiro, "President Obama's Arab Spring Nightmare," *Town Hall Magazine,* August 21, 2013; see also Julie Pace, "Egypt Challenges Obama's Arab Spring Philosophy," Associated Press, August 17, 2013.

28. "The Candidates on Democracy Promotion in the Arab World; Issue Tracker: Romney," Council on Foreign Relations, October 31, 2012.

29. C. Hart, "Obama Administration Draws Closer to Egypt's Muslim Brotherhood," *American Thinker,* July 23, 2012.

30. Tiffany Gabbay, "Was Romney Ahead of the Curve on Muslim Brotherhood?" *The Blaze,* May 9, 2012.

EPILOGUE

1. "Anti-Morsi Petition Gets 22 Million Signature;" *Huffington Post,* June 29, 2013; also "The Lead with Jake Tapper," CNN, July 2013.

2. David Kirkpatrick, "Visiting Republicans Laud Egypt's Force," *New York Times,* September 8, 2013. See also, Michele Bachmann, "Muslim Brotherhood, a History of Terror," *Daily News of Egypt,* December 17, 2013.

3. Ibrahim Qassem, "23.5 Million Egyptians Participated in the Referendum," *Yom Sabe',* January 16, 2014 (in Arabic). That was the highest level of popular vote in Egypt's history, with more than 90% approving the new constitution.

4. See Mohammed Sharif "The Obama Administration in a Difficult Position after Egypt Declares the Ikhwan a Terror Organization," *al Watan al Arabi,* December 25, 2013; "Masr Tabda'a tafkik imbaratoriat al Ikhawn" (Egypt begins disbanding the Ikhwan financial empire), *al Watan al Arabi,* December 30, 2013; also Ali Bin Tamim, "I'lan al Ikhwan Tanzim Irahabi fil Khaleej" (Declaring the Ikhwan a terror organization in the Gulf), 24 AE TV, December 28, 2013.

5. K. T. McFarland, "Egypt on the Brink: Country Needs Our Political, Financial and Moral Support," Fox News, October 14, 2013.

6. Holly Williams, "Syria Gov't, Opposition Trade Accusations Over Chemical Weapons Use," CBS, August 24, 2013.

7. Hamdi Alkhshali and Nic Robertson, "Syria Islamist Rebels Take Control of Historic Christian Town of Maaloula," CNN, September 8, 2013.

8. See "Stephen Sackur Speaks to Prince Reza Pahlavi, Spokesman for the Iran National Council." *BBC HARDtalk,* October 10, 2013; also "Iranian Dissidents Say Iran has Built Secret New Nuclear Site," Reuters, November 18, 2013; also

Hamid Yazdan Panah, "U.S. Should Help Iranian Dissidents," UPI, November 28, 2013; and "Maryam Rajavi: Crimes Against Humanity in Camp Ashraf and Mass Executions in Iran Should Not Be Ignored Under the Guise of Nuclear Negotiations," Foreign Affairs Committee of the Iranian National Resistance, also in *Consiglio Nazionale*, December 7, 2013.

9. Press releases in social media by Iranian opposition youth are found on "No Secret Deals with IRAN" Facebook page, https://www.facebook.com/NOSE-CRETDEAL, accessed November 2013. See also Sayeh Hassan, "The Deal with Iran Is a Dangerous Mistake: Canada Is Right in Being Skeptical and Refusing to Ease the Sanctions in Iran!" Shiro Khorshid blog, November 27, 2013.

10. "Tunisia's Army Arrests Militants after Gun Battle in City that Started the Arab Spring Revolutions," Associated Press, January 2, 2014.

INDEX